New Approaches to Religio

Series Editor

Joerg Rieger
Vanderbilt University Divinity School
Heidelberg
Baden-Württemberg
Germany

Aims of the Series

While the relationship of religion and power is a perennial topic, it only continues to grow in importance and scope in our increasingly globalized and diverse world. Religion, on a global scale, has openly joined power struggles, often in support of the powers that be. But at the same time, religion has made major contributions to resistance movements. In this context, current methods in the study of religion and theology have created a deeper awareness of the issue of power: Critical theory, cultural studies, postcolonial theory, subaltern studies, feminist theory, critical race theory, and working class studies are contributing to a new quality of study in the field. This series is a place for both studies of particular problems in the relation of religion and power as well as for more general interpretations of this relation. It undergirds the growing recognition that religion can no longer be studied without the study of power.

More information about this series at
http://www.springer.com/series/14754

Bruce Rogers-Vaughn

Caring for Souls in a Neoliberal Age

Bruce Rogers-Vaughn
Vanderbilt University
Nashville, Tennessee, USA

New Approaches to Religion and Power
ISBN 978-1-137-55338-6 (hardcover)   ISBN 978-1-137-55339-3   (eBook)
ISBN 978-1-349-71633-3 (softcover)
DOI 10.1057/978-1-137-55339-3

Library of Congress Control Number: 2016956960

Cover image © cryingjune / Getty Images

Printed on acid-free paper

This Palgrave Macmillan imprint is published by Springer Nature
The registered company is Nature America Inc. New York
The registered company address is: 1 New York Plaza, New York, NY 10004, U.S.A.

To my wife, Annette, with gratitude and love

And in loving memory for my son
Taylor Vaughn
1986–1995

And my mother
Doris Louise Vaughn
1933–2014

And forgive us our debts,
as we also have forgiven our debtors.

(Matthew 6:12)

Acknowledgements

As most authors are aware, books do not appear without a great deal of inspiration from and collaboration with others. I am particularly grateful to three professional associations of psychotherapists for opportunities to share my developing ideas concerning the social and political origins of the sufferings to which we collectively bear witness. The Southeast Region of the American Association of Pastoral Counselors and the Tennessee Association of Pastoral Therapists both graciously allowed me to speak to this issue during their annual conferences. I was also invited to offer a day-long workshop on this subject during the spring of 2015, hosted by the Nashville Psychotherapy Institute. The encouragement and lively dialogue I enjoyed during these meetings have been critical in the effort to keep my theorizing grounded in the distresses experienced by actual human beings and in the challenges faced by those who must listen and respond to them. Along similar lines, I wish to thank my clinical associates at the Pastoral Center for Healing in Nashville, Tennessee—Tom Knowles-Bagwell, Rod Kochtitzky, Annette Rogers-Vaughn, Gay Welch, and Elizabeth Zagatta-Allison. It has been a pleasure to know them as both friends and colleagues, and their support and ongoing companionship have contributed immeasurably to this project.

I have lived and worked not only in clinical settings, but in academic ones as well. Here, I must especially recognize my colleagues in the Society for Pastoral Theology (SPT). During June of 2014, I was honored to deliver a "work in progress" address to the full body of the society. Without the energetic feedback that followed, this book might not ever have matured to see the light of day. Several members of SPT have been regular conversation partners or have played pivotal roles in stimulating this work. These include Nancy J. Ramsay, Barbara J. McClure, Ryan LaMothe, Philip Browning Helsel, and Denise Dombkowski Hopkins. In parallel to my everyday associates in clinical work, I enjoy the company of esteemed scholars at Vanderbilt Divinity School, where I have been teaching for many years. My peers in the area of Religion, Psychology and Culture—Bonnie Miller-McLemore, Evon Flesberg, Jaco Hamman, Phillis Isabella Sheppard, and Volney P. Gay—have been a dependable source of encouragement and wise counsel. I am immensely indebted also to my students, especially those who enrolled in the course "Pastoral Care and Global Capitalism." These individuals were patient with me as I rolled out partially formed ideas, and were keen to point out elements that were either missing or not yet quite digestible. One of these students, Aaron Palmer, helpfully tracked down several much-needed references early in the project. Another former student, Morgan Watts, provided indispensable assistance proofing the manuscript and preparing it for final submission.

My deep appreciation goes out to Joerg Rieger, the series editor for the collection in which this volume appears, for inviting me to submit a proposal and for his valuable advice and stimulating conversations along the way. My thanks also to all the dedicated staff members at Palgrave Macmillan for their help in bringing this task to completion, especially to my editor, Phil Getz, and his assistant, Alexis Nelson, whose correspondences were always timely and beneficial.

Many of the souls whose presence accompanied me through every page of this book literally cannot be named. They are the many individuals who sought me out for a psychotherapy relationship over the past three decades. Working with them has enriched my life beyond measure and, I believe, has made me wiser than I could have otherwise become. I can only hope I have represented their struggles accurately and fairly.

Finally, I thank my family—Annette Rogers-Vaughn, Mackenzie Vaughn, and the twins, Blake and Huntley Rogers-Vaughn. Unfortunately, writing this book has often demanded too much sacrifice from them all. The currently eight-year-old twins' recurring inquiry—"Are you done with the book yet?"—has been one of the primary motivations to actually finish. Thanks largely to passing the days with these four precious souls, I know at least as much about joy as I do suffering.

CONTENTS

LIST OF FIGURES

CHAPTER 1

Introduction: Preface to a Post-Capitalist Pastoral Theology

How could it happen that a Baptist minister who grew up in the United States, in the Deep South no less, in a politically and religiously conservative milieu, ever wanted to author a book criticizing capitalism? I am aware of three sets of motives. First, from the mid-1980s to this day, I have worked as a pastoral counselor and psychotherapist. Aside from some adjunct teaching, this was my sole occupation from 1992 until 2010. Throughout my professional career, I have conducted approximately 30,000 counseling sessions. Sustaining such intimate acquaintance with people over time has permitted me to observe bewildering changes that have been occurring between and within human beings in my part of the world during these 30 years.

The average individual I encounter in the clinical situation today is not the same as the person who sat with me 30 years ago. Sometimes the changes are subtle. Often they are obvious. But they are pervasive and apparently widespread. There has been a marked increase in self-blame among those seeking my care, as well as an amorphous but potent dread that they are somehow teetering on the edge of a precipice. This is confounded by the appearance of a few individuals who seem far more self-assured and confident, even entitled or defiant, than I have previously witnessed. Somewhat mysteriously, these highly self-reliant souls seem more superficial and one-dimensional than their depressive or anxious cohorts. Meanwhile, addictive behaviors have become more prevalent and

© The Author(s) 2016
B. Rogers-Vaughn, *Caring for Souls in a Neoliberal Age*,
DOI 10.1057/978-1-137-55339-3_1

have quickly expanded into areas of life not usually associated with compulsivity. Relationships, even familial or romantic ones, seem to be becoming more ephemeral and contrived, almost businesslike. The people I now see tend to manifest a far more diffuse or fragmented sense of self, are frequently more overwhelmed, experience powerful forms of anxiety and depression too vague to be named, display less self-awareness, have often loosened or dropped affiliations with conventional human collectives, and are increasingly haunted by shame rooted in a nebulous sense of personal failure. I find myself more disquieted and even confused than I used to be while sitting with people, even less "myself." What has happened?

Puzzled by this, I began to investigate. I soon became aware that a number of clinicians, particularly psychoanalysts, had been making observations similar to mine. In a prescient set of reflections, Bollas (1987) had argued that a new sort of person was emerging that he called "normotic personality" (pp. 135–156). Such an individual suffers a numbing or erasure of subjectivity, experiencing herself as a commodity in a world of commodities. Samuels (2003/2006) noted that something happened during the period from 1980 to 1990 that began to alter his patients' presentations. Consulting with his analytic colleagues, he concluded: "We tended to put it down to the fact that, since the mid-1980s, the pace of political change in the world appeared to have quickened" (pp. 12–13). The analysts Layton, Hollander, and Gutwill (2006) pinned such changes to powerful shifts within capitalism as it was practiced in the United States, arguing that such alterations had produced a "traumatogenic environment" (pp. 1–5). Noticing that other clinicians' observations, like my own, were chiefly anecdotal, I looked around for additional sorts of evidence. Sure enough, careful scientific surveys and empirical studies were showing that depression, anxiety, and addiction were increasing, not only in the United States but globally. Simultaneously, I noticed that a number of sociologists and geographers were recognizing developments pointing to the erosion of communities and human collectives.

I returned to my therapy patients.[1] I listened ever more closely to their self-blame. Were there clues? My suffering subjects complained persistently about their situations or moods, but almost all (except the super-confident outliers) concluded they themselves were somehow the problem. If they had not made that fateful decision, or if they were more intelligent, or more motivated, or more beautiful, or more talented, and so on, then maybe they would not be in this mess. Many perceived their problems as rooted in their identities. Maybe if they were not a woman, or a man, or gay, or black, or white, or adopted, or an immigrant, or Catholic, and so on, things would be better for them. Many attributed their sufferings to childhood traumas, or parental or family dysfunctions. But even those who saw the roots of their psychic pain in their identities or in trauma still believed *only they could do anything about their problems.* If they had suffered so long and still were not making headway, they mused, perhaps they were doing something wrong; or, even worse, something was wrong with them. So in the end, they felt just as responsible as my other, ostensibly more fortunate clients. I was starting to understand why people were drinking more, taking more drugs, "veg'ing out" playing video games, retreating into their smartphones, social media, iPads, or otherwise losing themselves in some other manic activity or distraction. I was beginning to entertain it myself.

Then I began to notice how much blaming was occurring in our society, particularly toward those who were not succeeding in "the land of opportunity." On cable and online news outlets, pundits could be heard villainizing the less fortunate. Apparently if people were poor, or were struggling in some way, it was their own damned fault. Even those in the shrinking middle class were often portrayed as less than sufficiently successful, as deficient in some fundamental way. Television programs had become heavily populated by beautiful and well-off people, with the apparent suggestion that these are the ones we should emulate. The ever-popular "reality shows" had turned cut-throat competition into entertainment, thus normalizing the belief that it is natural for the world to contain a very few "winners" surrounded by multitudes of "losers."

The same themes were showing up in national and local politics. Many politicians, backed up by a number of theorists within the academy, interpreted growing inequality as either a temporary evil or the price of progress in a necessarily highly competitive market. It is inevitable, according to such experts, that some unfortunate ones are simply unable to keep up. Dominant economic ideologies increasingly paint the world in stark "survival of the fittest" terms. I began to wonder, along with the analysts I had been reading, if there might be a relationship between what I was seeing in the media, politics, and the economy, and what I was witnessing in the therapeutic space. I also started to suspect that "private" suffering was governed primarily by dynamics distal to the individual—in the broader social, economic, and political environment. I found this idea overwhelming, perhaps due to my own relatively privileged perspective as a professional white male, and decided to set it aside for later investigation.

However, I was unsuccessful. I could not leave it alone. Through the rearview mirror, I can see that my sensitivity to these matters has become more acute due to my having grown up in a working-class family and community. This has to qualify as another origin of my passion to write this book. My father was, at various times, a member of the United Automobile Workers and the International Union of Electricians. His father and grandfather were both life-long coal miners in Appalachia, and were active members of the United Mine Workers. My mother's family consisted chiefly of rural sustenance farmers, truck drivers, and factory hands. To this day, I support the right of workers to collective bargaining and union membership. If my father, by the time I was ten years of age, had not eventually earned union wages, I would never have been able to attend college.

The life circumstances of the working class are not just memories for me. Neither of my parents, nor my sister, and none of my cousins, uncles, aunts, grandparents, or great grandparents ever attended college. This was rarely even an option. Most have done jobs requiring hard physical labor, which has often meant that their bodies have worn out before they could reach retirement. Some have become prematurely disabled or died from work-related injuries. For over 30 years, my father worked on an assembly line, bending sheet metal at a General Electric factory. Today he is hearing impaired from sitting beside a hydraulic press for that period of time. Many in my extended family still struggle to sustain themselves. One cousin, now in his early 60s, has continued to work two jobs to make ends meet. He recently learned that his new boss, a college-educated individual less than half his age, moved him to another shift that will require him to quit one of his jobs. He will likely no longer earn a living wage. Another cousin, the one with whom I was most intimate during my childhood and youth, died a few years ago from a pulmonary embolus. His death was unnecessary. He had put off treatment for an infection in his leg, which was secondary to a serious work injury, because he had inadequate insurance and financial resources. Suffice it to say I have little patience for those who claim that the "underemployed" and the poor are happy to live off the government, or are lazy or unintelligent. My relatives, on the average, work as many or more hours than I do, and under conditions over which they have far less control. As such incidents suggest, recent changes within capitalism have not been kind to my relatives and friends back in my small hometown, or to most people in the remainder of the United States or the world for that matter. These developments will be illustrated, documented and untangled in this book.

So two motives for writing this book are already apparent. I am pushed by my allegiance to working-class people who brought me into this world, and I am pulled by curiosity as to what might explain the changes I have seen, over the last three decades, in the people coming to me for care. The third source concerns the *character* of my therapeutic practice as the *care of souls*. The focus of my clinical work has been two-fold: to alleviate pain and distress whenever possible, and, whether or not this is possible, to assist people in *hearing* their suffering. What is it calling them to do and/ or to understand? Often in the course of pastoral conversations, I have noted that physical pain, according to physicians and biological scientists, has a function. It calls for us to attend to it, and to take action to address a threat or problem. Psychological, relational, and spiritual suffering, as I have frequently indicated to those receiving my consideration, has a simi- lar function. At minimum these particular sufferings insist on finding a voice. And often they call upon their subjects to initiate a course of action. This action may be limited to their own material or psychological space, but most often also extends to their relational, communal, or even social or political spaces.

This method of attention has yielded practical wisdom, both for myself and for those I have served. I (and we) have learned that, when unheeded, pain produces and structures alienation, injustice, ignorance, division, and isolation into our individual and collective lives. As I have regularly said to those who seek my attention, much of our suffering comes from our efforts to avoid or deny suffering. I (we) have also learned that, when articulated and heard, pain may yield and structure connection, continu- ity, integrity, justice, and direction into our individual and collective lives.

Taken together, this type of attention and the wisdom it engenders constitute healing, the *care of soul*. In this context, soul refers neither to a supernatural or natural essence, nor to some dimension of self separate from the material. I understand soul, rather, as an aspect of the embodied self, namely *the activity of self-transcendence*, where this refers not to an act of individual rationality, but to that activity which holds individuals in relation with self, others, creation, and the Eternal (whether or not this ultimate value is recognized as God). While I will discuss soul in detail later in this book, I must note here that soul, by its very nature, cannot be confined within the individual. It is, rather, a fabric that embeds every one of us within all that is. It is our existence within the "living human web" (Miller-McLemore, 1996), and within creation. That said, souls do not simply become ill or fail to thrive from within. They wither or become disoriented when the fabric becomes torn or stained.

However, there is a growing discord between the care of souls and the cultural and political environment that has emerged since the early 1980s. This is now so acute that I believe the care of souls to be threatened. The field of counseling and psychotherapy, as well as other practices of care, has been colluding with these changes, and has itself been transformed by the now dominant paradigm. The emphasis on "measurable outcomes" and "empirically supported treatments" promoted by the "best practices" culture of mental health disciplines—all indicators of a neoliberalized attitude—insists on instilling *adaptation* to society (rather than *resistance*), *functioning* in accord with the values of production and consumption (rather than *communion* and *wholeness* in relation to others and the earth), on *symptom relief* (rather than *meaning-making*), and accepting *personal responsibility* (rather than *interdependent reliance* within the web of human relationships). Meanwhile, the now dominant ideology of the psychological disciplines, at least in the United States, identifies the source of personal distress as originating solely *within the individual* (rather than primarily the social and political environment), and thus exacerbates the self-blame that underlies much contemporary distress. Consequently, I see the currently prevailing practices of psychotherapy as sophisticated exercises in *blaming the victim*. Unfortunately, as we shall see, this general approach to care is no longer limited to professional counseling and related forms of care, but has infected the way we now understand care in all its manifestations.

The concerns and anxieties rooted in these three areas feed my appetite for this book. I will be contending that all these changes are driven by the transformation and global expansion of capitalism that has advanced steadily since the early 1980s. There is now growing evidence, produced across an array of disciplines, that this development—now widely known under the umbrella term "neoliberalism"—has been progressively and systematically undermining social, interpersonal, and psychological well-being. In accord with Antonio Gramsci's (1929–1932/1992–2007) notion of hegemony, *I will contend that neoliberalism has become so encompassing and powerful that it is now the most significant factor in shaping how, why, and to what degree human beings suffer.*

At the same time, no hegemony achieves complete and absolute control. If this were the case, there would be no hope for a form of care that could address the suffering it produces. My clinical experience leads me to have confidence that human longing is difficult to entirely suppress, and has a way of seeping up through the cracks of any system of domination.

The care of what has been called "soul"—that dimension of self that is sustained in communion with self, others, creation, and the Eternal—attends solicitously to this longing. Part of the structure of any hegemony is the character and location of its cracks, such that it also governs, even in its failures, practices of care. Any care that responds to the sufferings it generates, in other words, will necessarily seek out and respond to a hegemony's distinguishing fractures.

A corollary of the claim that neoliberalism is now globally hegemonic is that pastoral care, as well as other forms of the care of souls, must undergo revision in order to have some hope adequate for both healing and protest. In this book, I will argue that the theories corresponding to this care, including pastoral theology, are generally constrained within postmodern cognitive models, as well as dwelling largely within the fabric of neoliberal versions of identity politics. Any substantial innovation in the fields of pastoral theology and the care of souls today, therefore, will require us to reaffirm our commitment to a common ground that unifies us as diverse people, and to the public good. It will also demand that we extend our analyses and critiques of oppression due to difference (identity) to include the problems of domination intrinsic to capitalism. Indeed, it will mean that subjugations rooted in difference will now be understood, and appreciated more profoundly, in light of capitalism's current global hegemony. *The time has arrived, then, to work toward a post-capitalist pastoral theology, by which I mean a pastoral theology that does not assume the normativity of capitalism.*

In the remainder of this chapter, I will lay a foundation for the work of this book. In pastoral theology and other theories of care, it is customary to begin with a case or clinical vignette in order to ground succeeding reflections in human experience. I will follow this practice. However, I will be attempting to show throughout this book that no clear line exists between what we call public or social space, and what we usually refer to as personal or psychological space. In fact, I will argue that social and cultural dynamics, including the economic and political, are the most powerful forces shaping both interpersonal and psychological experience. The "case" I offer in the next section, therefore, is a summary of the changes occurring since 1980 within localities in the United States. Bits and pieces of individual and interpersonal experience, as we will see, arise organically within the discussion of this context. Following this, I provide a brief preliminary description of neoliberal capitalism as the overarching paradigm guiding these changes and experiences. I then inquire whether pastoral theology, as the theory that frames pastoral care, has been in collusion with the neoliberalization of society, and whether a post-capitalist pastoral theology is possible. Finally, I will offer an overview of the book in order to provide the reader with an orientation to the larger argument.

LIVING IN THE UNITED STATES AFTER THE SILENT REVOLUTION, 1980–2015

In his most recent book *Wages of Rebellion* (2015), Chris Hedges reports an interview he held with Avner Offer, an economic historian at Oxford University. Offer contends that "a silent revolution" in economics occurred during the 1970s, centered in the United States and the United Kingdom (pp. 76–80). This instigated political and cultural revolutions in both countries, also relatively quiet compared with typical revolutions, beginning with the elections of Margaret Thatcher and Ronald Reagan in 1979 and 1980. We continue to live in the deep shadows of this revolution, and today reside in a renovated economic, political, and cultural climate.

In the United States the transformations since 1980 have been chronicled by a number of scholars, but perhaps none of them are better known than the Harvard political scientist Robert Putnam. In *Our Kids: The American Dream in Crisis* (2015), Putnam documents the growing economic inequality in the United States and the effects on class, communities, families, and education. Putnam begins the book reviewing changes in Port Clinton, Ohio—population 6500—his hometown. When he graduated from high school in 1959, he observes: "Family or not, the townspeople thought of all the graduates as 'our kids'" (p. 3). During those days, Putnam recalls, the residents of Port Clinton exhibited a neighborhood mentality. People freely associated across class lines as they attended one another's weddings and birthday parties, worshipped in local churches, or collaborated in civic organizations. Children from poorer working-class families hung out with children of wealthy families. Upward mobility was quite apparent, as the community encouraged and supported adolescents from working-class families in their efforts to seek higher education. For instance, one of his classmates, Don, was quite poor. Neither of his parents completed high school, and his father worked two factory jobs to make ends meet. They owned neither a car nor television. Interviewed later as an adult, Don downplayed the class distinctions in Port Clinton: "I lived on the east side of town...and money was on the west side of town. But you met everyone as an equal through sports" (p. 4). Although his parents knew nothing about college, Don reported that a minister in the town saw potential in him and recommended him to the university, helped him get financial aid, and guided him through the admissions process. Later, Don completed seminary and became a minister himself.

Meanwhile, Frank, another classmate, was "from one of the few wealthy families in Port Clinton" (p. 5). In fact, Frank's parents were the wealthiest and best educated of the parents of the class of 1959. And yet Frank's parents were careful to minimize their wealth, putting relationships with others in the community above their own self-interests. They encouraged Frank to participate in activities with peers from less financially well-off families, and not to allow his social standing to make others uncomfortable. His grandfather once admonished his uncle: "If we're in Cleveland or New York, you can order whatever you want, but when you're with kids in Port Clinton, you do what they can do" (p. 5). This is not reflective of life in Port Clinton today. Putnam reflects:

> As my classmates and I marched down the steps after graduation in 1959, none of us had any inkling that change was coming .... But just beyond the horizon an economic, social, and cultural whirlwind was gathering force nationally that would radically transform the life chances of our children and grandchildren. For many people, its effects would be gut-wrenching, for Port Clinton turns out to be a poster child for the changes that have swept across America in the last several decades. (pp. 19–20)

Putnam then surveys the devastation: a decline in manufacturing employment from 55 % of jobs in 1965 to 25 % in 1995, a gradual decline in real wages, a stagnant population, longer commutes in search of better wages, a doubling of single-parent households, a quadrupling in the divorce rate, and a steep rise in rates of juvenile delinquency. Port Clinton has become a shadow of its former self:

> Most of the downtown shops of my youth stand empty and derelict, driven out of business partly by the Family Dollar and the Walmart on the outskirts of town, and partly by the gradually shrinking paychecks of Port Clinton consumers. (p. 20)

But that is only part of the story. The other is "the birth of the new upper class" (p. 21) in Port Clinton. Its picturesque location on the shores of Lake Erie began to attract wealthier professionals from nearby Cleveland

and Columbus, who settled in mansions and gated communities along those shores. In the lavish Catawba Island area of town, "Luxury condos ring golf courses and lagoons filled with opulent yachts" (p. 22). Meanwhile, though the child poverty rate remained practically zero in the Catawba section, child poverty throughout most of Port Clinton increased from below 5 % in 1990 to over 35 % between 2008 and 2012. Putnam observes that, driving east along East Harbor Road, the census tract to the left has a child poverty rate of 1 %, while the tract on the right side of the road has a rate of 51 % (p. 22).

On one side of the road lives Chelsea (pp. 24–26). Her mother, Wendy, an educator in private practice, has a graduate degree. She comes from a prominent family in Michigan. Her father, Dick, is a manager in "a major national corporation," and "travels a great deal for his business." Chelsea's parents make sure one of them is at home every day when she gets home from school. They throw her themed birthday parties every year, and build an expensive 1950s-style diner in the basement where she can hang out with her friends. Wendy is proud to be involved with Chelsea's education, and recalls an incident during the seventh grade when Chelsea received a low grade due to an incomplete assignment. Wendy appealed to the principal and ultimately the school board, who changed the grade and transferred the teacher. Despite their financial comfort, Wendy does not see their family as especially affluent: "Most parents around here are Midwest parents who work for their money .... It's not like Beverly Hills or the Hamptons." She makes sure her kids take part-time and summer jobs, noting "You have to work if you want to get rich." Wendy resents proposals to provide funding for educating poorer kids: "If my kids are going to be successful, I don't think they should have to pay other people who are sitting around doing nothing for their success." As Putnam clearly insinuates, Port Clinton has long since devolved from a community where "our kids" live, to one divided between "my kids" and "their kids."

On the other side of the road lives David (pp. 26–29). His father, a high school dropout, tries first to make a living driving a truck, then must settle for picking up temporary jobs. He ultimately ends up in prison. After his parents separate when he is little, David's mother moves out and he no longer knows exactly where she lives. David is tossed back and forth between staying with his paternal grandmother and his father, who continues to be in and out of prison. After a string of women enter and leave his dad's life, he finally settles down with a woman when David is around ten years of age. Though they never marry, David calls her his stepmother. She is addicted to drugs and alcohol, and finally leaves his dad for someone else. When this happens, says David, his dad "went off the deep end" with drugs and women. The undependability of adults leaves David with the sense that "nobody gave a shit" about him or his nine half-siblings. He copes by isolating himself and smoking marijuana. After circulating through several schools, he gets kicked out and ends up in a "behavior school." He eventually has a criminal record after breaking into a series of stores with some other kids, then violating probation by getting drunk and flunking a drug test. David nevertheless finishes high school, but then gets stuck in a series of dead-end jobs due to his juvenile record, which he cannot get expunged because he has no money to pay the necessary legal fees. Despite everything, David tells the interviewer: "I really want to get a higher education .... I need one. It's hard to get a job without one anymore." But he cannot get there. No one in the town has bothered to reach out and help. At the same time, he feels great respon-sibility for his half-siblings, who also have no stable adults to look after them. In fact, when Putnam first meets David in a public park in 2012, at the age of 18, he is "affectionately watching over an eight-year-old half-brother." That same year David's girlfriend becomes pregnant. Within two years she leaves him, and they are sharing custody of their daughter. David "lives paycheck to paycheck," but enjoys being a dad. The narra-tive closes with a Facebook update David posts in 2014, upset with his girlfriend's betrayal and frustrated with his hopeless job: "I always end up at the losing end ... I just want to feel whole again. I'll never get ahead! I've been trying so hard at everything in my life and still get no credit at all. Done...I'm FUCKING DONE!" Putnam concludes that this story is typical for present-day Port Clinton: "Compared to working-class kids in 1959, their counterparts today, like David, lead troubled, isolated, hope-less lives" (p. 30).

On one side of the road are family dinners, fancy parties, "helicopter parenting," and an abundance of adult support. On the other side, people are having trouble being families at all, and usually there is no one step-ping up to help. Putnam, summarizing his research for his book, notes that his hometown is only one example of a pattern that has spread across the United States:

> Port Clinton is just one small town among many, of course—but the rest of this book will show that its trajectory during the past five decades, and the divergent destinies of its children, are not unique. Port Clinton is *not* simply a

Rust Belt story, for example, although it is that. Subsequent chapters will trace similar patterns in communities all over the country, from Bend, Oregon, to Atlanta, and from Orange County, California, to Philadelphia. (p. 30, emphasis in original)

So, this has happened throughout the United States? I decided to check my own hometown—Fort Payne, Alabama—to compare with Putnam's. After all, Port Clinton is in "the North," and Fort Payne in "the Deep South." Might they be very different? Like Port Clinton, Fort Payne was far from perfect as I was growing up. Both towns were (and are) predominately white, and even after the schools integrated in the 1960s, Fort Payne remained otherwise quite racially segregated. Patriarchy dominated, and minorities were far from being treated fairly. Sexually, any individual other than a cisgender heterosexual remained deeply in the closet. And yet, as with Port Clinton, community life displayed fluidity across class boundaries. As the child of a factory worker and "housewife," I discovered several of my closest friend's parents were doctors, lawyers, or other professionals. I will never forget the first visit to my best friend's home, who was the son of a well-paid engineer and a school teacher. I had never been a guest in a house so spacious, and with features—such as a house-wide built-in intercom and a central vacuum system—that I had not even known existed. Teachers and other adults in the community just assumed, because my grades were good, that I was headed for college, despite the fact that no one in my family had ever done such a thing. My school guidance counselor encouraged me to apply to one of the better private colleges in the state, and then helped me navigate the application process, something about which my parents could know very little. Upon my graduation from high school, in 1974, the community gathered with obvious pride, as they did in Port Clinton in 1959, in "our kids."

But the same sorts of changes that swept through Port Clinton would not spare Fort Payne. Nestled between the hills of southern Appalachia, the town was once hailed as the "Official Sock Capital of the World." At their production height, around 2001, Fort Payne's 125 textile mills manufactured one of every eight pairs of socks sold on the planet, and close to half of those sold in the United States (Marshall, 2011; Martin, 2011). These mills employed about 8,000 people in a city of only 14,000 residents. One of every three jobs was related to making socks. However, the free trade policies aggressively implemented by the United States from the mid-1990s forward progressively eroded the success of the mills. The cost of labor in Fort Payne, with a non-unionized workforce already cheap by national standards, could not compete with labor costs at similar sock mills in Central America, and especially in Datang, China (Lee, 2005). As large international retailers, such as Walmart, pursued cheaper socks from abroad, demand for the town's main industry dried up almost overnight. By 2011 less than ten hosiery plants remained, employing fewer than 600 workers (Carter, 2011). An office manager at one of the remaining mills reported that residents were calling in every day, begging for jobs: "Every day, you get at least 20 calls from people wanting to know if they can come back to work." Another individual noted that, even if one was lucky enough to get called back, the jobs were not the same: "Used to be, you'd do one thing and that's what you did…Now, you do five jobs. That's what you do now. That's the times" (Marshall, 2011).

Although different from Port Clinton in some respects, the consequences in Fort Payne have been similar. Manufacturing jobs have declined from 43 % in 1980 to 28 % in 2013. The divorce rate has more than doubled during that same period. The unemployment rate has increased from less than 4 % to over 11 %. The number of college graduates living in the city has decreased from an already low 14.7 % to 10.7 %. The level of childhood poverty (the percentage of those 18 years of age and below living in households below the poverty level), within the five census tracts comprising the heart of Fort Payne, increased from 3.97 % in 1989 to 28.63 % in the period from 2008 to 2013.[2] As with Putnam's hometown, graphics of the child poverty rate, comparing the same census tracts from 1989 to 2013, vividly illustrates the increasing economic inequality in my hometown (see Fig. 1.1. The darker the area appears, the higher the poverty rate).

The child poverty rate in tract 9612, just north of downtown, has hardly changed at about 8 %. Meanwhile, just across the street in tract 9613, the rate has increased from 4 % to almost 46 % during the same period. The increasing class segregation visible here coupled with reductions in overall education levels, Putnam contends (2015, pp. 41–45), are critical indicators of social mobility. Whereas conventional methods measuring social mobility depend on "lagging indicators," class segregation and education levels of parents are reliable indicators of *future* social mobility. If Putnam is correct, then individuals in Port Clinton and Fort Payne—indeed throughout the United States—are increasingly destined to remain in the class into which they are born. In Putnam's words,

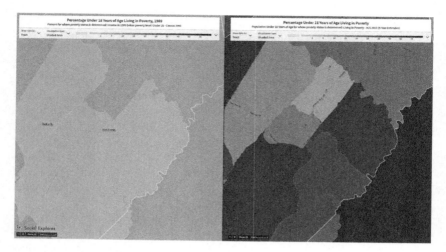

Fig. 1.1 Child poverty rate, Ft. Payne, Alabama (USA): 1989–2013. Comparison by census tract. ACS 2009–2013 (five-year estimates) data as compiled by Social Explorer, accessed through Vanderbilt University Library

social mobility "seems poised to plunge in the years ahead, shattering the American Dream" (p. 44).

Putnam concludes that what is apparent in Port Clinton (and Fort Payne) is pervasive across the United States: "the ballooning economic gap has been accompanied by growing de facto segregation of Americans across class lines" (2015, p. 37). Putnam observes that three trends emerge from this change. First, neighborhoods have become more separate: "More and more families live either in uniformly affluent neighborhoods or in uniformly poor neighborhoods," resulting in "a kind of incipient class apartheid" (pp. 38–39). Second, neighborhood segregation "has been translated into de facto class-based school segregation" (p. 39). Finally, people in such unequal circumstances "tend to marry others like themselves," especially in terms of educational level and class. Consequently, kin networks are ever more constricted along class lines (pp. 40–41). This leads to some rather unexpected results. Class segregation among African Americans, for example, has increased more than it has for whites. This is not lost on Putnam, who notes that "while race-based segregation has been slowly declining, class-based segregation has been increasing. In fact, the trend toward class segregation has been true *within* each major racial group" (pp. 38–39, emphasis in original).

My initiation of a pastoral care book with such collective "cases," rather than the customary vignettes confined largely to narrating the experiences of individuals or perhaps families, may seem odd to many people. What could this have to do with caring professions, and, in particular, any caregiving effort that stands in the "care of souls" tradition? As we will see in the following chapter, the socioeconomic shifts visible in the small towns of Port Clinton and Fort Payne since 1980, and indeed across the United States, have been accompanied by a massive deterioration of social well-being. These decades, marked by a rapid increase in economic inequality and class-based segregation, have seen a remarkable decline in the quality of social relations, along with steep increases in the incidence of depression, addiction (and "mental disorders" generally), violence and incarceration; decreased life expectancy; waning educational performance; and declining social mobility. Later, I will summarize how this extends to the weakening of human collectives, interpersonal relationships, including even the quality and exchange of human emotions, and the disintegration of human subjectivity. Stated theologically, these conditions are weakening the human soul, that connective tissue linking us together as a human community, as well as to creation and the Eternal. In other words, the transformations occurring in society are related to the full spectrum of human problems that have traditionally occupied the caregiving professions and human care as a whole, including the care of soul. Finally, by using such collective cases, I am anticipating a central claim of this book— that human relational and psychological sufferings are best understood as rooted primarily in material, social, and even political conditions, rather than simply in some underlying physiological process or in individual decisions or behaviors.

If these claims hold water—and I implore the reader to withhold judgment until considering the evidence and reflections presented in the remainder of this book—two questions come immediately to mind. First, is there some greater trend, process, or program that is fueling the changes in Port Clinton, Fort Payne, the United States, and indeed the world beyond, over these several decades? Second, if such a program can be identified, are those concerned with human care, and especially the care of souls, aware of or tending to this all-encompassing development?

AT THE HEART OF THE REVOLUTION: CAPITALISM UNHINGED

In the opening reflections of this chapter I have, of course, betrayed my hand. I do believe there is sufficient evidence for a larger pattern explaining the developments I have just mentioned. Social scientists in the academy are famously cautious about making claims concerning causes of the events they so carefully catalogue. This includes Putnam (2015). In *Our Kids*, he identifies several important markers or symptoms, but demurs when responding to the question as to why such changes are occurring (pp. 72–77). Given the enormous complexities of human relationships at all levels, I certainly respect such restraint. However, those who are directly involved in the social, relational, psychological, or spiritual care of human beings rarely have the luxury to wait for what might count as empirical proof. When dealing with such intricacies, we usually must settle for reasonable theories based on highly suggestive or strong correlations. The urgency to adopt a governing theory becomes critical when, as we are observing now, the impact on human suffering is broad, deep, and accelerating. In this book, I will argue that the best candidate for such a governing theory is that the doctrines and practices of neoliberal capitalism are grounding the transformations we are witnessing today. Although I will discuss the history and development of neoliberalism in some detail in the next chapter, perhaps I should summarize here what neoliberalization entails.

Though the complexity and local diversity of neoliberalism make simple definitions risky, it is important to attempt a description of its universal characteristics as the reigning grand narrative. Jones (2012) has offered perhaps the most succinct definition, describing neoliberalism as "the free market ideology based on individual liberty and limited government that connected human freedom to the actions of the rational, self-interested actor in the competitive marketplace" (p. 2). We should carefully notice here that freedom has been redefined on the market's terms, and that society has been replaced by isolated and competitive individuals. Moreover, the actions of these individuals emerge from conscious choices based on self-interest rather than the common good. Steger and Roy (2010) note that the policy practices flowing from this ideology follow the now familiar "D-L-P formula"—Deregulation, Liberalization, and Privatization (p. 14). The deregulation of the economy means that governments reduce or withdraw laws and rules requiring corporations to consider any purposes other than the pursuit of profit. This includes the reduction or removal of taxes on corporations and their wealthy owners, which by definition are levied for the public good rather than the benefit of corporations, and result in decreased profit. The consequent unbridled pursuit of profit and decline in public revenue necessarily leads to reductions in social services and welfare programs. Liberalization refers to the removal of trade barriers, such as taxes on imports that attempt to keep the playing field level for laborers. It also requires eliminating laws inhibiting the exchange of international currencies, effectively turning currency markets into a global casino for wealthy investors. Finally, privatization denotes removing properties and services from public control (i.e. from governments) and turning them over to the "private sector" (to corporations and their owners). To all this, Mann (2013) adds that what is unprecedented in neoliberalism, compared to prior versions of capitalism, is the degree of *globalization* and *financialization* (the trade of financial instruments rather than goods and services), both of which are facilitated by the nearly instantaneous movement of capital made possible by the internet and other advanced communications technologies (pp. 143–148).

Even a superficial consideration of this summary of neoliberalization makes it easier to imagine how the changes in Port Clinton and Fort Payne, and other places across the country, have come to pass and are ultimately tied together. Considered as a political and economic agenda, the D-L-P formula, constructed specifically to increase profits for corporate elites, reduces both jobs and wages for average workers and results in ever-increasing economic inequality. Meanwhile, the "rational choice theory" embedded in Jones's definition denies the importance, if not the existence, of the common good. This sort of belief, observe Häring and Douglas (2012), alleges "to show by means of scientific discourse that the concepts of 'the public' and 'public interest' or 'general welfare' [are] arbitrary and meaningless" (pp. 21–22). Thus the policies pursued by the D-L-P strategy intentionally attack the public good, both politically and economically. This is why David, interviewed by Putnam (2015), has no access to resources to help him gain legal assistance, education, or better employment. Finally, as Centeno and Cohen (2012) and others have shown, the process of neoliberalization is not limited to politics and economics. It is also a cultural project. It is a way of organizing human society based on the principles of individualism and competition (Brown, 2015; Dardot & Laval, 2009/2013, pp. 255–299; Davies, 2014). This subtly but steadily influences our attitudes and feelings toward ourselves, including our understanding of what it means to be a "self," as well as our dispositions and feelings toward others. Combined with the erosion of belief in the common good, this leaves us with a society in which each person increasingly looks after their own interests, and leaves others to look after theirs. Anyone not managing to compete is viewed with suspicion, if not with disdain. In the worst of cases, care itself, toward anyone but "one's own," becomes considered a weakness. This helps us understand why an otherwise reasonable individual such as Wendy, when interviewed by Putnam (2015), recoils at the thought of increasing public funding to help poorer kids in Port Clinton. She concludes: "If my kids are going to be successful, I don't think they should have to pay other people who are sitting around doing nothing for their success" (p. 25). This is how inequality turns into class segregation. If we consider that this same attitude can be directed toward oneself, it may also shed light on why those who seek my counsel are now so filled with shame and self-blame. Perhaps they suffer from segregation within the soul.

WE ARE ALL NEOLIBERALS NOW: PASTORAL THEOLOGY, CARE, AND THE NATURALIZATION OF CAPITALISM

Given the sweeping and disturbing political, economic, and cultural effects of neoliberalization, particular features of which I will discuss in succeeding chapters, how have professionals dedicated to caring for human beings responded? More to the current point, how have those who theorize such care responded? The answer, at least in the United States and the wealthiest countries, is by and large "not very well." The broader disciplines of psychology and psychotherapy have not only generally ignored these developments, but have largely served the interests of the new capitalism. I will not offer a critique of psychology and psychotherapy along these lines, for that has already been undertaken by the emergent field of critical psychology, especially as it is developing in the United Kingdom (e.g. Ingleby, 1980; Parker, 2007, 2015a, 2015b; Smail, 2005). Rather, I will focus here on my own field, pastoral care, and its theory, pastoral theology. Pastoral care and pastoral theology offer an interesting case, it turns out, for this discipline has historically been entrusted to articulate, preserve, and continually reinterpret the care of souls. Its deep roots in a religious tradition of care potentially enable it to gain some perspective on contemporary developments within capitalism.

And yet from the neoliberal transformation on, most of us, especially those like me who have spent their careers primarily in clinical practice, have regarded the sufferings of individuals as originating within themselves, as arising from their personal choices, feelings, individual biology, private relationships, and their unique, idiosyncratic unconscious lives. We have failed, as a rule, to explore the social, cultural, or political environment as a potentially greater determinant of such distresses. Rarely do we consider the so-called "individual unconscious" as also being intrinsically social and political. As for the academy, for at least two decades, pastoral and practical theologians have been increasingly exploring the sources of both individual and collective suffering within the cultural domain. We have become particularly sensitized to the problems of racism, sexism, heterosexism, and the politics of difference as sources of discrimination, violence, oppression, and a host of spiritual, relational, and psychological maladies. I suspect that for the majority of us, however, such differences constitute the bedrock of what we consider the social and cultural origins of suffering. Rarely do we think of such problems as currently being founded, sustained, and even transformed by dynamics endemic to developments within capitalism. Slavoj Žižek (2000) has admonished his progressive colleagues for their implicit "acceptance of capitalism as 'the only game in town,'" and "the renunciation of any real attempt to overcome the existing capitalist liberal regime" (p. 95). Likewise, feminist political theorist Wendy Brown (1995) has criticized academic theorists on the left for their "Theoretical retreat from the problem of domination within capitalism" (p. 14). *Pastoral theologians have participated in this retreat.* Any acknowledgment of the sufferings imposed by capitalism is often cursory, lacking thorough analysis and critique. Consequently, both pastoral care professionals and pastoral theologians are inhibited from fully comprehending the sources and the dynamics of the problems now occupying our attention, as well as proposing more effective ways of addressing them.

It is likely that pastoral theologians and caregivers, along with other theorists and practitioners over the course of the last three decades, have avoided attending to capitalism as a source of suffering simply because we have accepted it as normative. Thus the primary origins of such sufferings have sunk out of awareness and become part of our collective unconscious. Capitalism has become the air that we breathe, a dimension of our natural world. Extending her analysis, Brown (1995) has argued that activists and academics on the left have become entrenched in, if not captured by, American identity politics. This development, she contends, "would seem to be achieved in part *through* a certain renaturalization of capitalism that can be said to have marked progressive discourse since the 1970s" (p. 60, emphasis in original). Moreover, she asserts that this renaturalization of capitalism has shifted resentment originating in class-based oppression (which becomes invisible when neoliberalism is normative) onto the emotions and theorizing swirling around identities, such that "identity politics may be partly configured by a peculiarly shaped and peculiarly disguised form of class resentment, a resentment that is displaced onto discourses of injustice other than class" (p. 60).

Brown's analysis suggests the elision of *class* as a marker of suffering and oppression. Indeed, the power interests of neoliberal capitalism are quite comfortable with a discourse that emphasizes multiculturalism, diversity, and tolerance. One could argue that such a discourse improves corporate profits by extending the reach of markets. What these powerful interests cannot abide is any effort to shine a light on matters of class. Brown (1995), following the argument just mentioned, raises this concern: "Could we have stumbled upon one reason why class is invariably named but rarely theorized or developed in the multiculturalist mantra, 'race, class, gender, sexuality'?" (p. 61).

I am worried that pastoral care and theology are subject to this critique. Are we, too, implicitly accepting the normativity of capitalism, despite the now massive evidence of how it is initiating and escalating forms and transformations of suffering? Have we not undergone our own subjection to capitalism? Since its publication over ten years ago, I have regarded the essays collected in the book *Pastoral Care and Counseling: Redefining the Paradigms* (Ramsay, 2004) as something of a placeholder for progress in our discipline. These sophisticated and valuable essays attempt to chart the changes that occurred in the field since the publication of the *Dictionary of Pastoral Care and Counseling* in 1990. They highlight modifications in pastoral identity and method, as well as the ways in which dynamics of power and privilege, particularly around issues of race, gender, sexual orientation, and ethnic differences, have led to a paradigm shift in the field. And yet I cannot find in the entire collection more than a trickle of references to capitalism or the excesses of "free market" practices. One contributor, Christie Cozad Neuger (2004), acknowledges: "Class continues to be one of the most neglected perspectives in pastoral theology" (p. 76). She predicts: "Critiques of capitalism and general economic practices, class structures and distribution of wealth and resources" will become more prominent in the future trajectory of the field (p. 82). We are still awaiting the comprehensive realization of this expectation.

Precursors for the Critique of Capitalism
Within Pastoral Theology

What I find most striking about the essays in *Pastoral Care and Counseling: Redefining the Paradigms*, aside from the irony that many of the shifts in the field discussed in the book may best be understood as aspects of a burgeoning neoliberal hegemony, is that the authors are generally aware of precedents in the field that call for an in-depth analysis of capitalism, and yet remain for the most part silent on this subject. These same precedents constrain me from assuming a grandiose claim to originality for the project I have undertaken. I am certainly not the first to suggest that theories of pastoral care have neglected a thorough examination of the impact of capitalism. Indeed, pastoral theology has occasionally produced its own voices "crying in the wilderness." In *The Relational Self: Ethics & Therapy from a Black Church Perspective*, Archie Smith, Jr. (1982) sounds an alarm concerning the challenges presented by capitalism. Writing just as neoliberalism was beginning its rise to political dominance, Smith observes that conservative shifts in politics and religion then occurring in the United States had "helped to strengthen an uncritical commitment to the structural arrangements and social relations that underlie an expanding and exploitative economic system, namely profit-centered capitalism" (p. 167). A full 16 years passed before an entire book in our discipline would be devoted to responding to capitalism. In *No Room for Grace: Pastoral Theology and Dehumanization in the Global Economy*, Canadian theologian Barbara Rumscheidt (1998) poses the crucial question for our field today: "What does it mean to do pastoral theology in a world where people have been reduced to 'human resources'?" (p. x). Four years later, we saw the release of James Poling's *Render Unto God* (2002), in which he compellingly situates domestic violence within the context of global capitalism. An entire portion of his book (part three) is dedicated to documenting resistances to capitalism in Nicaragua, as well as among African Americans and women in the United States. In the second part, Poling summarizes the theories and practices of capitalism, and calls for a theological critique from the standpoint of the Christian tradition. In a cogent observation, Poling anticipates some of the analysis I attempt to undertake in this book: "The culture of capitalism dramatically affects how people understand themselves and one another" (p. 87).

A number of contributions in pastoral theology have not focused on capitalism as such, and yet have addressed issues relevant to an analysis and critique of capitalism. These include Pamela Couture's explorations of poverty (1991, 2007), Judith Orr's consideration of pastoral care with working-class people (1991, 1997, 2000), and Tom Beaudoin's *Consuming Faith* (2007). Barbara McClure (2010) decries the influence of individualism in pastoral care and counseling. Although she does not focus on capitalism, we will see later on that neoliberal capitalism is the most radically individualistic ideology we have yet encountered. The efforts of pastoral theologians working in a postcolonial vein, such as Emmanuel Lartey (2013), are also indispensable, given that neoliberalization is essentially a neo-colonizing process. An accounting of valuable cohorts for critiquing capitalism would be incomplete, as well, without reference to womanist pastoral theologians, such as Phillis Sheppard (2008, 2011), who have consistently focused on the intersection of class concerns with gender and race. In a more general way, Charles Gerkin's work broadened the scope of pastoral theology to include details of the social context of suffering. This is particularly apparent in his *Widening the Horizons: Pastoral Responses to a Fragmented Society* (1986). A collection of essays in his honor (Couture & Hunter, 1995), *Pastoral Care and Social Conflict*, illustrates the breadth of his influence. One of the essays, titled "The Future of Pastoral Care and Counseling and the God of the Market" (Couture & Hester, 1995), documents how this social turn can be aimed in the direction of capitalism. From this wide-angle view, most of the work by contemporary pastoral and practical theologians—which leads the field in the direction of public theology—touches upon matters related to capitalism, even when these efforts are not offered as assessments of capitalism. Indeed, if today's capitalism is truly hegemonic, as I will be arguing, then almost nothing we can discuss lies outside its reach. This means that the survey I undertake in this paragraph is necessarily abbreviated. My colleagues will no doubt be thinking of other authors I should have mentioned. Nonetheless, it remains true that none of these efforts, to my knowledge, endeavor to go beyond the issues at hand to tie them in a thoroughgoing way to capitalism, much less undertake a comprehensive critique of capitalism as a systematic production of suffering.

Only recently have works in pastoral theology mentioned neoliberalism by name. Couture (2007) questions whether "neoliberal economics" and "The Washington Consensus" are playing a role in the global increase of child poverty, yet seems undecided as to whether this new economic system is the cause or the solution to this problem, suggesting somehow that it may be both (pp. 97, 105–113). Subsequently, a handful of pastoral theologians have become categorically more critical. This is apparent in several articles authored by Ryan LaMothe (2016a, 2016b) and myself (Rogers-Vaughn, 2013a, 2013b, 2014, 2015). Recently two books have appeared. The first book in this discipline to address neoliberalism directly is by Philip Browning Helsel (2015). The initial chapter gets to the point of his monograph: "Social Class and Mental Illness in a Neoliberal Era" (pp. 19–52). Meanwhile, Cedric Johnson (2016) thoughtfully explores the impact of neoliberalism on African Americans in his work titled *Race, Religion, and Resilience in the Neoliberal Age*. My intention in the present volume has a broader scope, which is to consider how neoliberalization is both increasing and transforming suffering on a global scale, while simultaneously altering social, interpersonal, and psychological systems. In my judgment, the immensity of this impact summons the entire discipline to move toward a post-capitalist posture.

Is a Post-Capitalist Pastoral Theology Possible?

All of the publications I have mentioned that openly focus upon capitalism, beginning with Smith's (1982) *The Relational Self* until now, have called for a thoroughgoing critique of capitalism within pastoral theology. There is now a pressing need to revise this effort in light of the dramatic and accelerating shifts that have been occurring within capitalism. I am suggesting that what we now need is a post-capitalist pastoral theology. What does this mean? Emmanuel Lartey (2002) proposes that pastoral theology currently exists "in an era of 'post-phenomena'." The prefix "post," he asserts, does not merely indicate what follows or replaces the term it qualifies. Rather than simply designating what comes after a particular order or system, "it is a way of speaking about the condition of *being in critical vein* or *in questioning mode* concerning it" (p. 1, emphases in original). This is precisely the spirit in which I am using this prefix. Lartey contends that pastoral theology must *respond* in a time that is "post-modern, post-colonial, post-Christian, post-human and perhaps also 'post-pastoral'" (p. 1). However, I am conducting this analysis from the opposite direction. We are certainly *not* living in a "post-capitalist" era. In fact, as Fredric Jameson (2003) famously notes, "it is easier to imagine the end of the world than to imagine the end of capitalism" (p. 76). In an age of global and hegemonic capitalism, I argue that pastoral theology must *become* post-capitalist.

There is growing evidence, beyond the field of pastoral theology, that the time is now ripe for such a change. Within theological education generally, several scholars have begun to argue that advanced capitalism now poses the most significant threat to the human spirit, to civilization, and to the health of the planet. John Cobb (Cobb, 2010; Cobb & Daly, 1994), Rosemary Radford Ruether (2005), and Susan Brooks Thistlethwaite (2010), for example, have penned major treatises from this perspective. A new generation of scholars has undertaken a reorientation of liberation theology, bringing this important critical tradition to bear upon advanced capitalism as the current form of imperialism and colonialism. These include Joerg Rieger (2009), Jung Mo Sung (2007, 2011), Néstor Míguez (Míguez, Rieger, & Sung, 2009), and Kwok Pui-lan (Rieger & Pui-lan, 2012). Theological studies, however, have lagged behind other disciplines in the investigation of capitalism's effects. The relative neglect of neoliberalism in theology and religious studies, compared with the social sciences as a whole, is starkly visible in Fig. 1.2,

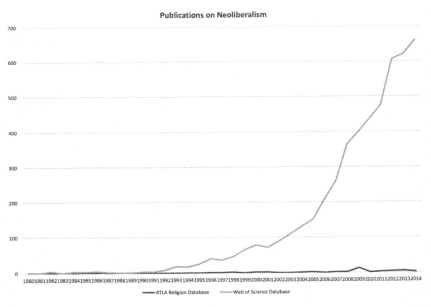

Fig. 1.2 Annual number of publications on neoliberalism, 1980–2014: Comparison between theological studies and the social sciences. Sources: Web of Science and ATLA religion databases, accessed through Vanderbilt University Library

which displays the number of publications on neoliberalism in each category, from 1980 to 2014[3]:

For some time, social scientists have focused rather narrowly on discrete aspects of capitalism, such as economic inequality, consumerism, and the decline of collectives. During the last 20 years, however, there has been a steady convergence of concerns, accompanied by a growing recognition of neoliberal hegemony. Social epidemiologist Roberto De Vogli (2013), in his recent book *Progress or Collapse*, describes these intersections:

> It is no coincidence that crises such as climate change and the rapid depletion of natural resources are occurring in combination with other symptoms of social breakdown: rising mental disorders, mindless consumerism, materialistic conformism, status competition, civic disengagement, startling economic inequalities, global financial instability and widespread political inertia. While these crises are usually studied in isolation, they are all interconnected. To some specialists, this claim may sound far-fetched. But this is only because they fail to connect the dots. Specialists have provided invaluable contributions to science, but they are often too attached to their microscopical views of society. (pp. xi–xii)

De Vogli concludes that "the market greed doctrine," which he identifies as the neoliberal paradigm, is the connection between these dots.

The current level of public restlessness and receptivity may be even more significant than academic trends as an indicator of the need for a pastoral theological revision. For example, a PRRI/RNS Religion News Survey (2011) shows that 44 % of US citizens believe that capitalism conflicts with Christian values, whereas only 36 % believe they are compatible. More recently, a Harvard Public Opinion Project (2016) survey reveals that more than half of young people in the United States oppose capitalism in its current form. Meanwhile, the distinctly anti-capitalist apostolic exhortation of Pope Francis (2013), *Evangelii Gaudium*, garnered significant publicity, leading US radio personality Rush Limbaugh to worry that the Vatican had been compromised by Marxist conspirators. Nonetheless, the popularity of this pope has continued to soar, both globally and within the United States. Finally, the presence of capitalism on the public mind is apparent in the popularity of French economist Thomas Piketty's *Capital in the Twenty-First Century* (2014), which reached number one on the *New York Times* best-seller list during May of 2014.

There are even some indications that resistance is emerging in current political developments. Most remarkable are recent events in the United States and Britain, where neoliberal policies were first embraced and from where they have spread around the globe. In 2015, Jeremy Corbyn, in a staggering upset, was elected leader of the Labour Party in Britain. He ran on an anti-austerity platform that opposed most of the neoliberal strategies Margaret Thatcher had promoted during the 1980s and that have held sway since then. The current presidential campaign cycle in the United States has been marked by a similar surprise: the rising popularity of Bernie Sanders, a self-proclaimed democratic socialist. Even though it appears that he will lose the Democratic Party nomination to Hillary Clinton, many analysts believe his relative success is the leading edge of a shift in politics in the United States. Like Corbyn, his strongest support has been among young people, who were born after the neoliberal revolution and have suffered the most economic impact. There are also signs of political stress in international financial institutions, which have been instrumental in imposing neoliberal "structural adjustments" on developing countries. For example, three leading researchers at the International Monetary Fund (IMF) have just released a report concluding that the austerity policies and the liberalization of flows of capital that typify neoliberal strategies have contributed to global inequality and instability. The researchers conclude: "In sum, the benefits of some policies that are an important part of the neoliberal agenda appear to have been somewhat overplayed" (Ostry, Loungani, & Furceri, 2016, p. 40). Considering the source, this is a startling admission.

In summary, seismic shifts are underway that are likely to place increasing pressure on a number of academic disciplines to undertake alterations in orientation or even major adjustments to their preferred theories. This includes pastoral theology. *If pastoral theology is about learning from and responding to human suffering, and if neoliberalism is now a hegemony that is governing and transforming suffering globally, then a revision of our discipline is in order.* Moreover, if we have the necessary theoretical tools to undertake this revision, and if hearts and minds are receptive, then the time for this work is upon us. I am not suggesting, of course, that we should focus on capitalism to the exclusion of the other important work we have been doing. The specific concerns that have occupied us remain critical, are constantly evolving, and demand our ongoing efforts. What I am proposing is that it is a mistake to ignore how the dominant paradigm, neoliberal capitalism, is grounding, sustaining, or transforming whatever discrete form of suffering we are exploring and attempting to alleviate. It is time, in other words, to "connect the dots."

In this book, I will attempt a synopsis of the evidence that the dots indeed connect, and in the process I will offer some thoughts about implications for change in the way we carry out pastoral care and theology. I must confess that the task I have set for myself is difficult and likely unattainable. A task like this calls for expertise in many disciplines, and my knowledge in many of these specialties is superficial at best. I will inevitably commit oversights. What I offer is bound to be both inadequate and incomplete. This work is part of a larger endeavor that calls for a community of inquirers, rather than sequestered individual thinkers. This project will also require time. It may be that our students, or our students' students, will be the generation of scholars to see this to fruition. Regardless, we are living at a time when the earth and all its inhabitants are at risk. We do not have the luxury of scholarship as usual, staying in our cubicles using narrow sets of theories on narrow sets of problems. There are patterns that only become visible using a wide-angle lens, thus this era demands a type of scholarship that is synthetical more than analytical. I am suggesting that we must now view suffering through the lens of the dominant paradigm. In science a paradigm is, by definition, a general theory of everything. Applied to culture, it is not only a theory, but an interactive nexus of thoughts, beliefs, images, behaviors, impulses, feelings, and desires that permeate every dimension of human organization, including the individual psyche. Thus, in the words of De Vogli (2013), "to understand how the world works, we need to know more and more about more and more until we know something about everything" (p. xii). What I offer here, therefore, are only preliminary and uncertain steps in what will likely be a long journey.

The Structure of the Book

In the following chapter, I will summarize the history and key features of neoliberalism, with particular attention to its character as a *cultural* project rather than simply an economic or political venture. In everyday life, the consequent society manifests a "survival of the fittest" spirit, with sadistic undertones. The imbrications between neoliberal culture and the condition commonly referred to as postmodernity mean that the postmodern critical theories now prevailing in the academy are already entangled with the ideology and circumventions of neoliberalism. This will require me to pause to consider this problem, and to address the methodological challenges it poses for my argument. The chapter concludes with evidence that one of neoliberalism's intrinsic attributes, economic inequality, is associated with a broad spectrum of social, interpersonal, and individual problems.

The third chapter goes beyond general support for a correlation between neoliberalism and human suffering by exploring specific consequences of contemporary capitalism for three entangled systems of human life: the social, the interpersonal, and the psychological. I will utilize William Connolly's (2013) notion that neoliberal capitalism "deflates" various self-organizing and entangled systems. I will propose that with regard to human systems, it accomplishes this deflation by two methods: *marginalization* (a reduction of the scope and power of these systems) and *corruption* (altering these systems to conform them to its own purposes). I will use particular examples to demonstrate how these methods are accomplished in each system. Because I cite the marginalization and corruption of religious collectives as an instance of the neoliberal deflation of social systems, I will pause along the way to discuss how secularization theory may divert attention from the cultural impact of neoliberalization.

I begin the fourth chapter with a broader perspective, summarizing evidence that neoliberalism is increasing human suffering and death globally, even when compared to previous historical regimes. I then turn to the notion of neoliberalism as a cultural *paradigm* that founds novel forms of suffering while mutating already existing types of suffering. Following the observations of Dufour (2003/2008), I will propose that neoliberalism introduces a new type of normative suffering corresponding to characteristics unique to its cultural manifestations: deinstitutionalization, desymbolization, and desubjectivation (what I call "the three D's"). I will designate this new normal as "third order suffering."

Third-order suffering inevitably becomes entangled with the already existing first- and second-order forms of suffering to such an extent that these new versions constitute unprecedented developments. Focusing on the subsequent alteration of second-order suffering, in the fifth chapter I suggest that the contemporary transformations of sexism, racism, and class struggle provide exemplary cases. Noting that neoliberalism adopts its own version of intersectionality theory, I offer an interpretation of this important theory as an inter-relationality of suffering that opposes the type of multiculturalism and diversity advocated by the market.

In the sixth chapter, I draw upon my clinical experience with pastoral psychotherapy to attempt a constructive turn. I open the chapter highlighting a feature of third-order suffering. This form of suffering is marked by a double unconsciousness: a dual lack of awareness that does not simply burden soul, but weakens or dis-members soul. Moreover, because soul is social–material in character, a way forward appears through a reversal of this double unconsciousness that simultaneously re-members soul. In other words, the indelible bonds between self, others, and the social and material world are restored to awareness and strengthened. I explore recent theoretical developments in critical psychology and psychoanalysis that yield insights into how this might occur. Utilizing these theories, I portray the clinical situation as a place where individuality becomes a window into the dialectics of soul. Here it becomes apparent that suffering, especially when returned to consciousness, is already a nascent resistance to the hierarchies and dynamics of power that characterize the neoliberal age. To illustrate this, I offer material from my clinical practice demonstrating how the undercurrents of a neoliberal world appear even in people's dreams. Work around such dreams is but one small instance of how the necessary increase of awareness and re-membering of soul may begin to come about. That being said, I close the chapter noting that the inherent limitations and fragility of psychotherapy prevent this form of care from becoming a sufficient response to the sufferings of a neoliberal age.

I carry forward the insights from the sixth chapter into the final section of the book, a series of three reflections I call "concluding theological postscripts." Any adequate reply to the sufferings of our age will necessarily involve the strengthening of human collectives, the nurture and increase of soul, and the amplification of hope. These three efforts, all profound activities of care, are inseparable and entangled. If we removed any one of them, the other two would either evaporate or suffer co-optation into a neoliberal strategy. As I will conclude there, soul inhabits a collective body, a body that exhales hope. This hope, once exhaled, expands to enfold our precious, entangled world, only to take it back in again. It aspires and inspires. Caring for souls in a neoliberal age will settle for nothing less.

NOTES

1. There is no term available to refer to people who see me for psychotherapy that completely pleases me. "Patients" can have the unfortunate connotation of passivity, and is strongly tied to the medical

model. However, "clients" is associated with consumerism, business contracts, and the very economic models I critique in this book, and thus disturbs me far more. The neologisms sometimes used as substitutes, such as "counselee" or "therapeut," seem convoluted or contrived. That said, the etymology of "patient" has ancient referents that, for me, remain meaningful. These are summarized by my pastoral theological colleague Pamela Cooper-White: "The reason for retaining this language of 'patient' is that it continues to carry the multiple meanings of soul and psyche; of suffering, passion, the pathos of the human condition (patient), and the meeting of this suffering at a profound level with a movement toward healing (*therapevo*)" (2007, p. 10, emphasis in original). For this reason, whenever I cannot avoid this sort of designation, I will, in this book, use the term "patient" rather than "client" or other alternates.

2. The figures cited in this paragraph were derived from the database available through Social Explorer (http://www.socialexplorer. com/), using data from the US Census Bureau and the American Community Survey (ACS).

3. Searches were limited to publications in English in which the terms "neoliberalism" or "neo-liberalism" appeared in the title, abstract, or keywords. Web of Science data include all covered publications within the social sciences. The term "capitalism" was not used for these searches because it is frequently used descriptively, whereas "neoliberalism" usually denotes a posture of critique.

REFERENCES

Beaudoin, T. (2007). *Consuming faith: Integrating who we are with what we buy.* Lanham, MD: Sheed & Ward.

Bollas, C. (1987). *The shadow of the object: Psychoanalysis of the unthought known.* New York, NY: Columbia University Press.

Brown, W. (1995). *States of injury: Power and freedom in late modernity.* Princeton, NJ: Princeton University Press.

Brown, W. (2015). *Undoing the demos: Neoliberalism's stealth revolution.* Brooklyn, NY: Zone Books.

Carter, K. (2011, February 2). Gildan to end remaining sock production in Fort Payne. *The Gadsden Times.* Retrieved June 23, 2016, from http://www. gadsdentimes.com/news/20110202/gildan-to-end-remaining-sock-production-in-fort-payne

Centeno, M. A., & Cohen, J. N. (2012). The arc of neoliberalism. *Annual Review of Sociology, 38,* 317–340.

Cobb Jr., J. B. (2010). *Spiritual bankruptcy: A prophetic call to action.* Nashville, TN: Abingdon Press.

Cobb Jr., J. B., & Daly, H. E. (1994). *For the common good: Redirecting the economy toward community, the environment, and a sustainable future.* Boston, MA: Beacon Press.

Connolly, W. E. (2013). *The fragility of things: Self-organizing processes, neoliberal fantasies, and democratic activism.* Durham, NC: Duke University Press.

Cooper-White, P. (2007). *Many voices: Pastoral psychotherapy in relational and theological perspective.* Minneapolis, MN: Fortress Press.

Couture, P. (1991). *Blessed are the poor? Women's poverty, family policy, and practical theology.* Nashville, TN: Abingdon Press.

Couture, P. (2007). *Child poverty: Love, justice, and social responsibility.* St. Louis, MO: Chalice Press.

Couture, P. D., & Hester, R. (1995). The future of pastoral care and counseling and the God of the market. In P. D. Couture & R. J. Hunter (Eds.), *Pastoral care and social conflict: Essays in honor of Charles V. Gerkin* (pp. 44–54). Nashville, TN: Abingdon Press.

Couture, P. D., & Hunter, R. J. (Eds.). (1995). Pastoral care and social conflict: Essays in honor of Charles V. Gerkin. Nashville, TN: Abingdon Press.

Dardot, P., & Laval, C. (2009/2013). *The new way of the world: On neo-liberal society* (Gregory Elliott, Trans.). London: Verso.

Davies, W. (2014). *The limits of neoliberalism: Authority, sovereignty and the logic of competition.* London: SAGE Publications.

De Vogli, R. (2013). *Progress or collapse: The crises of market greed.* London: Routledge.

DuFour, D.-R. (2003/2008). *The art of shrinking heads: On the new servitude of the liberated in the age of total capitalism* (David Macey, Trans.). Cambridge: Polity Press.

Gerkin, C. V. (1986). *Widening the horizons: Pastoral responses to a fragmented society.* Philadelphia, PA: Westminster Press.

Gramsci, A. (1929–1932/1992–2007). *Prison notebooks* (Vols. 1–3). New York, NY: Columbia University Press.

Häring, N., & Douglas, N. (2012). *Economists and the powerful: Convenient theories, distorted facts, ample rewards.* London: Anthem Press.

Harvard Public Opinion Project. (2016). *Executive summary: Survey of young Americans' attitudes toward politics and public service* (29th ed.). Cambridge, MA: Harvard University Institute of Politics Retrieved June 7, 2016, from http://iop.harvard.edu/sites/default/files/content/160425_Harvard%20 IOP%20Spring%20Report_update.pdf.

Hedges, C. (2015). *Wages of rebellion: The moral imperative of revolt.* New York: Nation Books.

Helsel, P. B. (2015). *Pastoral power beyond psychology's marginalization: Resisting the discourses of the psy-complex.* New York, NY: Palgrave Macmillan.

Ingleby, D. (Ed.). (1980). *Critical psychiatry: The politics of mental health.* New York, NY: Pantheon Books.

Jameson, F. (2003). Future city. *New Left Review, 21*(May/June), 65–79.

Johnson, C. C. (2016). Race, religion, and resilience in the neoliberal age. New York, NY: Palgrave Macmillan.

Jones, D. S. (2012). *Masters of the universe: Hayek, Friedman, and the birth of neoliberal politics.* Princeton, NJ: Princeton University Press.

LaMothe, R. W. (2016a). The colonizing realities of neoliberal capitalism. *Pastoral Psychology, 65*(1), 23–40.

LaMothe, R. W. (2016b). Neoliberal capitalism and the corruption of society: A pastoral political analysis. *Pastoral Psychology, 65*(1), 5–21.

Lartey, E. Y. (2002). Embracing the collage: Pastoral theology in an era of 'post-phenomena'. *The Journal of Pastoral Theology, 12*(2), 1–10.

Lartey, E. Y. (2013). *Postcolonializing God: An African practical theology.* London: SCM Press.

Layton, L., Hollander, N. C., & Gutwill, S. (2006). Introduction. In L. Layton, N. C. Hollander, & S. Gutwill (Eds.), *Psychoanalysis, class and politics: Encounters in the clinical setting* (pp. 1–10). London: Routledge.

Lee, D. (2005, April 10). The new foreign aid. *Los Angeles Times.* Retrieved June 23, 2016, from http://www.latimes.com/business/la-fi-socks10apr10-story.html

Mann, G. (2013). *Disassembly required: A field guide to actually existing capitalism.* Edinburgh: AK Press.

Marshall, M. (2011, April 19). The decline of the former 'sock capital of the world' is a story of lost jobs and empty mills. *The Huntsville Times.* Retrieved June 23, 2016, from http://blog.al.com/huntsville-times-business/2011/04/the_decline_of_the_hosiery_ind.html

Martin, T. W. (2011, February 22). Alabama sock town suffers as cotton soars. *The Wall Street Journal.* Retrieved June 23, 2016, from http://www.wsj.com/articles/SB10001424052748703803904576152712394690824

McClure, B. J. (2010). *Moving beyond individualism in pastoral care and counseling: Reflections on theory, theology, and practice.* Eugene, OR: Cascade Books.

Míguez, N., Rieger, J., & Sung, J. M. (2009). *Beyond the spirit of empire: Theology and politics in a new key.* London: SCM Press.

Miller-McLemore, B. J. (1996). The living human web: Pastoral theology at the turn of the century. In J. Stevenson-Moessner (Ed.), *Through the eyes of women: Insights for pastoral care* (pp. 9–26). Minneapolis, MN: Fortress Press.

Neuger, C. C. (2004). Power and difference in pastoral theology. In N. J. Ramsay (Ed.), *Pastoral care and counseling: Redefining the paradigms* (pp. 65–85). Nashville, TN: Abingdon Press.

Orr, J. L. (1991). Ministry with working-class women. *Journal of Pastoral Care, 45*(4), 343–353.

Orr, J. L. (1997). Hard work, hard lovin', hard times, hardly worth it: Care of working-class men. In C. C. Neuger & J. N. Poling (Eds.), *The care of men* (pp. 70–91). Nashville, TN: Abingdon Press.

Orr, J. L. (2000). Socioeconomic class and the life span development of women. In J. Stevenson-Moessner (Ed.), *In her own time: Women and developmental issues in pastoral care* (pp. 45–64). Minneapolis, MN: Fortress Press.

Ostry, J. D., Loungani, P., & Furceri, D. (2016). Neoliberalism: Oversold? *Finance & Development, 53*(2), 38–41.

Parker, I. (2007). *Revolution in psychology: Alienation to emancipation*. London: Pluto Press.

Parker, I. (2015a). *Psychology after the crisis: Scientific paradigms and political debate*. London: Routledge.

Parker, I. (2015b). *Psychology after psychoanalysis: Psychosocial studies and beyond*. London: Routledge.

Piketty, T. (2014). *Capital in the twenty-first century*. (Arthur Goldhammer, Trans.). Cambridge, MA: Belknap Press.

Poling, J. N. (2002). *Render unto God: Economic vulnerability, family violence, and pastoral theology*. Eugene, OR: Wipf & Stock.

Pope, F. (2013). *The joy of the gospel: Evangelii gaudium*. Washington, DC: United States Conference of Catholic Bishops.

Public Religion Research Institute, & Religion News Service. (2011). *Survey: Plurality of Americans believe capitalism at odds with Christian values*. Retrieved January 9, 2014, from http://publicreligion.org/research/2011/04/plurality-of-americans-believe-capitalism-at-odds-with-christian-values/

Putnam, R. D. (2015). *Our kids: The American dream in crisis*. New York, NY: Simon & Schuster.

Ramsay, N J. (Ed.). (2004). *Pastoral care and counseling: Redefining the paradigms*. Nashville, TN: Abingdon Press.

Rieger, J. (2009). *No rising tide: Theology, economics, and the future*. Minneapolis, MN: Fortress Press.

Rieger, J., & Pui-lan, K. (2012). *Occupy religion: Theology of the multitude*. Lanham, MD: Rowman & Littlefield Publishers.

Rogers-Vaughn, B. (2013a). Best practices in pastoral counseling: Is theology necessary? *The Journal of Pastoral Theology, 23*(1), 1–24.

Rogers-Vaughn, B. (2013b). Pastoral counseling in the neoliberal age: Hello best practices, goodbye theology. *Sacred Spaces, 5*, 5-45. Retrieved July 31, 2014, from http://www.aapc.org/media/127298/2_rogers_vaughn.pdf

Rogers-Vaughn, B. (2014). Blessed are those who mourn: Depression as political resistance. *Pastoral Psychology, 63*(4), 503–522.

Rogers-Vaughn, B. (2015). Powers and principalities: Initial reflections toward a post-capitalist pastoral theology. *Journal of Pastoral Theology, 25*(2), 71–92.

Ruether, R. R. (2005). *Integrating ecofeminism, globalization, and world religions.* Lanham, MD: Rowman & Littlefield Publishers.

Rumscheidt, B. (1998). *No room for grace: Pastoral theology and dehumanization in the global economy.* Grand Rapids, MI: William B. Eerdmans Publishing Company.

Samuels, A. (2003/2006). Working directly with political, social and cultural material in the therapy session. In L. Layton, N. C. Hollander, & S. Gutwill (Eds.), *Psychoanalysis, class and politics: Encounters in the clinical setting* (pp. 11–28). London: Routledge.

Sheppard, P. I. (2008). Mourning the loss of cultural selfobjects: Black embodiment and religious experience after trauma. *Practical Theology, 1*(2), 233–257.

Sheppard, P. I. (2011). *Self, culture, and others in womanist practical theology.* New York, NY: Palgrave Macmillan.

Smail, D. (2005). *Power, interest and psychology: Elements of a social materialist understanding of distress.* Ross-on-Wye: PCCS Books.

Smith, A., Jr. (1982). *The relational self: Ethics and therapy from a black church perspective.* Nashville, TN: Abingdon.

Steger, M. B., & Roy, R. K. (2010). *Neoliberalism: A very short introduction.* New York, NY: Oxford University Press.

Sung, J. M. (2007). *Desire, market and religion.* London: SCM Press.

Sung, J. M. (2011). *The subject, capitalism, and religion: Horizons of hope in complex societies.* New York, NY: Palgrave Macmillan.

Thistlethwaite, S. B. (2010). *Dreaming of Eden: American religion and politics in a wired world.* New York, NY: Palgrave Macmillan.

Žižek, S. (2000). Class struggle or postmodernism? Yes, please! In *Judith Butler, Ernesto Laclau, & Slavoj Žižek, Contingency, hegemony, universality: Contemporary dialogues on the left* (pp. 90–135). London: Verso.

CHAPTER 2

Neoliberalism, Inequality, and the Erosion of Social Well-being

In this chapter, I will identify key features of neoliberalism that provide a foundation for the work of subsequent chapters. In a fashion analogous to the story of an individual human life, the history of neoliberalism is a narrative of an uneven and somewhat unpredictable process that nevertheless exhibits discernable enduring patterns as it progressively occupies economic, political, and cultural spaces. Recognizing neoliberalization as a cultural process is particularly critical to understanding the way it transforms the social, interpersonal, and psychological dimensions of our lives. The neoliberal renovation of culture requires an appreciation of how it is intertwined with the condition called postmodernity. This presents some methodological challenges, as it calls into question some of the conventions of postmodern critical theories—theories which are nonetheless necessary for developing a comprehensive analysis and critique of neoliberalization. These challenges must be addressed if I am to successfully navigate the argument of this book. Finally, I will highlight a central characteristic of neoliberalism—increasing economic inequality—as a powerful sign of its erosion of individual and social well-being. As a general marker of the depth and breadth of human suffering produced by neoliberalization, the global escalation of economic inequality calls for the more detailed analyses conducted in subsequent chapters.

© The Author(s) 2016
B. Rogers-Vaughn, *Caring for Souls in a Neoliberal Age*,
DOI 10.1057/978-1-137-55339-3_2

Historicizing Neoliberalism

In the previous chapter, I indicated something about the basic character of neoliberalism by repeating the brief description of Daniel Stedman Jones (2012) and the "D-L-P formula" outlined by Steger and Roy (2010). The problem is that the actual complexity of neoliberalism resists simple definitions or reduction to easy acronyms. Efforts at straightforward or minimal definitions leave the impression that neoliberalism is a monolithic, static strategy that is then imposed without differentiation across space and time. During the 1990s, the designation "neoliberal" was widely used in this fashion as a vague slogan of political protest, even within the academy. Thus Boas and Gans-Morse (2009) introduce their critique with a curt declaration: "Neoliberalism has rapidly become an academic catchphrase" (p. 138). They proceed to document the loose and vacillating usage of the term. Likewise, Jones (2012) objects that "the term neoliberalism is used with lazy imprecision in both popular debate and academic scholarship" (p. 10). A succinct definition may not even be possible, as Jamie Peck (2010) flatly concludes: "Crisply unambiguous, essentialist definitions of neoliberalism have proved to be incredibly elusive" (p. 8). There is currently an emerging consensus that the term does not refer to an entity at all, but to a *reflexive process*. In this vein, geographer Simon Springer (2010) argues that "neoliberalism," which implies a static thing, should be replaced by "neoliberalization," a process word that "recognizes neoliberalism's hybridized and mutated forms as it travels around our world" (p. 1026). A better way to approach neoliberalization, therefore, is to tell its story. By historicizing neoliberalism, we can get a sense not just of its fluctuating content but also of its dynamics and its conflicted and contested features. Indeed, this is the intention of the recent histories written not just by Jones (2012) but also by Peck (2010), Dardot and Laval (2009/2013), and Brown (2015), among others.

Jones (2012), in his comprehensive history *Masters of the Universe*, contends that neoliberalism has progressed in three distinct phases. During the first, from the 1920s until around 1950, the conceptual structure began to form. The term "neoliberalism" was first introduced at the Colloque Walter Lippmann meeting in Paris in 1938, as designating an alternative not only to state-planned economies, its archrival, but also to the laissez-faire character of classical liberal economics. Unlike liberal economies, in which the state and markets occupied separate concerns, neoliberalism envisioned governments taking an active role to guarantee the protection and free functioning of markets. The chief intellectual during this period was the Austrian political scientist Friedrich von Hayek, author of the influential *Road to Serfdom* (1944/2007). In 1947, Hayek gathered with like-minded men (all European and North American) in Switzerland to form the Mont Pelerin Society (MPS), which became the first institute for developing and promoting these ideas. We should note that throughout this time, indeed until the mid-1970s, neoliberal ideology was considered radical or even dangerous by then mainstream economists (George, 2000). Capitalistic societies were dominated during this time by the theory of British economist John Maynard Keynes (1936/2008), who believed that markets might implode under their own weight if not carefully regulated by governments for the sake of the public good. We must also understand that there was never a time when neoliberal thought was unitary, even in the MPS. This is not a story of an original pure idea, hatched by a closed circle of intellectuals, which was then applied uniformly and autocratically to states worldwide. As Peck (2010) notes, "there is no neoliberal replicating machine" (p. 6). The MPS included a hodge-podge of thinkers— the German Ordoliberals, centered in Freiburg; American economists, especially the "Chicago School" led by Milton Friedman; and Hayek and his followers, among others (Peck, 2010, Chap. 2). Key debates hinged on the type and extent of government involvement needed for the new approach. The Ordoliberals believed it was a mistake to view markets as entirely autonomous, arguing that states would still need to play a key role in their management. The Americans held out for a spontaneous, self-organizing market, with a minimal role for the state. In the middle was Hayek, trying to hold it all together. Peck concludes: "Neoliberalism was a transnational, reactionary, and messy hybrid right from the start. Neoliberalism has many authors, many birthplaces" (p. 39). Nevertheless, participants remained united by their determination "to *remake* laissez-faire for twentieth-century conditions" (p. 39, emphasis in original).

The second phase Jones (2012) identifies extends from 1950 until the political ascendency of neoliberalism during the Reagan and Thatcher administrations around 1980. Neoliberalism was effectively promoted during this period through cleverly embedded marketing strategies that had first been cultivated by Bernays in the 1920s (Bernays, 1928/2005; Tye, 1998). An important leader throughout this interval was Milton Friedman, a founding member of the MPS and chair of the economics department at the University of Chicago. Friedman (1951) initiated this phase with the publication of his paper, "Neo-liberalism and Its Prospects."

It was during this phase, notes Jones (2012), that the "moderate tone" set by Hayek was eclipsed by a "more strident" attitude, which "coalesced into a complete rejection of economic planning, social democracy, and New Deal liberalism" (p. 8). This shift was abetted by the establishment, in the 1950s and 1960s, of think tanks in the USA, such as the Institute of Economic Affairs (IEA) and the American Enterprise Institute (AEI). These organizations fostered a harsher version of neoliberal thinking. "For example," Jones asserts, "bodies like the IEA and the AEI argued that social and economic inequality was necessary as a motor for social and economic progress" (p. 9). It was primarily this Americanized mindset that was then successfully spread through the establishment of international think tanks, many of which published their own academic journals. This institutionalization process continues to this day. Peck (2010) notes that there are now over 275 free-market think tanks in 70 countries (p. 171).

Ironically, by the conclusion of this era, the term "neoliberalism" had largely fallen out of use by its proponents (Jones, 2012, pp. 6–7). Jones suggests that part of the reason was that the word did not resonate in an American context. Indeed, today the term typically appears among academics and activists outside the USA. But Boas and Gans-Morse (2009) identify a more compelling reason. In the mid-1970s, intellectuals in Chile successfully tied the term to the draconian economic reforms of the Pinochet dictatorship (pp. 139, 149–150). The word became, in short, a public relations problem. Thus from this point forward, neoliberalism turned into a negative term used primarily by its critics, in much the same way that critics of psychoanalysis might today use the term "Freudian." One consequence, Boas and Gans-Morse contend, "is that virtually *no one* self-identifies as a neoliberal" (p. 140, emphasis in original). Present-day neoliberal proponents prefer to simply consider themselves advocates of freedom, which is redefined as the unimpeded functioning of markets.

Jones (2012) asserts that the third phase of neoliberalism began in 1980 and continues to the present. During the 1990s, neoliberal policies were grouped under what became widely known as "the Washington Consensus." These policies became consolidated as the norm in Western Europe and North America, while expanding globally chiefly through the infamous "structural adjustments" of international financial institutions such as the International Monetary Fund (IMF), the World Trade Organization (WTO), and the World Bank. These are guided, in turn, by international "free trade" agreements, such as the North American Free Trade Agreement (NAFTA) (Jones, 2012, p. 8). Two other installments of such agreements are currently being negotiated, largely in secret. One is between officials in the USA and the European Union. Called the Transatlantic Free Trade Agreement (TAFTA), it would, among other things, hold member nation states liable for the financial losses of large corporations due to government regulations, such as those intended to protect the environment (Wallach, 2013). The other is the Trans-Pacific Partnership (TPP). Both the actions of the international financial institutions and the trade agreements enforce what Steger and Roy (2010) call the "D-L-P formula," thus suppressing the wages of workers and redistributing capital to global elites. These developments make it possible for us now to speak, in economic terms, of living in a "neoliberal world."

The temporal dynamics of these expansionist policies warrant comment. Implementation typically begins with "roll-back" processes that dismantle collectives and institutions that have the potential to obstruct neoliberalization. In Peck's words,

> Often prosecuted in the name of deregulation, devolution, and even democratization, this offensive is typically associated with attacks on labor unions, planning agencies, entitlement systems, and public bureaucracies, by way of the now familiar repertoire of funding cuts, organizational downsizing, market testing, and privatization (2010, p. 22).

This is followed by a "roll-out" phase, typically in response to pushback against deregulation, public austerity, and market failures. This is, in effect, a reregulation that "differs substantially from the preceding politics of retrenchment" (Peck, 2010, pp. 22–23). The purpose of this active intervention is to conform social and political processes to the governance of the market. Springer (2010) notes that this amounts to "an invasive social agenda centered on urban order, surveillance, and policing" (p. 1032). Peck argues that this may now be supplemented by a "rolling with" phase in which the market order is normalized. Or, alternatively, it may be described as a "*roiling* neoliberalism ... a still-dominant but deeply flawed 'settlement,' increasingly buffeted by crises" (2010, pp. 24–25, emphasis in original). In this phase, now current in the USA and most "developed" economies, neoliberalism repeatedly encounters its limits and evidences that contradict its assumptions. Nevertheless, as Mirowski (2013) has convincingly demonstrated regarding responses to the Great Recession that began in 2008, neoliberalism has become a "theory of everything" that finds a way to overcome and incorporate even its own failures and contradictions. Peck (2010) calls this a "failing forward," in which "manifest inadequacies have—so far anyway—repeatedly animated further rounds of neoliberal invention" (p. 6).

Meanwhile, the global economy has been "financialized," meaning that it increasingly depends less on the trade of material goods and services, and more upon the movement of capital using financial instruments engaged in the trading of securities, including esoteric instruments such as credit default swaps (CDSs). Mann (2013) notes that finance capital now accounts for 40 % of corporate profits in the USA, and this continues to increase (pp. 154–155). This is the system some are referring to as "casino capitalism." The consequence is that we are progressively haunted by a virtual economy that appears disconnected from any real, embodied human labor or consumption. Due to advanced information technologies, all this occurs "in the increasingly short 'instant,' the unit of neoliberal time" (Mann, p. 148). This leads to the "space-time compression" that Harvey (1990) discusses as a key feature of neoliberal culture. Rushkoff (2013) refers to the experienced effect as "digiphrenia," the alienation of our digital selves from our analog bodies (pp. 69–129). Theologians might detect in such developments a contemporary revival of Gnosticism, as the political, economic, and cultural dimensions of life become increasingly removed from the material world.

Finally, a number of scholars have argued that global neoliberalization might not have succeeded were it not aided by the imperial aspirations of the USA. In the late 1990s, John Gray (1998), a former conservative in Great Britain who influenced Margaret Thatcher, reversed course in his book *False Dawn*. Here he warns: "Only in the United States is the Enlightenment project of a global civilization still a living political faith.... In the post-communist era it animates the American project of a universal free market" (p. 101). Subsequently, the role of American imperialism in the dissemination of neoliberal thought and practice has been meticulously documented by award-winning journalist Naomi Klein's popular book, *The Shock Doctrine* (2007). More recently, in their thorough review *The Making of Global Capitalism*, Panitch and Gindin (2012) have argued that the USA has become an "informal empire" that has succeeded in its efforts to restructure other states in order to create a global habitat for competitive markets. This was effectively symbolized, they observe, on the cover of *Time* following the USA's interventions to ameliorate the 1997–1998 Asian financial crisis, which was itself one of what has become a series of global crises created by the excesses of neoliberalization. The cover featured a photo of Federal Reserve director Alan Greenspan, along with the US Treasury Department's Robert Rubin and Lawrence Summers, beneath a banner hailing them as "The Committee to Save the World" (p. 18).

This has not resulted, however, in a world in which every state and culture looks like a copy of the USA. Neoliberalization has a remarkable capacity, as many expert observers have noted, to merge with particular geographies and cultures, creating indigenous forms everywhere it goes. Some of these have been summarized in a volume edited by Saad-Filho and Johnston (2005). I have already referred to Springer's (2010) observation that neoliberalization hybridizes and mutates as it spans the globe, as well as Mirowski's (2013) reflections on its capacity to absorb its own failures and incongruities. This turns neoliberalization into an incredibly adaptive ongoing process, as it quickly morphs to outmaneuver its critics and opponents. In his insightful analysis in *Cool Capitalism* (2009), McGuigan explores particular instances in the cultural dimension where neoliberalization incorporates disaffection, literally turning opposition into novel paths to corporate profits. This point is also forcefully made by French sociologist Luc Boltanski and management theorist Eve Chiapello in their monumental book *The New Spirit of Capitalism* (1999/2007). Capitalism, they argue, has evolved from its first spirit, epitomized in Weber's description of liberal capitalism, through a second phase called "organized capitalism," which dominated during the mid-to-late twentieth century, to the "new spirit," which emphasizes creativity, networking, and the shift of labor from conventional employment to project work. This new spirit, which emerged during the period from 1965 to 1995, incorporates the zeitgeist of the global rebellions of the 1960s into its agenda, emphasizing the autonomy and creativity of individual laborers while simultaneously capturing their efforts in the service of the new capitalism. In the USA, according to Peck's assessment (2010, Chap. 5), this appears most clearly in the immense popularity of Richard Florida's book *The Rise of the Creative Class* (2002/2012), and the attendant "cool cities" movement, with the characteristic "hipsterization strategies" of cities attempting to attract highly educated and technologically savvy younger workers. The individual residents of the "cool cities," in turn, bear the features of the new spirit of capitalism. These new subjects oddly resemble the postmodern self, described so well by psychoanalyst Stephen Mitchell (1993). They manifest a psyche that is "multiple, discontinuous, and fluid"—a point to which I will return in the next chapter.

We are left then with a new world order unlike any we have seen before. It is, in brief, a global hegemony that does not look like a hegemony, one that claims to be a liberator of humankind even as it shackles the human soul. This order is aptly summarized by Wendy Brown (2015):

> Thus the paradox of neoliberalism as a global phenomenon, ubiquitous and omnipresent, yet disunified and nonidentical with itself. This dappled, striated, and flickering complexion is also the face of an order replete with contradiction and disavowal, structuring markets it claims to liberate from structure, intensely governing subjects it claims to free from government, strengthening and retasking states it claims to abjure (pp. 48–49).

NEOLIBERALISM AS A CULTURAL PROJECT

The preceding overview of the history of neoliberalization focuses on the political and economic dimensions of this process. However, as the last two paragraphs already insinuate, this is not all there is to say about neoliberalism. Sociologists Centeno and Cohen (2012) have argued that neoliberalism is not just an economic and political project but also a *cultural* project. Indeed, if this were not the case, my explorations in the next chapter into the ways neoliberalism has transformed the social, interpersonal, and psychological spheres would not be conceivable. For now, I will simply comment on the manner in which neoliberalism is a cultural project.

We must first understand that cultural transformation was part of the neoliberal impulse from its very inception. As Davies (2014) observes: "A defining trait of neoliberalism is that it abandons this liberal conceit of separate economic, social and political spheres, evaluating all three according to a single economic logic" (p. 20). Hayek, in *The Road to Serfdom* (1944/2007), proclaims: "This is really the crux of the matter. Economic control is not merely control of a sector of human life which can be separated from the rest; it is the control of the means for all our ends" (pp. 126–127). This was concisely formulated by Margaret Thatcher in a famous 1981 interview published in London's *Sunday Times* (Butt, 1981): "Economics are the method; the object is to change the heart and soul." Foucault (1979/2008), in a prescient analysis of neoliberalism in his final set of lectures, saw this clearly: "So it is not a question of freeing an empty space, but of taking the formal principles of a market economy and referring and relating them to, of projecting them on to a general art of government" (p. 131). Extending Foucault's spirit to the present, Wendy Brown (2015) encapsulates the ultimate successes of the market's governmentality:

> Neoliberalization is generally more termitelike than lionlike ... its mode of reason boring in capillary fashion into the trunks and branches of workplaces, schools, public agencies, social and political discourse, and above all, the subject. Even the termite metaphor is not quite apt: Foucault would remind us that any ascendant political rationality is not only destructive, but brings new subjects, conduct, relations, and worlds into being (pp. 35–36).

It is possible, once again, to historicize this development. Whereas Marxist revisionists, such as Duménil and Lévy (2011) and Harvey (2005), trace the emergence of neoliberal power to a capitalist "crisis of accumulation" that led to "stagflation" in the 1970s, the culture of neoliberalism largely evolved, in parallel and overlapping the economic crisis, from the sociopolitical upheavals that spanned the globe in 1968. This observation has been put forward by several scholars, including Dufour (2003/2008, p. 157), McGuigan (2009, pp. 20–30), Harvey (2005, pp. 41–42), Boltanski and Chiapello (1999/2007, pp. 167–202), and Jones (2012, p. 15). These broad social engagements, which corresponded in the USA with the civil rights movement, the anti-war movement, and second-wave feminism, emphasized individual freedoms and distrusted the state and other collective forms of authority. This was surely a crisis also for neoliberal interests, with their dependence on social stability and "law and order." However, we may justifiably see this as an original instance of neoliberalism's ability to overcome and incorporate opposition. As briefly mentioned in the previous section, the response of neoliberalization was to co-opt the libertarian spirit of these protest movements, merging them into its own project of radical individualism and anti-collectivism. The result was a new way of organizing society. Thus Dardot and Laval (2009/2013), drawing upon Foucault, assert: "Neo-liberalism does not only respond to a crisis of accumulation: it responds to a crisis of governmentality" (p. 11). They conclude: "at stake in neo-liberalism is nothing more, nor less, than the *form of our existence*—the way in which we are led to conduct ourselves, to relate to others and to ourselves" (p. 3, emphasis in original).

What is this neoliberal form of existence? Dardot and Laval (2009/2013), Davies (2014) and Brown (2015) are in general agreement: neoliberal societies are founded upon the principles of *competition* and *inequality*.

Dardot and Laval contend that neoliberalism is not simply an economic policy or ideology, but is a global *rationality* that organizes all of life "in accordance with the universal principle of competition" (p. 4). Likewise, Brown (2015) reiterates Foucault's observation that neoliberalism is a radical departure from previous versions of capitalism, in that "competition replaces exchange as the market's root principle and basic good" (p. 36). She continues: "This subtle shift from exchange to competition as the essence of the market means that all market actors are rendered as little capitals (rather than as owners, workers, and consumers) competing with, rather than exchanging with each other" (p. 36).

In such a society, every individual becomes an entrepreneur, managing and marketing the self as a personal enterprise and investment. This is evident in the world of social media such as Facebook and LinkedIn, as well as dating websites, where one's profile becomes a personal form of self-marketing. It is even apparent in the academy:

> The best university scholars are characterized as entrepreneurial and investment savvy, not simply by obtaining grants or fellowships, but by generating new projects and publications from old research, calculating publication and presentation venues, and circulating themselves and their work according to what will enhance their value (Brown, 2015, pp. 36–37).

Moreover, because each person must depend on their own creativity and effort alone, "we have no guarantee of security, protection, or even survival." Each individual subject "is at persistent risk of failure, redundancy and abandonment through no doing of its own, regardless of how savvy and responsible it is" (Brown, 2015, p. 37). Social and corporate risks are shifted onto vulnerable individuals, who are then left to their own fate. Due to the dismantling of social-security programs by neoliberal policies, "this jeopardy reaches down to minimum needs for food and shelter" (p. 37). This helps explain why my psychotherapy patients today, compared to those during the mid-1980s, experience themselves as living on the edge of a precipice.

In a system in which competition replaces exchange, Brown asserts, "inequality replaces equality" (p. 64). In the words of Davies (2014), "To argue in favour of competition and competitiveness is necessarily to argue in favour of inequality, given that competitive activity is defined partly by the fact that it pursues an unequal outcome" (p. 37). Davies contends that this eventually results in "*multiple inequalities*": "The inequality that occurs within the market sphere is separate from the inequality that occurs within the cultural sphere, which is separate from the inequality that occurs within the political sphere, and so on" (p. 35, emphasis in original). We will see this in the following chapter, where it will become apparent that inequality is recapitulated in the social, interpersonal, and even psychological spheres.

Finally, founding society upon competition and inequality necessarily enhances the level of violence within society. Society is reconceived as an arena where the "survival of the fittest" is the order of the day. Brown (2015) notes: "Competition yields winners and losers; capital succeeds by destroying or cannibalizing other capitals" (p. 64). This is an order, she argues, where the tenet of self-interest has finally been supplanted by the law of self-sacrifice: "In short, *homo oeconomicus* today may no longer have interest at its heart, indeed, may no longer have a heart at all" (p. 84). Generally, scholars critical of neoliberalism have highlighted the "Darwinian" character of neoliberal culture, with its emphasis on isolated individualism and competition. Some, such as Susan Searls Giroux (2010), have gone further, suggesting that neoliberal culture is Sadean, referring to the work and demeanor of the French radical philosopher Marquis de Sade (from whose infamy we have derived the word sadism). She concludes:

> The essential plot ingredients of Sade's malevolent, imaginary universe are uncannily recapitulated in the hard realities of a racially driven neoliberalized society that I have already sketched above: ruthless, efficient instrumentalization; the severing of all social bonds; compulsory amoralism; violence transvalued as pleasure, luxury, indulgence, spectacle; icy, emotionless judgement duly capable of producing endless corpses; erotic excess that hardens into indifference and apathy; relentless social fragmentation and violent isolation; the dissolution of thought; the exercise of force and domination that quickly betrays itself as masochistic self-destruction. A tale of two sovereignties—the sadistic and the neoliberalized—both predicated on absolute negation (p. 17).

Giroux laments: "one wonders if today Sade could elicit a blush from a child" (p. 17). Giroux is not alone. The American Pulitzer Prize–winning journalist Chris Hedges (2009) surveys the cultural climate in the USA and declares: "Sadism dominates the culture. It runs like an electric current through reality television and trash-talk programs, is at the core of pornography, and fuels the compliant, corporate collective" (p. 92). If neoliberal culture is even a fraction as malevolent as Giroux and Hedges contend, alert pastoral theologians and others who care for souls will sit up and take notice. What they are proposing is that the neoliberal paradigm is generating immense suffering at every level of society, and responding to suffering defines what we are about.

LOOKING AWAY (I): POSTMODERN THEORIES AS DIVERSIONS

Discussing the cultural dimensions of neoliberalism brings me to the first of two sections in this book I call "looking away." These sections concern complex issues that function either to obscure our vision or to avert our gaze as we attempt to critically assess the processes of neoliberalization and their effects. I must address these matters because, in my judgment, they make it more difficult to identify what caring for souls demands of us in the current age. This particular section focuses on the ways neoliberalism has co-opted postmodern discourse so that the ideals of such discourse have become, perhaps unwittingly, complicit in what Dardot and Laval (2009/2013) call the neoliberal "global rationality" or "world-reason" (p. 3).

I must confess this is a section I had rather not write. It produces in me a vertigo that arises whenever I am about to rush in where angels fear to tread. This anxiety has two sources. First, I am no expert in postmodern philosophies. I find the primary sources—the writings of French intellectuals such as Derrida, Lyotard, Foucault, Deleuze, and others—difficult to read, much less fully comprehend. So I am usually left to rely on colleagues who understand their thought far better than I do. Second, these theories have shaped the work of at least an entire generation of academics, especially in the humanities. This includes religious studies and theology. And it includes my own work. Indeed, the spirit of Foucault (though not necessarily his vocabulary) infuses the next chapter of this book, particularly his explorations of governmentality. Thus criticizing these theories can feel like a betrayal of one's parents, and causes me to fear (perhaps neurotically so) the disapproval of my academic peers. I will begin by pointing to historical markers of the emergence of this postmodern–neoliberal alignment, follow up by articulating a false binary that facilitated this collusion, then inviting several theorists who have addressed this complicity to speak. Finally, I will conclude by identifying an approach that may help us move past this theoretical gridlock.

In the previous section, I recalled that an initial example of the neoliberal capacity to incorporate the opposition was its transformation of the social protests that broke out internationally in 1968. Harvey (2005) notes that these movements "had social justice as a primary political objective." However, they also "were strongly inflected with the desire for greater personal freedoms" (p. 41). Harvey argues that there was an uneasy tension between these motives: "Pursuit of social justice presupposes social solidarities and a willingness to submerge individual wants, needs, and desires in the cause of some more general struggle" (p. 41). Neoliberal rhetoric, he continues, was able to exploit this tension, and succeeded in driving a wedge between the "libertarianism, identity politics," and "multiculturalism" of these movements and "the social forces ranged in pursuit of social justice" (p. 41). Harvey then concludes:

> Neoliberalization required both politically and economically the construction of a neoliberal market-based populist culture of differentiated consumerism and individual libertarianism. As such it proved more than a little compatible with that cultural impulse called 'post-modernism' which had long been lurking in the wings but could now emerge full-blown as both a cultural and an intellectual dominant. This was the challenge that corporations and class elites set out to finesse in the 1980s (p. 42).

Boltanski and Chiapello (1999/2007) contend that the "new spirit of capitalism" grew out of these same movements, as the new leaders of corporate management drew upon the leftist sentiments of their youth:

> Thus, for example, the qualities that are guarantees of success in this new spirit—autonomy, spontaneity, rhizomorphous capacity, multitasking, ... conviviality, openness to others and novelty, availability, creativity, visionary intuition, sensitivity to differences, listening to lived experience and receptiveness to a whole range of experiences, being attracted to informality and the search for interpersonal contacts—these are taken directly from the repertoire of May 1968 (p. 97).

The similarities here to Deleuzean descriptions of rhizomatous becoming are striking, a fact not lost on the authors (pp. 144–145, 454–455). Dufour (2003/2008) likewise observes that when neoliberalism was first emerging into cultural prominence, "Deleuze thought he could outflank capitalism." He then concludes: "What Deleuze failed to see was that, far from making it possible to get beyond capitalism, his programme merely predicted its future. It now looks as though the new capitalism has learned its Deleuzean lesson well" (p. 11).

The characteristics of postmodernity are apparent in contemporary media outlets and the politics of those who support neoliberal agendas. Jodi Dean (2009) argues that the "academic left" won the culture wars only to find its methods adopted by the political right:

> The victory of the academic left in the culture wars should be understood along similar lines: the prominence of politically active Christian fundamentalists, Fox News, and the orchestrations of Bush advisor Karl Rove all demonstrate the triumph of postmodernism. These guys take social construction—packaging, marketing, and representation—absolutely seriously. They put it to work (p. 7).

Dennis Loo (2011) comments on this same scene: "Postmodernists are not fans of George W. Bush, but they share his worldview regarding empirical data and objective reality" (p. 4). In a world where "there is nothing outside the text" (Derrida), politicians can create reality at will.

The same goes for an economy in which desire is created by marketing and capital depends on financial investments rather than labor. Eagleton (1996), observing the congruity between postmodern theory and financial markets, notes:

> Its nervousness of such concepts as truth has alarmed the bishops and charmed the business executives, just as its compulsion to place words like "reality" in scare quotes unsettles the pious *Bürger* in the bosom of his family but is music to his ears in his advertising agency. It has floated the signifier in ways which cause the autocrats to reach for their banal certitudes, and in doing so found itself mimicking a society founded on the fiction of credit in which money spawns money as surely as signs breed signs. Neither financiers nor semioticians are greatly enamoured of material referents (p. 28, emphasis in original).

Meanwhile, Lisa Duggan (2003) notes that progressive social movements in the 1960s and 1970s combined multicultural and identity concerns with emphases on class conflict and labor. Beginning with the rise of neoliberal dominance in the 1980s, however, the progressive left was increasingly divided into opposing factions by an "economics/culture split" (pp. xvi–xx). On the "culture" side of this binary, Duggan observes: "the identity politics camps are increasingly divorced from any critique of global capitalism" (p. xx). The "identity politics" dimension of the left currently dominates leftist political discourse and theory (Dean, 2009). This camp typically rejects Marxist analysis, and its consideration of class conflict, as "essentialist." Intellectuals on this side of the divide are taken with postmodern theories, which focus upon cultural and identity-specific forms of knowledge and discourse. Espousing slogans such as "the personal is political," which appear undeniably true, they nonetheless tend to collapse the political into the personal. This evacuates the realm of conventional politics, concerned as it is with the formation of common interests, public policy, and the public good (Dean, 2009). On the "economics" side of the binary, Duggan continues, "critiques of global capitalism and neoliberalism ... attack and dismiss cultural and identity politics at their peril" (p. xx). This divide between economics and culture has become so apparent to scholars across disciplines that many are suggesting a range of strategies to mend this rift in the left. In addition to Duggan, these include Brown (1995), Connolly (1999), Dean (2009), Fraser (1997), and Springer (2012). The point here is that postmodern theories tend to fall down firmly on the "culture" side of this binary. One consequence has been that social justice is now routinely identified with cultural and identity issues, which means that justice is reduced almost entirely to undoing discrimination. In the meantime, the concern for economic justice and equality, with its attention to class, slips from view. This happens to suit neoliberal powers just fine. I will return our attention to this false binary at the conclusion of this section.

Turning to others who perceive an alliance between postmodern theories and neoliberalism, we look first to those we might expect to take such a stance—the Marxist revisionists. These include not only Harvey (1990, 2005), but Fredric Jameson (1991) and Terry Eagleton (1996). Jameson (1991), for example, observes how postmodern critical theories have inadvertently supported neoliberal agendas. He effectively accuses these methodologies of Gnosticism in their approach to theory building, in which "the deeper logic of the postmodern ... imperceptibly turns into its own theory and the theory of itself" (p. xii). The title of his book—*Postmodernism, or, The Cultural Logic of Late Capitalism*—reveals his conclusion: that late capitalism is the embodiment of postmodernity. Eagleton, for his part, acknowledges that postmodern critical theories have succeeded in gaining a hearing for marginalized voices and many of the world's downtrodden. At the same time, he argues, such theories have often committed "egregious excesses" (p. 24). And so, what are these "excesses"? First, they tend to re-create orthodox binaries. Eagleton (1996) contends:

> For all its vaunted openness to the Other, postmodernism can be quite as exclusive and censorious as the orthodoxies it opposes. One may, by and large, speak of human culture but not human nature, gender but not class, the body but not biology, jouissance but not justice, post-colonialism but not the petty bourgeoisie. It is a thoroughly orthodox heterodoxy, which like any imaginary form of identity needs its bogeymen and straw targets in order to stay in business (p. 26).

Second, the excesses of postmodernism may include a cultural relativism. In their more radical forms, such theories emphasize the incommensura-bility of local cultures to the degree that they lose ethical import. In their fear of affirming common humanity (much less the dreaded human "uni-versals"), they can lose moral standing. Again I channel Eagleton (1996):

> But in seeking to cut the ground from under its opponents' feet, postmod-ernism finds itself unavoidably pulling the rug out from under itself, leaving itself with no more reason why we should resist fascism than the feebly prag-matic plea that fascism is not the way we do things in Sussex or Sacramento (p. 28).

Later Eagleton notes: "Culturalism is quite as much a form of reduction-ism as biologism or economism, words at the sound of which all stout postmodernists have been trained to make the vampire sign" (p. 74).

Finally, postmodern theory exhibits a complicity, however unintended, with the peculiar character of neoliberal hegemony. Such theories tend to emphasize "hybridity" and pluralism regarding culture. However, as Eagleton (1996) observes: "Capitalism is the most pluralistic order his-tory has ever known, restlessly transgressing boundaries and dismantling oppositions, pitching together diverse life-forms and continually overflow-ing the measure" (p. 133). The position of the Marxist revisionists may best be summed up by geographer Hans van Zon (2013), who states: "*Postmodernism disarmed the left with respect to neoliberalism.* Both ideolo-gies helped to focus people on themselves (or sub-culture) rather than the public good" (p. 112, emphasis added).

But lately such criticism has not been limited to Marxist revisionists. It is also emerging in quarters that have been dominated by postmodern critical theories, such as postcolonial theories and critical feminist theories.

Neil Lazarus (2011) excoriates his postcolonialist colleagues for their rigid adherence to poststructuralist orthodoxy, a devotion he believes at times causes them to overlook the claims upon common humanity made by indigenous artists and writers in previously ignored or diaspora populations. Using specific examples, he demonstrates that, while interviewing these artists or reviewing such literature, many postcolonial scholars simply miss the elements within such work that do not fit into the postmodern sensibility (pp. 21–88).

Lazarus (2011) also notes that postcolonial theory developed in parallel with neoliberalism, in the late 1970s, and, like neoliberalism, came to full flower in the 1990s. Furthermore, he asserts: "Especially after the collapse of historical communism in 1989, it was disposed to pronounce Marxism dead and buried also" (p. 9). For Homi Bhabha, Lazarus observes: "'Postcolonial criticism,' as he understands and champions it, is constitutively anti-Marxist … it disavows nationalism as such and refuses an antagonistic or struggle-based model of politics in favour of one that emphasises 'cultural difference'" (p. 12). In other words, in terms of the economics/culture split Duggan (2003) and others describe, the postcolonial critics Lazarus reviews are committed to the "culture" side of the divide. Accordingly, they have largely declined to criticize capitalism. As Lazarus avows: "Within postcolonial studies, it is notable that the core concepts of 'colonialism' and even 'imperialism' are routinely severed from the concept of 'capitalism'" (p. 36). This includes attention to class. In Lazarus' words: "Although it is ubiquitously cited in passing … the category of class is seldom afforded sustained or specific attention in mainstream postcolonial criticism" (p. 36). Again, Lazarus is suggesting that a postmodern lens has prevented many postcolonial theorists from criticizing neoliberal capitalism.

Among feminists, Nancy Fraser (1997, 2009, 2013a) is an exemplar of those who are re-assessing the feminist movement in light of neoliberal developments. Fraser campaigns against feminist theory's exclusive reliance on poststructuralist analysis, arguing this must be supplemented with retrievable aspects of Marxist theories. Like Duggan, she perceives that neoliberal ascendancy has produced a division between "the social left" and "the cultural left," a situation she terms "the 'postsocialist' condition" (1997, p. 3). She calls upon critical theorists to "rebut the claim that we must make an either/or choice between the politics of redistribution and the politics of recognition" (1997, p. 4). To accomplish this, she argues, feminist theorists must go beyond the refusal of all normative or "totalizing" thinking based on a commitment to "postmodernism" or "deconstruction" (p. 4). In a column written for *The Guardian* (2013b), she employs this integrative style of thinking to show that contemporary feminism has unfortunately become "entangled in a dangerous liaison with neoliberal efforts to build a free-market society" (para. 2).

Some Foucault scholars are now advising a rapprochement between the "economics" and "culture" sides of the current impasse. Wendy Brown's *Undoing the Demos* (2015) may be the best example. First, while drawing on Foucault's insights to demonstrate how neoliberalism governs society, human relationships, and even the subject, Brown highlights deficiencies in Foucault's method vis-à-vis its ability to confront the excesses of neoliberalization. Exploring Foucault's analysis of neoliberalism in his final set of lectures, Brown remarks on "his odd neglect of capital as a form of domination" (p. 73). She concludes:

> Foucault averted his glance from capital itself as a historical and social force. Appearing with striking infrequency in these lectures, when capital is mentioned, it is usually to heap scorn on the idea that it follows necessary logics or entails a system of domination (p. 75).

Second, Brown observes that Foucault's focus on governmentality excludes attention to the political as such: "There is no *political* body, no demos acting in concert ... there are few social forces from below and no shared powers of rule or shared struggles for freedom" (p. 73, emphasis in original). Thus Foucault's methodology contributes to the split Duggan and Brown identify between cultural analysis (which is concerned solely with governed and resisting subjects and identities) and political/economic activity. Brown (2015) attributes this to Foucault's "antagonism to Marxism" (p. 74), and then points the way toward the required approach:

> The point here is not to correct Foucault with Marx, but to bring forward certain dimensions of Marx's analysis of capitalism that would have to be welded to Foucault's appreciation of neoliberal reason to generate a rich account of neoliberal dedemocratization (p. 77).

Such an integrated method is precisely what is now necessary if we are to adequately understand neoliberalism's production and transformation of human suffering, as well as how the care of souls may respond to today's circumstances. Geographer Simon Springer (2012) articulates the method quite well. Poststructuralism and Marxism, he argues, are complementary rather than incommensurable. Springer notes that even Derrida, Foucault, and Deleuze were not entirely anti-Marxist, but rather attempted a reinterpretation that in some ways parallels Marxist analysis (pp. 139–140), a point that is expounded at length by Peters (2001). It would not be fair or accurate, therefore, to say that these important thinkers are "neoliberals in disguise," or even that they imagined any complicity between their philosophies and capitalism, much less neoliberalization. The problem, rather, may have more to do with the ways their theories have been appropriated by what Jodi Dean (2009) calls "the academic and typing left" (p. 4) and by popular culture at large. The critical issue, Springer notes, is to use discourse analysis to understand how neoliberal rationality shapes human subjects and relationships, while also recognizing how neoliberalization effects "material practices on the ground," such as "state formation and policy and program implementation that characterize the specificities of 'actually existing neoliberalism' … or neoliberalization in practice" (p. 141). In keeping with my use of Connolly's (2013) theory in the next chapter, I see cultural processes of subject (identity) formation and economic/political processes of state and policy formation as self-regulating systems that are nevertheless highly entangled. I must agree with Springer, then, that "a considered understanding of how power similarly operates in both a Gramscian sense of hegemony and a Foucauldian sense of governmentality points toward a dialectical relationship" (p. 143). In the next chapter, therefore, I will examine how neoliberalism forms social, interpersonal, and psychological systems in ways that are congruent with Foucault's notion of governmentality (though without taking Foucault as the point of departure), while in Chap. 4, I will explore how neoliberalism as a hegemony, or sociopolitical paradigm, operates in a normative fashion to form and transform human suffering. I do not consider these approaches to be irreconcilable or necessarily in conflict.

By rejecting the aforementioned economics/culture dichotomy, I believe my colleagues in pastoral theology and all those involved in the care of souls can better avoid unwitting complicity with neoliberal hegemony. Stated positively, we could, for example, do a better job addressing the uneven attention we have given to the dynamics of patriarchy compared to those of class conflict. Few of us, I suspect, would tolerate passing references to "the evils of patriarchy" without conducting in-depth and meticulous analyses of exactly how sexism pervades society, religious and other institutions, personal relationships, and the individual psyche. The same goes for racism and other forms of discrimination. And yet for too long, we have settled for oblique allusions to class-based forms of oppression without comparable attention to the intricate ways this sort of suffering is perpetrated through all dimensions of society—institutional, interpersonal, and psychological.

Finally, I must add that clarifications around methodology—such as undertaken in this section—do not ultimately constitute the identities of pastoral theologians or caregivers. We do not undertake our theory building or caregiving because we are postmodern thinkers or Marxist ideologists, regardless of how useful we may occasionally find such analytic tools. As Crossley (2012) has observed, opposition to contemporary capitalism no longer emanates solely from Marxism, but emerges from "a range of ideological perspectives which are not necessarily Marxist, such as human rights activism, direct action, anarchism ... environmentalism, certain feminist movements, animal rights activism, certain church and religious movements and so on" (p. 25). For pastoral theologians and caregivers who are Christian, the motivation and inspiration for our work arise from a historical community and interpretive tradition that locates its origin in the movement that gathered around Jesus. That neoliberal rationality and practice are profoundly incongruent with the Jesus portrayed in the Gospels should already be apparent. I will take this up in more detail later in the book, especially in the postscripts.

Neoliberalism and Economic Inequality

Economic inequality as an inescapable consequence of neoliberalization has been emphasized primarily, though not exclusively, by Marxist revisionists, such as Duménil and Lévy (2011) and Harvey (2005). Theorists engaging neoliberalism from the standpoint of governmentality or discourse analysis are often critical of such a perspective. Dardot and Laval (2009/2013), for instance, determine that Harvey "continues to adhere to an explanatory schema that is decidedly unoriginal" (p. 8). It is important to notice, however, that neither Dardot and Laval nor other Foucauldians, such as Wendy Brown (2015), deny that economic inequality has been a widespread result of neoliberal processes. They simply argue that attention to the rationality and discourse of neoliberalism offers a better way to see what is truly original about its way of constructing society. This is a good place to understand the necessity of rejecting the either/or thinking of the economics/culture divide discussed in the previous section. Neoliberalism is *both* a form of hegemonic control that serves the interests of financial elites *and* a form of governance that adapts to local circumstances and shapes individual subjects and their personal relationships. We do not have to choose. If we devalue the viewpoints of Marxist theorists, we will fail to comprehend critical aspects of the neoliberal project, as well as envisioning possibilities for opposition. Making a similar point, Springer (2012) concludes:

> Thus neoliberalism as a concept allows poverty and inequality experienced across multiple sites to find a point of similitude, whereas disarticulation undermines efforts to build and sustain shared aims of resistance beyond the micro-politics of the local (p. 136).

Stuart Hall (2011) states the matter succinctly: "Hegemony is a tricky concept and provokes muddled thinking. No project achieves 'hegemony' as a completed project. It is a process, not a state of being" (p. 26). Still, he reasons: "However, in ambition, depth, degree of break with the past, variety of sites being colonised, impact on common sense and shift in the social architecture, neoliberalism does constitute a *hegemonic project*" (p. 27, emphasis in original).

In the remainder of this chapter, as well as Chap. 4, my analysis builds mainly on this notion of neoliberalism as a hegemony or paradigm, whereas in Chap. 3, I will depend primarily on the perspective of neoliberalism as a form of governance and rationality.

I have already commented on the emergence of inequality as part of the narrative of neoliberalization. There can be little doubt that economic inequality was an integral presumption of the neoliberal project from its inception. Concerning Hayek's prototypical vision, Jones (2012) remarks:

> It also implied a fundamental acceptance of substantive inequality—an essential feature of neoliberal ideas throughout all three phases of its history. An understanding of inequality as unavoidable, even desirable, gets at the crux of the conflict between neoliberal ideals and those of the New Deal liberals or social democrats—there was an acceptance of the rectitude of different outcomes for different individuals for neoliberal theorists (p. 63).

At the level of theory, inequality is deemed an essential ground for motivating individuals to work hard and inspiring them to act creatively and ambitiously. Inequality, too, is essential to the notion of competition, which presupposes the existence of winners and losers. Friedman (1970) famously argued, at the beginning of the neoliberal revolution, that the only social responsibility of corporations is to increase shareholder profits. Inequality is the unavoidable result of such an ideology. Eventually, increasing profits necessitates either increased unemployment or decreased wages, or both. Others have maintained that neoliberalism began as a deliberate reclamation of economic and political power by wealthy elites. Duménil and Lévy (2011) assert, for example, that neoliberalism has been a reassertion of upper-class dominance from the outset. Harvey (2005), echoing this view, concludes: "Redistributive effects and increasing social inequality have in fact been such a persistent feature of neoliberalization as to be regarded as structural to the whole project" (p. 16).

The impact on public policy is well-known by now: decreased taxes for large corporations and the wealthy, regressive taxes that shift the financial burden to the middle and working class, regulations that restrict collective bargaining for laborers, deconstruction of the social safety net, an overall lessening of public goods and services, and so on. Using data provided by the Internal Revenue Service, Piketty and Saez (2003) graphically record the consequent increase of income inequality in the USA. Saez (2015) recently updated this data through 2014 (Fig. 2.1), demonstrating that inequality has continued to increase since the start of the Great Recession in 2008.

The graph displays the percentage of total household annual income in the USA that is captured by the top 10 % of wage-earning households. The most noteworthy figure is represented by black triangles, which designates income including capital gains (a prominent form of income for wealthier families). Here we see that in 1929, on the eve of the Great Depression, the top 10 % garnered almost 50 % of the total household income. With the implementation of the New Deal, this rate fell precipitously, and hovered near the 35 % level until the initiation of neoliberal policies in the early 1980s. Since that point, inequality has soared back to levels even higher than the 1920s, during "the first Gilded Age" (Fraser, 2015). This has just been confirmed in a separate study by researchers at the Economic Policy Institute (Sommeiller, Price, & Wazeter, 2016). Between 2009 and 2013, they record, the top 1 % of income-earning households in the USA garnered 85.1 % of the total income growth (p. 1). Sadly, even these figures fail to tell the whole story, which is revealed when we consider the distribution of total accumulated wealth in the USA during this "second Gilded Age" (Fraser, 2015). Currently, the top 1 % of US households controls 40 % of the total wealth, with the top 0.1 % accounting for most

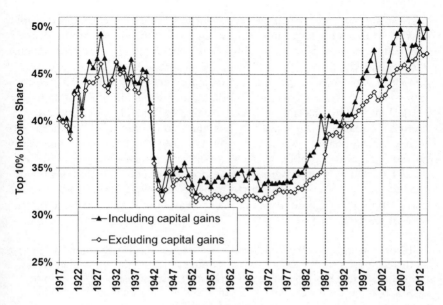

Fig. 2.1 Increasing income inequality in the USA, 1917–2014. Income is defined as market income (and excludes government transfers). In 2014, top decile includes all families with annual income above $121,400

of the recent gains (Saez & Zucman, 2014). Meanwhile, the bottom 80 % is getting by on a mere 7 %.[1]

The growing economic inequality in the USA has now been abundantly documented, most recently by Gilbert (2015), who traces its effects on "the American class structure." Like many academics in the USA, however, Gilbert summarily attributes increasing inequality to an array of issues reflecting "big changes in the economy," without identifying neo-liberalization, or even capitalism generally, as the culprit (pp. 264–265). However, in their recent joint effort, *The New Class Society: Goodbye American Dream?*, American sociologists Wysong, Perrucci, and Wright (2014) do not hesitate to name neoliberalism as the overarching rationale for changes in "the new economy" (pp. 45–47). Similarly, political scientists Hacker and Pierson (2010) argue that the role of technological change in the workplace, financial globalization, and inequality of education has been exaggerated. Instead, they document evidence that the primary cause for increasing inequality is a takeover of US politics orchestrated by powers committed to a radicalized "free market" capitalism. The details regarding this seizure of state power, with massive inequality as the consequence, have also been documented by Gilens (2012) and Gilens and Page (2014).

Comparable global usurpations of state power by free-market interests have been traced by many scholars, including Häring and Douglas (2012) and William Davies (2014). Again, as Reid-Henry (2015) documents, inequality is not simply the inevitable outcome of globalization or technological change. Rather, its origin is political. Economic inequality appears across the globe, wherever neoliberal policies are implemented. A 2011 report by the Organisation for Economic Co-operation and Development (OECD), a consortium of several of the world's most prosperous countries, noted that inequality was on the rise in most of the nations it represents:

> Income inequality followed different patterns across OECD countries and there are signs that levels may be converging at a common and higher average. Inequality first began to rise in the late 1970s and early 1980s in some Anglophone countries, notably in the United Kingdom and the United States, followed by a more widespread increase from the late 1980s on. The most recent trends show a widening gap between poor and rich in some of the already high-inequality countries, such as Israel and the United States. But countries such as Denmark, Germany and Sweden, which have traditionally had low inequality, are no longer spared from the rising inequality trend: in fact, inequality grew more in these three countries than anywhere else during the past decade (p. 6).

The timing of these developments—"from the late 1980s on"—indicates their relationship to the globalization of neoliberalism. A subsequent OECD study (2012) confirmed the continuation of these trends. Similarly, the World Economic Forum (2011) predicted that inequality would prove to be the most critical global problem for at least the next decade.[2]

INEQUALITY AND SOCIAL WELL-BEING

Inequality is not only a prominent feature of neoliberal societies; it is also a key indicator of social health. In a masterful study demonstrating the connection between economic equality and social well-being, British researchers Richard Wilkinson and Kate Pickett (2009) conducted a metastatistical analysis of empirical studies from a span of several decades. Though the average level of wealth within countries did not predict social well-being (once basic material needs were met), Wilkinson and Pickett determined that the extent of economic inequality was highly predictive of social well-being. Focusing on the 23 richest economies, they examined the relationship between inequality and nine measures of social well-being: level of trust, mental illness (including addiction), mortality rates, obesity, children's educational performance, teenage births, homicides, rates of incarceration, and social mobility (p. 19). Averaging these indicators, they displayed the statistical correlation between poor social well-being and inequality (Fig. 2.2)[3].

The steep gradient of the line of statistical significance indicates a high correlation between inequality and these nine measures. This illustrates that the USA, though wealthier than other countries in terms of gross domestic product (GDP), has—among other things—significantly shorter average life spans, more mental illness and obesity, and higher rates of

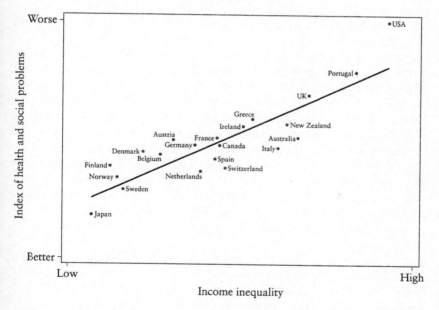

Fig. 2.2   Income inequality and social well-being: The world's 23 wealthiest countries

incarceration than any of the other countries. Wilkinson and Pickett discovered the correlation to hold true for all nine measures, even when
considered separately. The correlation for mental illness and drug use was
even higher than most other indicators (2009, pp. 63–72). Given the high
level of inequality in the USA, Wilkinson and Pickett looked more closely
at this country, and determined that inequality continued to predict social
well-being even when they analyzed each of the 50 states individually.
Again, states with higher inequality had lower scores on social well-being,
regardless of how wealthy the state might be.

However, Wilkinson and Pickett (2009) did not conclude that inequality is a direct *cause* of low levels of social well-being; they regarded it
as an *indicator* of decreased well-being. Inequality's relationship to well-
being, in other words, is overdetermined. It represents an intricate web of
interwoven factors. For example: societies with a high degree of inequality also tend to be more hierarchical and stratified, leading to increased
shame for individuals who perceive themselves as less successful. These
findings are similar to those of widely renowned epidemiologist Michael
Marmot (2004), who argues that inequality denotes a complex interre-
lationship between status, income, and power. Working independently
from Wilkinson and Pickett, Marmot discovered that individuals living in
highly stratified societies have worse physical, psychological, and relational
health, as well as higher mortality rates. Two other findings deserve close
inspection. First, like Wilkinson and Pickett, Marmot found that it is not
just the poor who suffer more in unequal societies. Rather, individuals in
every class suffer more in more unequal societies. Second, Marmot carefully studied the effects of social standing *within* particular societies, and
concluded that *where* individuals live on the social gradient predicts their
level of health. In a given society, people who are in lower classes have
worse health than those in higher classes. This holds true not just when
comparing the rich with the poor. It is also the case, for example, when
comparing individuals in the middle class to those in the upper class.

In summary, the neoliberalization of a society leads to increased levels
of inequality, which in turn signals an increase in human suffering of all
types. I cannot help but think that the immense implications of this will
astonish pastoral theologians, pastoral caregivers, and all others involved
in the care of souls. In light of the preponderance of evidence that neoliberalism is increasing suffering on a global level, we must question how
pastoral care and theology—which take their cues from human suffering—
have paid so little heed to contemporary capitalism. The correspondence

between economic inequality and human suffering is just the beginning of the story, however. Inequality, as I have argued, is merely a general (if complex) marker indicating a relationship between neoliberalism and the scope and intensity of human suffering. Investigating the specifics of how today's capitalism impacts suffering is a task that remains. We must still, in other words, connect the dots. Further examination will suggest that neoliberalism not only increases suffering but also is shaping *how* we are suffering. This will occupy our attention in the following chapter and beyond.

NOTES

1. A video illustrating US wealth distribution is available at http://www.youtube.com/watch?v=QPKKQnijnsM&list=FLucdX5GEDe 5ykVaPeXI-HGQ. References for the data are provided at the conclusion of the video.
2. The global increase of economic inequality over the last five decades has been visually summarized by a series of maps created by the University of Texas Inequality Project (UTIP). The maps are available at http://utip.gov.utexas.edu/. Last accessed August 3, 2015.
3. Slides based on the research in *The Spirit Level*, including one similar to the graphic used here, are open access and are available from The Equality Trust: http://www.slideshare.net/equalitytrust. Last accessed August 3, 2015.

REFERENCES

Bernays, E. (1928/2005). *Propaganda*. Brooklyn, NY: Ig Publishing.

Boas, T. C., & Gans-Morse, J. (2009). Neoliberalism: From new liberal philosophy to anti-liberal slogan. *Studies in Comparative International Development, 44*(2), 137–161.

Boltanski, L, & Chiapello, E. (1999/2007). *The new spirit of capitalism* (Gregory Elliott, Trans.). London: Verso.

Brown, W. (1995). *States of injury: Power and freedom in late modernity*. Princeton, NJ: Princeton University Press.

Brown, W. (2015). *Undoing the demos: Neoliberalism's stealth revolution*. Brooklyn, NY: Zone Books.

Butt, R. (1981, May 1). Mrs. Thatcher: The first two years. *The Sunday Times*. Retrieved August 6, 2015, from http://www.margaretthatcher.org/document/104475

Centeno, M. A., & Cohen, J. N. (2012). The arc of neoliberalism. *Annual Review of Sociology, 38,* 317–340.

Connolly, W. E. (1999). Assembling the left. *Boundary, 2, 26*(3), 47–54.

Connolly, W. E. (2013). *The fragility of things: Self-organizing processes, neoliberal fantasies, and democratic activism.* Durham, NC: Duke University Press.

Crossley, J. G. (2012). *Jesus in an age of neoliberalism: Quests, scholarship and ideology.* Sheffield: Equinox Publishing.

Dardot, P., & Laval, C. (2009/2013). *The new way of the world: On neo-liberal society* (Gregory Elliott, Trans.). London: Verso.

Davies, W. (2014). *The limits of neoliberalism: Authority, sovereignty and the logic of competition.* London: SAGE Publications.

Dean, J. (2009). *Democracy and other neoliberal fantasies: Communicative capitalism and left politics.* Durham, NC: Duke University Press.

DuFour, D.-R. (2003/2008). *The art of shrinking heads: On the new servitude of the liberated in the age of total capitalism* (David Macey, Trans.). Cambridge: Polity Press.

Duggan, L. (2003). *The twilight of equality? Neoliberalism, cultural politics, and the attack on democracy.* Boston, MA: Beacon Press.

Duménil, G., & Lévy, D. (2011). *The crisis of neoliberalism.* Cambridge, MA: Harvard University Press.

Eagleton, T. (1996). *The illusions of postmodernism.* Malden, MA: Blackwell Publishing.

Florida, R. (2002/2012). *The rise of the creative class: Revisited.* New York, NY: Basic Books.

Foucault, M. (1979/2008). In M. Senellart (Ed.), *The birth of biopolitics: Lectures at the College de France, 1978-1979* (Graham Burchell, Trans.). New York, NY: Picador.

Fraser, N. (1997). *Justice interruptus: Critical reflections on the "postsocialist" condition.* New York, NY: Routledge.

Fraser, N. (2009). Feminism, capitalism and the cunning of history. *New Left Review, 56*(March/April), 97–117.

Fraser, N. (2013a). *Fortunes of feminism: From state-managed capitalism to neoliberal crisis.* London: Verso.

Fraser, N. (2013b, October 13). How feminism became capitalism's handmaiden—And how to reclaim it. *The Guardian.* Retrieved February 28, 2016, from http://www.theguardian.com/commentisfree/2013/oct/14/feminism-capitalist-handmaiden-neoliberal

Fraser, S. (2015). *The age of acquiescence: The life and death of American resistance to organized wealth and power.* New York, NY: Little, Brown and Company.

Friedman, M. (1951). Neo-liberalism and its prospects. *Farmand, 17,* 89–93 Retrieved May 17, 2015, from http://0055d26.netsolhost.com/friedman/pdfs/other_commentary/Farmand.02.17.1951.pdf.

Friedman, M. (1970, September). The social responsibility of business is to increase its profits. *The New York Times Magazine*. Retrieved January 11, 2014, from http://www.stthomas.edu/cathstudies/cst/facdevelop/missiondriven-cit/Friedman1stpage.pdf

George, S. (2000). A short history of neoliberalism: Twenty years of elite economics and emerging opportunities for structural change. In W. Bello, N. Bullard, & K. Malhotra (Eds.), *Global finance: New thinking on regulating speculative capital markets* (pp. 27–35). London: Zed Books.

Gilbert, D. (2015). *The American class structure in an age of growing inequality* (9th ed.). Los Angeles, CA: SAGE Publications.

Gilens, M. (2012). *Affluence & influence: Economic inequality and political power in America*. Princeton, NJ: Princeton University Press and the Russell Sage Foundation.

Gilens, M., & Page, B. I. (2014). Testing theories of American politics: Elites, interest groups, and average citizens. *Perspectives on Politics, 12*(3), 564–581.

Giroux, S. S. (2010). Sade's revenge: Racial neoliberalism and the sovereignty of negation. *Patterns of Prejudice, 44*(1), 1–26.

Gray, J. (1998). *False dawn: The delusions of global capitalism*. New York, NY: The New Press.

Hacker, J. S., & Pierson, P. (2010). *Winner-take-all politics: How Washington made the rich richer—And turned its back on the middle class*. New York, NY: Simon & Schuster.

Hall, S. (2011). The neoliberal revolution: Thatcher, Blair, Cameron—The long march of neoliberalism continues. *Soundings, 48*, 9–27.

Häring, N., & Douglas, N. (2012). *Economists and the powerful: Convenient theories, distorted facts, ample rewards*. London: Anthem Press.

Harvey, D. (1990). *The condition of postmodernity: An enquiry into the origins of cultural change*. Cambridge, MA: Blackwell Publishing.

Harvey, D. (2005). *A brief history of neoliberalism*. Oxford: Oxford University Press.

Hayek, F. A. (1944/2007). In B. Caldwell (Ed.), *The road to serfdom: Text and documents, the definitive edition*. Chicago, IL: University of Chicago Press.

Hedges, C. (2009). *Empire of illusion: The end of literacy and the triumph of spectacle*. New York, NY: Nation Books.

Jameson, F. (1991). *Postmodernism, or, the cultural logic of late capitalism*. Durham, NC: Duke University Press.

Jones, D. S. (2012). *Masters of the universe: Hayek, Friedman, and the birth of neoliberal politics*. Princeton, NJ: Princeton University Press.

Keynes, J. M. (1936/2008). *The general theory of employment, interest and money*. La Vergne, TN: BN Publishing.

Klein, N. (2007). *The shock doctrine: The rise of disaster capitalism*. New York, NY: Metropolitan Books.

Lazarus, N. (2011). *The postcolonial unconscious*. Cambridge: Cambridge University Press.

Loo, D. (2011). *Globalization and the demolition of society*. Glendale, CA: Larkmead Press.

Mann, G. (2013). *Disassembly required: A field guide to actually existing capitalism*. Edinburgh: AK Press.

Marmot, M. (2004). *The status syndrome: How social standing affects our health and longevity*. New York, NY: Times Books, Henry Holt and Company.

McGuigan, J. (2009). *Cool capitalism*. London: Pluto Press.

Mirowski, P. (2013). *Never let a serious crisis go to waste: How neoliberalism survived the financial meltdown*. London: Verso.

Mitchell, S. A. (1993). *Hope and dread in psychoanalysis*. New York, NY: Basic Books.

Organization for Economic Co-operation and Development. (2011). *Growing income inequality in OECD countries: What drives it and how can policy tackle it?* Paris, France: OECD Publishing.

Organization for Economic Co-operation and Development. (2012). *Divided we stand: Why inequality keeps rising*. Paris, France: OECD Publishing.

Panitch, L., & Gindin, S. (2012). *The making of global capitalism: The political economy of American empire*. London: Verso.

Peck, J. (2010). *Constructions of neoliberal reason*. Oxford: Oxford University Press.

Peters, M. A. (2001). *Poststructuralism, Marxism, and neoliberalism: Between theory and politics*. Lanham, MD: Rowman & Littlefield Publishers.

Piketty, T., & Saez, E. (2003). Income inequality in the United States, 1913-1998. *Quarterly Journal of Economics, 118*(1), 1–39.

Reid-Henry, S. (2015). *The political origins of inequality: Why a more equal world is better for us all*. Chicago, IL: University of Chicago Press.

Rushkoff, D. (2013). *Present shock: When everything happens now*. New York, NY: Current.

Saad-Filho, A., & Johnston, D. (Eds.). (2005). *Neoliberalism: A critical reader*. London: Pluto Press.

Saez, E. (2015, June). Income inequality in the United States: Tables and figures updated to 2014 in Excel format. Retrieved August 8, 2015 from http://eml.berkeley.edu/~saez/

Saez, E., & Zucman, G. (2014, October). *Wealth inequality in the United States since 1913: Evidence from capitalized income tax data*. (Working Paper 20625, National Bureau of Economic Research). Cambridge, MA: National Bureau of Economic Research. Retrieved August 8, 2015, from http://gabriel-zucman.eu/files/SaezZucman2014.pdf

Sommeiller, E., Price, M., & Wazeter, E. (2016). Income inequality in the U.S. by state, metropolitan area, and county. Washington, DC: Economic Policy

Institute. Retrieved June 18, 2016, from http://www.epi.org/files/pdf/107100.pdf

Springer, S. (2010). Neoliberalism and geography: Expansions, variegations, formations. *Geography Compass, 4*(8), 1025–1038.

Springer, S. (2012). Neoliberalism as discourse: Between Foucauldian political economy and Marxian poststructuralism. *Critical Discourse Studies, 9*(2), 133–147.

Steger, M. B., & Roy, R. K. (2010). *Neoliberalism: A very short introduction.* New York, NY: Oxford University Press.

Tye, L. (1998). *The father of spin: Edward L. Bernays and the birth of public relations.* New York, NY: Henry Holt and Company.

van Zon, H. (2013). The unholy alliance of neoliberalism and postmodernism. *Vlaams Marxistisch Tijdschrift, 47*(2), 110–114.

Wallach, L. M. (2013, December). The corporation invasion: Government by big business goes supranational. *Le Monde Diplomatique* [English edition]. Retrieved January 11, 2014, from http://mondediplo.com/2013/12/02tafta

Wilkinson, R., & Pickett, K. (2009). *The spirit level: Why greater equality makes societies stronger.* New York, NY: Bloomsbury Press.

World Economic Forum. (2011, January). *Global risks 2011* (6th ed.). Geneva: Author.

Wysong, E., Perrucci, R., & Wright, D. (2014). *The new class society: Goodbye American dream?* (4th ed.). Lanham, MD: Rowman & Littlefield Publishers.

CHAPTER 3

Going Viral: The Neoliberal Infiltration of the Living Human Web

Tracing the paths by which late capitalism penetrates and alters the various domains of human experience, yielding corresponding types of suffering, requires me to address another complex problem I had rather avoid, specifically, how to name these domains without thereby distorting the very character of what I attempt to describe. To identify categories of human experience and to call them "spheres," "domains," "levels," and so on, and then attempt to portray their relationships to each other, evokes images of the overlapping circles of the common Venn diagram. Unfortunately, this suggests independent structures, or organizations, of human life that may, either through happenstance or through predictable interactions, intermingle so as to produce shared consequences. Such a portrayal entirely misses the point. Even to limit their number to three is a didactic convenience rather than a description of firm boundaries natural to human life. What I wish to describe, rather, are various environments of human existence within what pastoral theologian Bonnie Miller-McLemore (1996) has called "the living human web." Staying with the pedagogical usefulness of a tripartite depiction, I suggest that we exist within this complex interactive web as: (a) relatively large collectives (institutions: e.g. governments, corporations, schools, religions, labor unions, cooperatives, and organizations), (b) smaller groups of face-to-face relations (friendships, intimate groups, marriages, families, lovers, etc.), and (c) individuals. *I am referring to these dimensions or ecologies of human relationships as the social,*

© The Author(s) 2016
B. Rogers-Vaughn, *Caring for Souls in a Neoliberal Age*,
DOI 10.1057/978-1-137-55339-3_3

the interpersonal, and the psychological. Although they are distinct types of human systems, they are not exactly separate domains, but ways of living that interpenetrate and are interdependent. One does not exist without the others, and what happens in one dimension affects the others.

Although he does not limit his analysis to human ecologies, political scientist William E. Connolly (2013) argues that the entire cosmos, including human systems, is *"composed of innumerable, interacting open systems with differential capacities of self-organization set on different scales of time, agency, creativity, viscosity, and speed"* (p. 25, emphasis in original). This helps us to avoid reductions that, for example, would perceive social institutions as simply aggregates of individuals, or individuals simply as social constructions. Moreover, not only might we now understand these three ecologies of human experience as dimensions of a larger system ("the living human web"), but also as systems within themselves. Thus sociologists, political scientists, and geographers, among others, may describe entire regional populations, ethnic subsets, and human institutions as displaying their own patterns, dynamics, agency, or other characteristics that distinguish them from other human systems. Likewise, interpersonal systems such as families (e.g. Bowen, 1978) manifest their own distinctive features. Family therapists, for example, regard families as being more than the sum of their parts: as homeostatic systems, even as having their own agency, or "a mind of their own." Finally, individuals do not appear as uniform, static monads. Psychoanalytic object relations theories, for instance, understand the individual psyche as constituted by the "internalization" of all the intersubjective experiences, from birth onward, that have affective significance for that individual. In effect, the individual is a system of relationships in dynamic relation. The individual is a community, yet manifesting her own agency. Recent object relations theorists have contended that internalizations forming the psyche are not limited to private and familial relationships, but include the entire social and political environment (e.g. Peltz, 2006; Rustin, 1991).

The question for us now is: how does neoliberal governance infiltrate and modify these various dimensions of human experience, producing, among other effects, corresponding forms of suffering? Connolly (2013) observes that neoliberalism, given its hegemonic scope, forces a binary choice: *"It thus inflates the self-organizing power of markets by implicitly deflating the self-organizing powers and creative capacity of all other systems"* (p. 31, emphasis in original). Given that all systems manifest "a degree of entanglement," in which "each impinges upon others, and some may become partially infused into others" (p. 81), how does neoliberal ideology and practice impinge upon and transform human systems? Connolly's observations suggest that neoliberal rationality and methods reduce the self-organizing, creative capacities of all human systems *except* the market. I will assert that this reduction is accomplished by processes of *marginalization* and *corruption* of these systems. *Marginalization*, in these instances, refers to how neoliberalism restricts the size, power, or scope of human systems within its hegemonic influence. It endeavors, in other words, to eliminate or overpower its competition. *Corruption* refers to how neoliberal rationality transforms human systems to conform to its discourse, ideology, and agendas; or, in other terms, how it co-opts the reduced human systems that remain. Furthermore, Connolly's reflection that systems are "entangled" applies particularly to human systems, implying that the infusions between them reinforce the forms of their marginalization and corruption.

It is essential to comprehend, before moving into particulars, the enormous import for pastoral theology and the care of souls of the assertion that neoliberalism now dominates human systems. I have already noted Centeno and Cohen's (2012) observation that neoliberalism is not simply an economic or political reality, but a *culture*. Raewyn Connell (2010), likewise, confirms that in neoliberal societies "a deep transformation of culture is at work" (p. 27). Moreover, the neoliberal transformation of culture is not a historical accident, but, as I noted in Chap. 2, was envisioned among its founding philosophers. "For Hayek and Mises," Jones (2012) observes, "the economy could not be separated from other arenas of social and political life. Economic freedom created the conditions for all other freedoms" (p. 69). The eventual success of neoliberalism in its global transformation of human culture has been widely documented, especially by the notable sociologist Zygmunt Bauman (e.g. 2001, 2003, 2004a, 2004b). As pastoral theologians, I believe we have not fully appreciated the triumph neoliberal capitalism has enjoyed in its constitution of culture. Thus, in keeping with the economics/culture split discussed in Chap. 2, we have usually explored the cultural origins of suffering as an area somewhat separated from economics and politics, and thus from capitalism generally. Duggan (2003) asserts, in a fashion consistent with this observation, "neoliberalism is generally associated with economic and trade policy; the cultural politics of neoliberalism are considered and debated relatively rarely" (p. 11).

The broad participation of the theological disciplines in this economics/culture divide has generally insulated neoliberal capitalism from pastoral theological assessment and critique.

An aspect of the "DNA" of neoliberalism that is highly manifest in transforming culture, and thus human systems—social, interpersonal, psychological—is its insistence upon privatization. Duggan (2003) asserts that *privatization* and *personal responsibility* are the "key terms" of neoliberal cultural governance: "These terms define the central intersections between the *culture* of neoliberalism and its economic vision, in the U.S. and abroad" (p. 12, emphasis in original). These terms echo the infamous dictum of Margaret Thatcher, that there is "no such thing as society, only individual men and women" (Harvey, 2005, p. 23). This logic betrays its origin in what Elliott and Lemert call *The New Individualism* (2009). While an emphasis on "rugged individualism" has characterized culture in the United States from its beginnings, Elliott and Lemert note that neoliberalism has radicalized individualism in three significant ways (pp. 38–42). First, individuals have become *commodities* in a market of labor and consumption. They are reduced to "human resources" in an exchange market. Second, the new individualism exists within "a new conservatism and reactionary intellectual consciousness" dedicated to dismantling public space (p. 39). Finally, Elliott and Lemert understand privatization as endemic to the new individualism: "Privatization ... concerns the spread of neo-liberal economic doctrines into the tissue of our social practice itself. *This process expands market deregulation into personal and intimate life, producing in turn isolating, deadening, calculating forms of life*" (pp. 40–41, emphasis added). Following the common description of pre-neoliberal capitalism as "embedded capitalism," I prefer to think of individualism prior to its transformation by neoliberal governance as "embedded individualism," or individualism that retains elements of interpersonal commitment and group loyalty. This new form is *disembedded individualism*, and retains no such obligations. The social space fragmented by this brand of individualism is what Zygmunt Bauman has called *The Individualized Society* (2001).

This radical individualism is not the only ingredient of the neoliberal DNA. Aside from its aversion to obligation or commitment within collectives of any kind, the new individualism thrives in an environment where everything is *economized*. Dardot and Laval (2009/2013) observe that the economization of life was a critical dimension of Hayek's original vision: "This aspect of Hayek's position is insufficiently stressed: the market order is not *an* economy, but is composed of 'economic relations' ... and these economic relations are *at the root of the social bond*" (p. 125, emphasis in original). This does not mean that all human relations are monetized, or reduced to purely financial values. Rather, as Dardot and Laval explicate, individuals are converted into *entrepreneurs*, agents who are dedicated to self-management and who view social and interpersonal exchanges largely in terms of assets and liabilities (pp. 101–119). Wendy Brown (2015) summarizes:

> To speak of the relentless and ubiquitous economization of all features of life by neoliberalism is thus not to claim that neoliberalism literally *marketizes* all spheres .... Rather, the point is that neoliberal rationality disseminates the *model of the market* to all domains and activities—even where money is not at issue—and configures human beings exhaustively as market actors, always, only, and everywhere as *homo oeconomicus*. (p. 31, emphases in original)

Furthermore, the transformation of human subjects into entrepreneurs requires them to order their lives "in accordance with the universal principle of competition" (Dardot & Laval, 2009/2013, p. 4). Brown (2015), following Foucault, emphasizes that neoliberal rationality, contrary to prior forms of capitalism, *replaces exchange with competition*. This necessarily means also that *equality is replaced by inequality*:

> This is another of those seemingly trivial replacements that is a tectonic shift, affecting a range of other principles and venues. Most importantly, equivalence is both the premise and the norm of exchange, while inequality is the premise and outcome of competition. Consequently .... inequality becomes legitimate, even normative, in every sphere. (p. 64)

Thus Davies (2014) insists that under neoliberalism, inequality is not limited to the economy, but pervades every field of human activity: "This means that there are *multiple inequalities*, with multiple, potentially incommensurable measures" (p. 35, emphasis in original).

The challenge of this chapter, then, is to summarize how these transformations are now manifest within social, interpersonal, and psychological systems. The strategic features of neoliberal rationality—privatization, entrepreneurship, competition, inequality—are not limited to economic or political ventures. They are imposed upon culture, and dominate our daily lives.

The Marginalization and Corruption of Social Systems

I begin with the most encompassing of these systems—the social. Jones (2012, pp. 73–84) traces how neoliberal ideology emerged out of a visceral distrust of all forms of socialism. Braedley and Luxton (2010) note: "This rejection of socialism in neoliberal thought surfaces as an almost complete rejection of collectivism" (p. 9). The outcome, as Elliott and Lemert (2009) observe, is that the new individualism has been "responsible for destroying human communities and solidarity on a scale not previously witnessed" (p. 39). Likewise, the notable philosopher Pierre Bourdieu (1998) has described neoliberalism as "*a programme of the methodical destruction of collectives*" (para. 4, emphasis in original). This fragmentation of social institutions began to be apparent as soon as neoliberalism assumed political power during the Reagan and Thatcher administrations. Both of these leaders almost immediately became known for their systematic dismantling of labor unions and collective bargaining for workers. They also railed against "big government" as they sought to reduce the public sector by reassigning many government functions to private corporations. While the anti-union and anti-government views of free market advocates are well known, most people are less aware that neoliberalism, as it becomes the cultural norm, weakens all forms of human collectives and institutions. This has been thoroughly documented by political scientists Robert Lane (2000) and Robert Putnam (2000), who also correlate the erosion of communities with depression and a general "loss of happiness."

As an aside, I should note that neoliberalization in practice produces an uneven outcome on collectives. In Chap. 2, I cited Peck's (2010) differentiation between the "roll-back" and "roll-out" dimensions of neoliberalization. During the "roll-back" phase, neoliberalism diminishes the reach and power of collectives that threaten resistance to its agendas. But during the "roll-out" process, it actually enhances the power of collectives that serve its purposes, particularly large corporations and the functions of government that insure the requisite order, surveillance, and policing. This highlights one of the many incongruities of neoliberal rationality. Promoted in the name of trimming the size of government and increasing corporate efficiency, it actually contributes to the construction of enormous and unwieldy government and corporate bureaucracies, a phenomenon documented by David Graeber (2015) in his recent book *The Utopia of Rules.* The upshot of these processes is that human collectives are placed into competition with one another in the marketplace of power. Laws and rules are established that increase the size and power of neoliberal-friendly collectives, while reducing the reach and power of virtually all others. The consequence is another instance of the "multiple inequalities" mentioned by Davies (2014).

One exhibit of this broad dismantling of collectives is the continuing decline of religious institutions in the United States, a steady erosion that signifies the general *marginalization* of religious collectives under neoliberal governance. For some time, with respect to Christian traditions, the decline of mainline Protestant churches was widely interpreted solely as a function of something endemic to those congregations and denominations. Recently, however, we are witnessing declines in evangelical, charismatic, and other conservative religious groups (Bass, 2012). This development transcends the erosion of Christian institutions, extending to religion in general. The General Social Survey (GSS), conducted by the National Opinion Research Center (NORC), an independent research institute at the University of Chicago, is widely considered to be the most reliable source of information on social trends in the United States.[1] Sociologists from the University of California, Berkeley, and Duke University have analyzed the GSS regarding religion, noting that the number of people not identifying with institutional religion has increased dramatically (Hout, Fischer, & Chaves, 2013). One of the researchers, in an interview with *The Huffington Post*, observed that the number claiming "no religion" held steady from the time it was first measured, in the 1930s, at around 5 %, increasing to only 8 % by 1990 (Bindley, 2013). From that year the increase has been dramatic, hitting 20 % by 2012. A graph from an updated study by Hout and Fischer (2014, Fig. 3.1) illustrates this phenomenal escalation in the GSS data:

In an earlier study, again using the GSS, two of these researchers (Hout & Fischer, 2002) combed the data and concluded that the increase of "nones" is not due to secularization, because there was little difference in the religious beliefs of those who claimed no religion and those who were religiously identified. Rather, they concluded, "The most distinctive fact about the people with no religious preference is their lack of participation in organized religion" (p. 174). Later, after in-depth research subsequent to the 2012 GSS data, Hout and Fischer conclude: "There is still almost no evidence of secularization" (2014, p. 424). Significantly, in both studies, they also discovered that the "nones" also show less attachment to

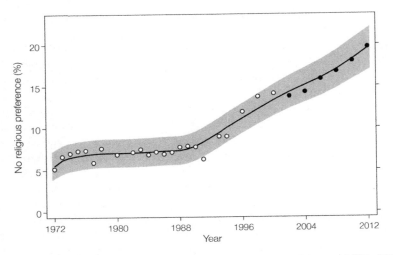

Fig. 3.1 Percentage preferring no religion by year, United States: 1972–2012. *Note*: Data smoothed using locally estimated regression (loess); trend line shown in *black*. *Circles* show raw data. *Source*: General Social Surveys, 1972–2012

social institutions *other than* religion, a finding that supports my thesis. They observe, regarding those who claim no religion:

> They belong to fewer nonreligious organizations and are significantly less likely to vote than persons with a religious affiliation. People with no religious preference are not totally inactive—they are more likely to attend concerts, see movies, and spend an evening with friends at a bar than are people with religious affiliations, but they are less likely to spend an evening with relatives or neighbors. They also reported having fewer friends. … We have shown that the people with no religious affiliation are unlikely to have a compensating attachment to other social institutions but do participate in cultural consumption. (2002, p. 176)

Given these findings, it is remarkable that these researchers do not locate the decline of religious participation within a larger context of deinstitutionalization in the United States during the period under study. Further, the comment that nonreligious people in the USA "do participate in cultural consumption" vaguely alludes to a possible connection with the neoliberal expansion occurring during this same period of time, yet this is also not pursued in the study. Instead, Hout and Fischer conclude that the dramatic increase of those claiming no religion is due to the desire of many people to distance themselves from the prominent political activities of the Religious Right. I have no argument with this conclusion, except to note that it ignores the imbrications between neoliberal hegemony and neo-conservative religion in the United States. Connolly (2008) has argued persuasively that neoliberalism has aligned itself with a stream of spirituality within Christianity that emphasizes power, fear of others, individualism, and revenge.

In a more recent study, Hout and Fischer (2014) determine that generational differences account for the rise of "nones" better than political reactivity. Here they note that the political backlash against conservative Christianity and generational differences are "both rooted in cultural changes and conflicts in the 1960s." People who grew up during the 1960s and after, they assert, "also mistrust authority and value autonomy more than those who came of age earlier" (p. 424). In their conclusion, they expand this finding beyond religion, observing that those coming of age during the 1960s and beyond "put the individual in the center and leave little margin for any authority—scientific, religious, judicial, political—to dictate a worldview" (p. 444). This recalls the connection between neoliberal ascendancy and the revolutions of the 1960s that I discussed in Chap. 2. As Harvey (2005) contends, regarding these cultural revolutions: "Any political movement that holds individual freedoms to be sacrosanct is vulnerable to incorporation into the neoliberal fold" (p. 41). My own conclusion is that Hout's and Fischer's findings are incisive, but should be placed into the larger framework of the neoliberalization of society for a full and complete interpretation.

Meanwhile, the Religious Right examined by Hout and Fischer (2002) represents a segment of Christianity that has undergone alteration under neoliberal hegemony. It is radicalized and drained of any remaining compassion toward those who are different, including and especially the poor, and made to conform to what Elliott and Lemert (2009) call the new individualism. It is surely no coincidence that the rise of the Religious Right in the United States paralleled the rise of neoliberalism. Neoliberalism does align with theological themes already present in this stream of Christian ideology, a stream strongly influenced by its roots in American frontier revivalism. As theologian Joerg Rieger (2009) observes, neoliberal rationality takes advantage of the "top-down images" of God in this stream (pp. 79–82). It is nonetheless the case that such Christianity also suffers what I have called a measure of *corruption* as it is co-opted by neoliberalization. At its extreme, this co-optation yields varieties of "Prosperity Gospel" (Rieger, 2009, p. 79), and now publicly dominant forms of Christianity that Connolly (2008) calls "the evangelical-capitalist resonance machine" (pp. 39–67).

Moreover, a second stream of Christianity identified by Connolly (2008, pp. 59–62, 119–146), one that he notes is agonistic, inclusive, and tolerant of ambiguity, has been *marginalized*. Rieger (2009) implicitly appeals to this stream when he notes:

> These images of God at work from the top down are in stark contrast with images of the Judeo-Christian God, who elects a people enslaved by an ancient empire in Egypt ... and who becomes human in Jesus Christ, whose life's work is in constant tension with the Roman Empire and it vassals, and with the religious establishment that lends supports to these powers. (p. 80)

Hout and Fischer do not explicitly investigate this segment of Christianity, except to note: "The increase in 'no religion' responses was confined to political moderates and liberals" (2002, p. 165). It appears to me that religious people within the agonistic stream of Christianity identified by Connolly would likely be identified as moderates and liberals in the current political climate of the United States. If so, then this is precisely the area of Christian faith and practice, according to Hout and Fischer's data, that has suffered the most erosion. Notably, this is also the sort of Christianity that engages in social justice activities that undermine neoliberal interests.

One aspect of the analysis offered by Hout and Fischer (2002) deserves special attention, because it illustrates how neoliberalism both *marginalizes* and *corrupts* religion, Christian or otherwise. Hout and Fischer document, contrary to the secularization hypothesis, that most people in the United States who claim "no religion" remain believers. They refer to these as "unchurched believers" (p. 165). A more familiar designation for this group is the "spiritual but not religious." Ammerman (2013) is no doubt correct when she argues against any strict dichotomy between "religious" and "spiritual," noting "that there is actually a good deal of overlap between spirituality and religion, at least in the American population" (p. 259). Nonetheless, under the neoliberal paradigm, it appears that religion is "out," while spirituality is most definitely "in." However, as I have stated elsewhere (Rogers-Vaughn, 2013a):

The replacement of religion with spirituality is perhaps the most pervasive, effective, and malignant strategy neoliberalism uses to marginalize theology and neutralize its prophetic threat. I intend to be quite clear on this point: *In the context of global neoliberalism, spirituality is not part of the solution. It is part of the problem.* (p. 5, emphasis in original)

Carrette and King (2005) argue that the spirituality inherent in the "spiritual but not religious" represents the *commodification* of religion that has occurred under neoliberal capitalism. They summarize:

Let us imagine that "religion" in all its forms is a company that is facing a takeover bid from a larger company known as Corporate Capitalism. In its attempt to "downsize" its ailing competitor, Corporate Capitalism strips the assets of "religion" by plundering its material and cultural resources, which are then repackaged, rebranded and then sold in the marketplace of ideas. This reselling exploits the historical respect and "aura of authenticity" of the religious traditions .... while at the same time, separating itself from any negative connotations associated with the religious in a modern secular context (rebranding). This is precisely the burden of the concept of spirituality in such contexts, allowing a simultaneous nod towards and separation from "the religious". The corporate machine or the market does not seek to validate or reinscribe the tradition but rather utilizes its cultural cachet for its own purposes and profit. (pp. 15–16)

Not only does this marginalize religious institutions, it corrupts what remains ("spirituality") by leaving aside the search for shared truth, the commitment to maintaining a common life, and concern for social justice that has often characterized traditional religious communities. The result, according to Webster (2012), is that "contemporary spirituality makes us stupid, selfish and unhappy."

The erosion of organized (institutional) religion, as I have said, is only one instance of the crumbling of social systems. The relationship between such social fragmentation and human suffering may not be immediately apparent, especially when many progressive theorists have imagined the escape from traditional institutions as liberating. Yet today many scholars are asserting that it founds novel forms of human misery. Dufour (2003/2008) has observed: "The great novelty of neoliberalism, as compared with earlier systems of domination, is that the early systems worked through institutional controls, reinforcements and repression, whereas the new capitalism runs on deinstitutionalization. Foucault probably did not see this coming" (p. 157). Consequently, Dufour insists, quoting Arendt: "we have a tyranny without a tyrant" (p. 166). Essentially, Dufour contends that this social fragmentation is grounding the disintegration of the individual, which I will discuss later in this chapter.

Looking Away (II): Secularization Theory as Diversion

My use of the erosion of religion as an exhibit of the dismantling of human collectives brings up another example—again, as with postmodern thought, especially in the academy—of a theory or set of theories that may distract us from noticing the destructive effects of neoliberalization. To some of my colleagues, it may appear that I am over-extending the reach of neoliberalism to explain secularization. I actually have little interest in explaining secularity. I mentioned secularization in the previous section only because Hout and Fischer (2002, 2014) insisted that the rise of the "nones" was not explained by secularization because their beliefs were not significantly different from those who remained religiously affiliated. In the strictest sense, I do not see neoliberalization and secularization as *competing* theories simply because they are talking about different things. In theories examining the neoliberalization of society, unlike secularization theories, the big story is neither a general decline of religion nor the diversification and reflexivity of personal religious expression, but the *erosion of human collectives*. Here the decline of "institutional religion" is regarded as just one dimension of this more encompassing destruction of public life. However, I do see the secularization thesis and the analysis of neoliberalism as genuinely *alternative* interpretations regarding the transformations that are occurring in religion today. *Indeed, they may occupy different paradigms.*

My intention in this section, then, is a bit more radical. I wish to interrogate the very notion of secularity from a post-capitalist theological perspective that peers through the lens of neoliberal rationality and practice. I begin with a quote. Buddhist philosopher David Loy (1997) has asserted that "our present economic system" has become "our religion." He concludes:

> The discipline of economics is less a science than the theology of that religion, and its god, the Market, has become a vicious circle of ever-increasing production and consumption by pretending to offer a secular salvation. ...

the Market is becoming the first truly world religion, binding all corners of the globe more and more tightly into a worldview and set of values whose religious role we overlook only because we insist on seeing them as "secular." (p. 275)

A bit later Loy states that "market capitalism ... has already become the most successful religion of all time, winning more converts more quickly than any previous belief system or value-system in human history" (p. 276). I will unpack these statements in two directions. First, without suggesting that this is the intent of secularization theorists, I will explore Loy's insinuation that the idea of the "secular" leads us to "overlook" the character of today's actually existing capitalism. This must include a deconstruction of secularization in which we ask, in the manner of Foucault, whose interests the idea of secularity might serve. What motivations or powers might it help to conceal and thus to immunize against criticism? Second, I will consider the claim that advanced capitalism functions as a religion. In agreement that it is a type of religion, I will argue that it is therefore subject to *theological* assessment and critique, and that such critique is not only an option, but an obligation.

At the outset, I should note that the term "secularization" is, if anything, more hotly contested than neoliberalization. Many scholars may question the meaning or scope of "neoliberalism," but few now question that it exists. The situation is otherwise with secularization. Renowned sociologist of religion Peter Berger was once known as a strong proponent of the secularization hypothesis. However, in his introductory essay to a volume he edited in 1999, *The Desecularization of the World*, Berger famously reverses course. There he flatly states, "the assumption that we live in a secularized world is false .... This means that a whole body of literature by historians and social scientists loosely labeled 'secularization theory' is essentially mistaken" (1999, p. 2). The empirical evidence, he argues, shows that religion is "resurgent" throughout the world. Since that time many scholars have arrived at similar conclusions. In his most recent book (2014), Berger reflects back on his 1999 essay and observes: "I was also not alone in my change of mind. Almost everyone studying contemporary religion has replicated it. There is a relatively small group of scholars who continue to defend secularization theory" (p. x). Berger notes that there are two exceptions to his "desecularization" thesis, one of which will presently be important to my interrogation. Rather than a secularization view, Berger concludes that the major shift in religion is pluralization, especially

at the level of individual consciousness and practice. However, in my estimation, Berger does not take sufficient account of the decline of religious
collectives that I explored in the previous section. Others have acknowledged this decline, but also explore the increased interest and diversity
in personal religious expression that Berger describes. Bass (2012), while
documenting the attrition of religious institutions, goes so far as to cel-
ebrate what she sees as a widespread spiritual renewal. This is reflected
in the title of her book: *Christianity After Religion: The End of Church
and the Birth of a New Spiritual Awakening.* Ammerman (2013), while
not denying a broad erosion of religious collectives, helpfully explores the
intersection and overlap between those who consider themselves religious,
and the "spiritual but not religious." Similar to Berger and Bass, she is
attentive to the increasing diversification and reflexivity of religion at the
individual level.

Secularization theory, however, is far from dead. The notion of secularization rejected by Berger (1999), "is simple: Modernization necessarily
leads to a decline of religion, both in society and in the minds of individuals" (p. 2). However, in his massive tome *A Secular Age*, Charles Taylor
(2007) brilliantly salvages the idea of secularization even as he critiques the
idea of secularity Berger espouses. Taylor is not very interested in the type
of secularization Berger has rejected. James K.A. Smith (2014) summarizes Taylor's perspective: "Secularization theorists (and their opponents)
are barking up the wrong tree precisely because they fixate on *expressions* of
belief rather than *conditions* of belief" (p. 20, emphasis in original). Taylor
(2007) argues that we are all now living within what he calls "the immanent frame" (pp. 539–593), a "social imaginary" (pp. 171–176) that no
longer depends upon any reference to transcendence: "this frame constitutes a 'natural' order, to be contrasted to a 'supernatural' one, an 'immanent' world, over against a possible 'transcendent' one" (p. 542). This
remains true even if one happens to believe in transcendence. Moreover,
this imaginary "is common to all of us in the modern West" (p. 543). In
this version of a "secular age," two things are new. First, religious belief has
not so much diminished as it has become "contestable." It is one option
among others. We are aware, in other words, that our religious faith and
practice is a *personal choice* among other possible choices. Second, "exclusive humanism" becomes a possibility:

> For the first time in history a purely self-sufficient humanism came to be a
> widely available option. I mean by this a humanism accepting no final goals

beyond human flourishing, nor any allegiance to anything else beyond this flourishing. Of no previous society was this true. (2007, p. 18)

I believe it is in reference to just such an imaginary that Eagleton (2014) remarks, with a bit more levity than Taylor might extend:

> Societies become secular not when they dispense with religion altogether, but when they are no longer especially agitated by it .... As the wit remarked, it is when religion starts to interfere with your everyday life that it is time to give it up. In this, it has a certain affinity with alcohol. (p. 1)

Eagleton concludes that in this sort of world, religious faith "dwindles to a kind of personal pastime, like breeding gerbils or collecting porcelain, with less and less resonance in the public world" (p. 1).

I happen to be a fan of Taylor's work. He offers an exquisite portrayal of human experience within a certain cultural domain. My critique is not so much that he is wrong, but that his interpretation of secularity is not grounded well enough in materiality (in other words, in a political or economic context). Berger (2014) applauds Taylor's contribution, but concludes: "However, the title of the book is misleading. The phrase 'secular age' hardly describes the empirical state of affairs in most of the contemporary world" (p. 73). Commenting on Taylor's rendition of the "immanent frame," Berger states:

> Taylor is a philosopher, and the process he analyzes occurs primarily in the realm of ideas .... This is a perfectly valid way of looking at this history, but it is important to understand that the course of human events is not primarily a history of ideas .... the plausibility of ideas is decisively influenced by developments that have nothing to do with ideas *but have an affinity with much coarser political and economic interests.* (p. 51, emphasis added)

Berger follows with an investigation of religious pluralism, but I will take his comment in another direction. Giving both Marx and Foucault their due, I invite the reader to consider whether the social imaginary Taylor describes coincides with the culture shaped by neoliberalization, and then to ask the question as to what powers or interests are served by such a narrative of secularity.

Let us begin with the first question. There is not enough space in this book for a full exposition of the intersections between Taylor's narrative and that of neoliberal rationality. But I wish to offer just enough here to hopefully intrigue the reader. Some of my reflections here must, unfortunately, assume the reader's familiarity with Taylor's work. Although Taylor locates the roots of today's immanent frame deep in history, he argues that it clicks into place during what he calls "the age of authenticity" (pp. 473–504). He dates the dawn of this age during the 1960s. This is congruent with the observations of Harvey (2005), among others, that neoliberalism is heir to the libertarian sentiments of that decade. So both the theories of neoliberalization and Taylor's narrative of secularity occur within the same time frame. That could be considered coincidence were it not for the similar content of these descriptions.

Taylor's analysis of the "expressive individualism" of this age, which he acknowledges is different from the individualism of earlier times, is deeply congruent with the "disembedded individualism" of neoliberal culture that I described earlier in this chapter. Occasionally, Taylor overtly associates this age with consumerism and a "kind of capitalist sub-culture" (p. 478), but the references to capitalism are so uncommon that the term fails to make the index of the book (although consumerism does appear). Similarly, Taylor aligns the emergence of the secular age with three modern social imaginaries, one of which he identifies as the economy (pp. 176–185). He even cites two works by Adam Smith, and concludes regarding his idea of the "invisible hand" of the market: "There is no collective agent here, indeed, the account amounts to a denial of such. There are agents, individuals acting on their own behalf, but the global upshot happens behind their backs" (p. 181). Taylor calls the separation of individual identity from collectives "the great disembedding" (pp. 146–158), and argues that in "the age of authenticity," individuals try to form an identity outside "the sense of belonging to large scale collective agencies" (p. 484). James K.A. Smith (2014) summarizes Taylor's "great disembedding" as a shift "in which society will come to be seen as a collection of individuals" (p. 45). This brings to mind Margaret Thatcher's famous neoliberal dictum, that there is "no such thing as society, only individual men and women" (Harvey, 2005, p. 23). Moreover, in the "live and let live" world of this age, Taylor observes: "The sin which is not tolerated is intolerance" (p. 484). This appears to concur with Wendy Brown's argument (2006) that the elevation of tolerance has an underside, in that it serves to consolidate the dominant class under contemporary capitalism.

Then there is Taylor's description of the self as experienced within the immanent frame, which he calls the "buffered" self. In this schema, Smith

(2014) notes: "Significance no longer inheres in things; rather, meaning and significance are a property of minds who perceive meaning internally" (p. 29). Taylor calls this self "buffered" because, according to Smith (2014), it is "insulated and isolated in its interiority" (p. 30). This self is engaged in "giving its own autonomous order to its life" (Taylor, 2007, pp. 38–39). The buffered self is an isolated self: "Indeed, this understanding lends itself to individuality, even atomism; sometimes we may wonder if it can be made hospitable to a sense of community. The buffered self is essentially the self which is aware of the possibility of disengagement" (Taylor, pp. 41–42). Is this not reflective of neoliberalism's emphasis on "the actions of the rational, self-interested actor in the competitive marketplace?" (Jones, 2012, p. 2). As in neoliberalism, Taylor observes that the age of authenticity elevates "bare choice as a prime value, irrespective of what it is a choice between, or in what domain" (2007, p. 478). Is such a self not, in the end, completely responsible for its own fate, as we see in Dardot and Laval's (2009/2013) depiction of the "neoliberal subject," described in the last section of this chapter? Furthermore, Taylor extends the primacy of choice to religious expression. The fragmentation of religious life creates a "nova effect" (2007, pp. 299–304) in which there is a seemingly infinite array of options from which the individual may choose. So, we now not only have a "marketplace of ideas," but a "marketplace of religious belief and practice." How is this not shaped by contemporary capitalism?

Finally, I have already noted that within the immanent frame, Taylor sees "no final goals beyond human flourishing" (2007, p. 18). Human "flourishing" has become a virtual code word for the purpose of life under neoliberal governance. It especially constitutes the meaning of life within the "creative class" (Peck, 2010, pp. 192–224). Dardot and Laval (2009/2013) describe the neoliberal subject as guided by this singular goal: "The self's new norm certainly consists in flourishing. To succeed, you must know yourself and love yourself. Hence the stress on the magical expression 'self-esteem,' key to all success" (p. 274). Furthermore, the social imaginary of the secular age, according to Taylor, downplays human vulnerability (2007, pp. 36–37). Individuals are not perceived as vulnerable to forces beyond themselves, as they were in ancient times. This is also congruent with neoliberal rationality, which portrays individuals as perfectly capable of managing their own lives without external assistance.

I am suggesting that the intersections between Taylor's portrayal of the secular age and neoliberal culture raise an important question. Is Taylor's revised narrative of secularization better understood as a dimension of neoliberalization, particularly the impact of contemporary economic and political forces on questions of meaning and value? *I propose that today's actually existing capitalism is the material body within which Taylor's immanent frame lives, and without which it might not exist.* If this is so, we might wonder what difference it makes. The difference, if we allow secular discourse to remain idealistic, is that once again capitalism is shielded from direct criticism. It does not have to answer for its consequences, as Loy insinuates in the quote that opened this section. This brings up the Foucauldian question. What powers or interests might the discourse of secularization serve?

I mentioned earlier that Peter Berger (1999) sees two exceptions to his desecularization thesis. One is Western Europe, a situation he regards as unclear and up for debate. The other exception, Berger contends, is not so ambiguous:

> There exists an international subculture composed of people with Western-type higher education, especially in the humanities and social sciences, that is indeed secularized. This subculture is the principle "carrier" of progressive, Enlightened beliefs and values. While its members are relatively thin on the ground, they are very influential, as they control the institutions that provide the "official" definitions of reality, notably the educational system, the media of mass communication, and the higher reaches of the legal system. They are remarkably similar all over the world today, as they have been for a long time. (p. 10)

Berger then places this intelligentsia within the context of contemporary religious movements: "In country after country, then, religious upsurges have a strongly populist character. Over and beyond the purely religious motives, these are movements of protest and resistance *against* a secular elite" (p. 11, emphasis in original). I find Berger's comments provocative, for he is essentially arguing that secularization theories participate in *class conflict*. And the parties they serve are the dominant classes, those who get to "define reality." This certainly accords with the social mobility I have experienced. As I moved from the working class of my upbringing, underwent the formation of higher education, and entered the professional and academic world, I experienced the struggles with faith and dislocation that Taylor so exquisitely describes. Thus I easily find myself in his work. But, despite Taylor's claim that "the immanent frame is common to all of us in the modern West" (2007, p. 543), I do not believe it accurately reflects the world occupied by most of my friends and relatives back in Alabama. The "simple," uncontested faith of my parents and family has endured. This has meant that, as I "left" this world, we generally have been unable to communicate on matters touching upon religious faith. This remains true even though both my father and I are ordained ministers. And it is a primary source of pain, not only for me, but for my family. Following Berger's assertion, I believe most of the earth's inhabitants are more like my family than myself. Consequently, those of us who have been privileged to receive higher education tend to theorize in rather idealized ways. We have, in effect, peered into the well of humanity and seen our own faces. And, perhaps especially because we are not aware, our theories often serve those in power. I suppose this should come as no surprise to us, given that the tuitions and grants that fund our salaries and research originate predominately in the elite classes.

Having said all this, I will conclude this section by asserting that the very idea of secularity is illusory. For example, though this is chiefly apparent through theological analysis, the religious character of capitalism has long been evident to theorists other than theologians. As early as 1921, Walter Benjamin, in a fragment titled "Capitalism as Religion" (1921/1996), contended: "A religion may be discerned in capitalism—that is to say, capitalism serves essentially to allay the same anxieties, torments, and disturbances to which the so-called religions offered answers" (pp. 288–291). Benjamin concluded that capitalism is "an essentially religious phenomenon" (p. 288). More recently, economist Robert H. Nelson (2001), in his book *Economics as Religion*, begins with these words:

> Economists think of themselves as scientists, but as I will be arguing in this book, they are more like theologians. The closest predecessors for the current members of the economics profession are not scientists such as Albert Einstein or Isaac Newton; rather, we economists are more truly the heirs of Thomas Aquinas and Martin Luther (p. xv).

Nelson proceeds to assert: "Beneath the surface of their formal economic theorizing, economists are engaged in an act of delivering religious messages" (p. xx). He then spends the remainder of this lengthy text prying into the details of particular economic theories to substantiate his claim.

I must note that, in the process, it becomes clear that Nelson is not using the terms "theology" or "religion" rhetorically. He means them literally. In fact, he contends that a new field of study is needed, one he calls "economic theology" (p. xvii).

This straightforward use of the term "theology" also appears in philosopher Philip Goodchild's book *Theology of Money* (2009). Goodchild describes contemporary capitalism as a system in which both human life and religion are economized. Money is the heart of this system. But money is neither a physical object nor does it have intrinsic value. Rather, it is "a promise of value" (pp. 115–116), an abstraction exchanged on the basis of a wager on its future value. As such, its nature is essentially eschatological. Goodchild makes us doubt whether Taylor is correct when he states that the immanent frame is an imaginary vacated by transcendence. "Money," he observes, "exercises a spectral power that exceeds all merely human powers." He continues, "the value of money is transcendent. It is a promise, taken on faith" (p. 12). But this does not mean that money is an ideality that floats above the earth. It is, instead, mired deeply in the material world. Wendy Brown (2015) has argued that "the neoliberal subject is granted no guarantee of life (on the contrary, in markets, some must die for others to live), and is so tethered to economic ends as to be potentially sacrificible to them" (p. 111). Goodchild would agree. He asserts that, not only is capitalism a religion, but it is a religion that demands human sacrifice. For example,

> When one comes to consider who ultimately staked their flesh and blood to ensure the profitability of the ventures undertaken by the eighteenth-century English merchants who profited most from the new credit economy, one quickly comes to sailors, Irish navvies, and African slaves (2009, p. 235).

Things are no different today. Goodchild proclaims: "The credit economy is a network of contracted servitude." He concludes:

> Whenever one spends money, one spends a portion of the substance, wealth, and life of those who have undertaken loans. Yet the value of money is also backed by profitability, including the drudge of labor in sweatshops and factories, the exclusion from the formal economy of those who are not employed profitably, the consumption of natural resources, and the erosion of ecosystems and societies. The value of money is still paid for in flesh and blood. (p. 236)

Such a system, then, is maintained "at the expense of existing structures of social dependence, provision, and care" (p. 222). It has to be sobering to vocational theologians, particularly pastoral theologians, that a capitalist system such as we now have opposes the value of care. This requires that pastoral theology must today also be an *economic theology*. Finally, after perusing his analysis, it is not surprising to find that Goodchild rejects any division between religion and the secular (p. 203). Life is religious through and through. Such a distinction is not only false but hazardous, for it hides the current system from criticism.

Although theology has tended to avoid the subject of capitalism in recent years, there have certainly been theologians who have spoken up. Joerg Rieger (2009), in *No Rising Tide*, observes: "The problem is not secularization—as is often assumed—but a kind of hidden religiosity that promotes the worship of the gods of the free market" (p. 68). In a 1999 article in *The Atlantic*, theologian Harvey Cox (in the business section, no less!) reports that, when he started reading *The Wall Street Journal* and the business sections of *Time* and *Newsweek*, he found himself in familiar territory. These texts, he observes,

> bear a striking resemblance to Genesis, the Epistle to the Romans, and Saint Augustine's City of God. Behind descriptions of market reforms, monetary policy, and convolutions of the Dow, I gradually made out the pieces of a grand narrative about the inner meaning of human history, why things had gone wrong, and how to put them right. Theologians call these myths of origin, legends of the fall, and doctrines of sin and redemption. (para. 2)

Cox then traces out contemporary views on the omnipotence, omniscience, and omnipresence of this "Market God," even expounding on a "market doctrine" he calls "reverse transubstantiation," in which "the human body has become the latest sacred vessel to be converted into a commodity" (para. 10). Such revelations do little to enhance our confidence in the category of secularity.

Catholic theologian Nicholas Lash (1996), in *The Beginning and the End of 'Religion'*, refuses both the categories "religion" and "secularity," arguing they are intertwined and mutually dependent ideas. The term "religion," he notes, was first coined in seventeenth-century England and came to represent a segment of life thought to be separate from other parts, such as art, science, politics, and economics. Lash argues that what we have called "religions" are best thought of as "schools," and that they draw the whole of human existence, indeed all that exists, into their purview. He contends: "Christianity and Vedantic Hinduism, Judaism and Buddhism and Islam are schools … whose pedagogy has the twofold purpose—however differently conceived and executed in the different traditions—of weaning us from our idolatry and purifying our desire" (p. 21). Later Lash asserts: "The secularity of our culture is an illusion, and a dangerous one at that" (p. 110). Why dangerous? Lash responds that human beings are "spontaneously idolatrous," meaning that we inevitably "set our hearts" on some mundane thing. Lash warns: "And none of us is so self-transparent as to know quite where, in fact, our hearts are set" (p. 21). Removing the ancient disciplines we call "religions" from "the realm of truth," Lash concludes, "leaves our propensity for idolatry unchecked and unconstrained, with devastating consequences" (p. 110). A similar point is made by Edward Farley (1990), who locates the origin of human evil in idolatry. Once we identify some mundane person, place, thing, or state of being with the "eternal horizon," he claims, we are then prepared to sacrifice anything—self, others, creation—to protect whatever we have made sacred. It does not matter, in this view, whether the idol is identified as "religious" or "secular."

Finally, as one more example among what could be many, this happens to accord with the theology of Paul Tillich (1957). As theologian Francis Ching-Wah Yip (2010) has observed, Tillich's description of faith as "ultimate concern" amounts to a rejection of the secular/religious divide. Yip surveys Tillich's work from the time he was writing in Germany through his "existentialist" years in the United States, showing his consistent criticism of capitalism and his belief that it constituted a modern form of religion. Technically, Tillich regarded capitalism as a "quasi-religion." The only thing absent from a "quasi-religion" that exists in what is usually identified as religion, according to Tillich, is that the former lacks an internal criticism to check its idolatrous tendencies and its susceptibility to what Tillich called the "demonic." And this, Tillich concluded, makes capitalism especially dangerous, despite all the benefits it may have brought with it.

So, why this long discursus on secularization and secularity? Aside from the reasons already mentioned, I will simply list three other implications of this section for pastoral care and pastoral theology. First, the religion/secularity dichotomy greatly diminishes the potential for pastoral care to exist as a *political* activity to reduce suffering. Pastoral care must not be limited to the care of individuals, but must include the care of collectives.

Moreover, this care cannot be confined only to congregations or other "religious" bodies, but must be extended to other collectives that harbor the capacity to resist oppressive power hierarchies. This is an urgent problem because, as I am claiming in this book, neoliberal hegemony is increasing and transforming suffering globally and will require collective action in order to be contained.

Second, much of what I have said is congruent with current efforts in pastoral and practical theology to act and speak as a "public theology." I take this to mean that pastoral theology not only speaks *to* the public, but that it *interprets what is occurring in the world* from a theological perspective, not limited to areas that may be designated as specifically "religious" or "spiritual." However, if this section is combined with the previous one, we must attend to the fact that, under neoliberal governance, "the public" is itself suffering erosion. We appear to want to "go public" just as the public to which we appeal as a frame for conversation and debate is quickly disappearing. Under the impact of neoliberalization, the area of human life designated as "public" has been diminished, corrupted, and called into question. Whether we speak of public policy, public goods, public interest, or simply the "common good," we are assuming a shared space exists for the voices of individuals and groups to be heard concerning policies and actions that directly impact the quality of their lives. Indeed, this constitutes the very meaning of the word "politics." But as the process of neoliberalization reaches every corner of the globe, we can no longer comfortably assume that the words "public" or "democracy" or "politics" denote something that exists in reality. This is a prominent conversation within the post-capitalist literature. Recent contributions on this theme include Jodi Dean's *Democracy and Other Neoliberal Fantasies* (2009) and Wendy Brown's *Undoing the Demos* (2015). This conversation builds upon Nancy Fraser's seminal essay "Transnationalizing the Public Sphere," first published in 2007. Fraser openly questions whether anything remains of the Habermasian description of the "public sphere," now that the authority of nation states has been eclipsed by the power of international markets and corporations. This may put pastoral and practical theologians in the uncomfortable position of having to help create and sustain the very public sphere to which they appeal. Otherwise the desire to be a "public theology" may prove futile, if not delusional.

Third, this section suggests that *theology matters*. If contemporary capitalism rests on theological assumptions, as some have claimed, then theology has not only the ability but an *obligation* to assess it. Goodchild

(2009) writes: "To refuse theology is to practice a cruel and unreflective theology. The fundamental problem is this: what is worth the sacrifice of flesh and blood, of time, attention, and devotion?" (p. 239). Elsewhere, he implores:

> To what will one devote one's life? What authority will one call on for one's decisions to bear credit? These are inescapable theological questions. Moreover, the dichotomy between the religious and the secular does not merely prevent secular thought from engaging with the most significant problems, for insofar as theology accepts this division of labor and concerns itself with the realms of belief, meaning, individual faith, and ecclesial tradition, it concedes much effective social authority to purely secular relations mediated by money. (p. 203)

Given this urgency, we must ask why theology has largely been so reticent in recent years to comment on the hegemonic power of neoliberalism. Yip (2010) observes: "Although capitalism in its early inception can be said to have emerged from Christian soil, as Max Weber has suggested, it was not welcomed by Christian thinkers" (p. 13). Karen Vaughn (1992), an economist, notes that it is "difficult to think of a major Christian theologian who wrote from 1920 through 1960 who regarded capitalism with favor" (p. 1). In light of this, my call for a post-capitalist pastoral theology appears neither original nor radical.

THE MARGINALIZATION AND CORRUPTION OF INTERPERSONAL SYSTEMS

I turn now to the impact of neoliberal governance on interpersonal systems, exploring first how it has *marginalized* intimate relationships. Zygmunt Bauman (2003) asserts that relationships in a world dominated by free market radicalism have become "liquid"—fragmented, discontinuous, opportunistic, tenuous, and lacking stability. He observes: "*Homo oeconomicus* and *homo consumens* are men and women *without social bonds*. They are the ideal residents of the market economy and the types that make the GNP watchers happy" (p. 69, emphasis in original). A comprehensive discussion would include how this appears as the erosion of face-to-face communities, friendships, romantic attachments, and working relationships. For the sake of brevity, however, I will use marriage as a marker for these alterations. Marriage has the advantage, moreover, of being a social institution while individual marriages are interpersonal relationships, thus illustrating the inseparability of these systems.

So, is neoliberalism *marginalizing* marriage? This would perhaps be a counterintuitive claim, given that in the United States, the conservative politics most visibly allied with neoliberal policies identifies itself as a defender of "family values." Yet, this is exactly what the evidence shows. Jennifer Silva (2013), a sociologist, commenting on variances in divorce rates, observes that economic inequality is now reflected in marital inequality:

> While these statistics may be read as a commentary on the declining value of marriage and family, a closer look reveals that they are more accurately a story of inequality—not only of the economic benefits of marri[age] such as pooled material resources, but also of symbolic and emotional goods such as lasting ties, trust, and love itself. (p. 58)

Silva adds, "since the 1970s, marital dissolution rates have fallen dramatically among highly educated men and women but remained steady among those with lower education" (p. 58). Furthermore, in a phenomenon social scientists call "assortative mating," economic inequality reduces the probability of marriage across class divides, thus adding further to inequality. This leads Andrea Garcia-Vargas, a commentator on this data, to conclude: "The rich marry rich and get richer. The poor marry poor and get poorer" (as cited by Pizzigati, 2014, para. 5–6). Thus we may legitimately see this as another example of the *multiple inequalities* produced culturally by neoliberalization (Davies, 2014, p. 35).

The larger story is revealed not by divorce rates, but changes in rates of marriage. If neoliberal culture is marginalizing marriage, we should see a significant change in the rate of marriage beginning between 1970 and 1980, or soon afterwards. This is indeed evident in the data. Recently the National Center for Family & Marriage Research (NCFMR),[2] located at Bowling Green State University, tabulated and compiled data on the marriage rate in the United States from 1890 through 2011 (Cruz, 2012). The study notes that the US marriage rate has declined almost 60 % since 1970. Other studies have linked this decline directly to the increase in economic inequality. Sociologists Corse and Silva (2013), using interview and survey data involving 300 people, documented the impact of inequality on the marriage rate. They note: "For people with insecure work and therefore few resources, little stability, and no sense of a foreseeable future, concerns for one's own survival threaten the ability to imagine being able to provide materially and emotionally for others" (p. 22). Similar findings appeared in a detailed and definitive examination of declining marriage rates in ten US cities (Gould & Paserman, 2003). Another US study, titled The Hamilton Project, demonstrated that *the entire* decline in the marriage rate since 1970 has occurred in the middle- and lower-income brackets. During this period, marriage rates actually *increased* for wage earners in the top 5 % (Greenstone & Looney, 2012).

This increasing inequality in family life has been reviewed most recently by Carbone and Cahn (2014) in their book *Marriage Markets: How Inequality is Remaking the American Family*. They observe: "economic inequality is remaking the American family along class lines" (p. 1). More pointedly, they argue that in the United States, marriage increasingly participates in class conflict: "The increase in marital stability at the top is related to the disappearance of marriage at the bottom" (p. 49). So we now have a small marital elite at the top, separated from a larger population who are struggling to be married at all.

Although I have focused on changes to marriage in the United States, I should note that marriage rates have been falling across the globe throughout this same period. The Organisation for Economic Co-operation and Development (2014), an economic organization comprising over 30 countries, has presented data demonstrating that marital rates have fallen precipitously in almost all of its member nations between 1970 and 2009. This suggests that the transformations of marriage summarized in the preceding paragraphs have been following the advances of neoliberalization. I believe it is safe to conclude that neoliberal policies introduced since the 1970s and 1980s have indeed marginalized marriage, which has followed upon the inequalities neoliberalism has produced in the economic sector.

Has the culture of late capitalism also *corrupted* marriages? Has it, in other words, altered the actual dynamics of marriage, as a preceding quote by Silva indicates? The idea of corruption assumes, naturally, a prior state that is to be more highly valued. In older, classical traditions, and certainly in Christian theologies, the most valued human relationships were based upon love, which was understood as intending the well-being of the other rather than purely self-interest. This sort of love was recognized as a *gift*. This view is apparent in what Robert Johann (1966) has called "disinterested love." "When love is interested," observed Johann, "when the attraction is based on a motive of profit or need, it has no difficulty in finding words to justify itself." Disinterested love, however, cannot explain itself: "Why do I love you? Because you are—*you*. That is the best it can do. It is indefensible" (p. 19, emphasis in original). Eva Illouz (2007), citing the work of sociologist Jorge Arditi, makes a similar point:

> Arditi suggests that to love means to apprehend the other directly and entirely. It means that no social or cultural object lies between the lover and the beloved, that is, that no element of the intellect plays any part in the experience of loving. These are well-known romantic ideas but I don't think they should be dismissed just because they are romantic. (p. 111)

Such a love was once widely understood as the glue of good-enough marriages, and intimate relationships generally. The culture of late capitalism, as I have noted, is suspicious of any value not based on rational self-interest. The privatization invoked by the new individualism entails a notion of marriage as a contract engaged for mutual self-benefit. Silva (2013), in field interviews with 100 individuals in their 20s and early 30s, observed a core ambivalence in their desires for marriage:

> They long for enduring relationships, based not solely on personal happiness but also on transcendent roles and obligations that ensure stability over time …. On the other hand, respondents speak of a desire to form therapeutic or "pure" relationships that nurture their deepest selves, meet their personal needs, and, most important, do not weigh them down with emotional or financial obligations. (p. 59)

Silva concludes: "Caught between two impossible ideals of love, many find themselves unable to forge romantic relationships that are both satisfying and lasting." Recoiling, these individuals numb themselves "by embracing cultural ideals of self-reliance, individualism, and personal responsibility." As a result, "*they become acquiescing neoliberal subjects*" (p. 149, emphasis added).

Perhaps the keenest analyst to date of the status of romantic attachments under neoliberal governance is the sociologist Eva Illouz (2007). Central to her analysis is the notion of *emotional capitalism:*

> Emotional capitalism is a culture in which emotional and economic discourses and practices mutually shape each other, thus producing what I view as a broad, sweeping movement in which affect is made an essential aspect of economic behavior and in which emotional life—especially that of

the middle classes—follows the logic of economic relations and exchange. Inevitably, the themes of "rationalization" and "commodification" (of emotions) are recurrent topics running throughout all three lectures. (p. 5)

Consequently, "market-based cultural repertoires shape and inform interpersonal and emotional relationships" (p. 5). These repertoires, she argues, alter the very meaning of emotions, yielding what she calls an "emotional ontology" (p. 36). This "gives rise to the idea of 'pure emotion,' the idea that emotions are definite discrete entities and that they are somehow locked and trapped inside the self," and that they "can be detached from the subject for control and clarification" (p. 33, 36). Notice the subtle shift that has occurred here. Emotions are no longer experiences that we undergo, or even that may overwhelm us. Instead, they become *subject to control*, and *rational* control at that. This makes it possible for the individual subject to be intentionally *responsible* for her emotions, a feature that is now almost universal in psychological discourses.

Moreover, as discrete entities, emotions can and should be packaged in a linguistic exchange of information. This is the new significance of "communication" within intimate relationships defined by emotional capitalism. As such, "emotions have become entities to be evaluated, inspected, discussed, bargained, quantified, and commodified" (Illouz, 2007, p. 109). The communication that thus characterizes these relationships is conscious, reasoned, unambiguous, and controlled, which is what leads Illouz to refer to them as "cold intimacies." Such an understanding of emotions, Illouz contends, is not truly congruent with intimate relationships. "Emotions," she asserts, "are by their very nature situational and indexical; they point to the ways in which the self is positioned within a particular interaction" (p. 38). I take this to mean that she understands emotions to be *co-created* by persons in relation, rather than residing *inside*, and thus belonging to the individual as her property. They are primarily unconscious, ambiguous, and even paradoxical, and thus best grasped by intuitive encounter rather than linguistic exchange. In the communication of emotional capitalism, the best one can do is "validate," "recognize," or "mirror" the other's emotions. Thus emotions "do not require any higher justification than the fact that they are felt by the subject. To 'recognize' another means precisely not to argue with or contest the ground for one's feelings" (pp. 35–36). This sort of recognition manifests an artificiality that fails to achieve a genuine meeting. It is an exchange of bits of objectified information rather than an encounter between whole persons. What is missing is the deep mystery and ambiguity of authentic encounters. Such encounters are not welcomed in the hyper-rational and controlled world of neoliberalism. Illouz concludes with a nod to Butler: "I am not sure this is conducive to recognition for, as Judith Butler puts it, 'recognition begins with the insight that one is lost in the other, appropriated in and by an alterity that is and is not oneself'" (p. 39).

The capitalistic character of this "cold intimacy" is also disclosed in its preoccupation with the language of "rights," "needs," and "wants." It is subject to the familiar cost/benefit analysis:

> This new model of intimacy smuggled the middle-class liberal and utilitarian language of rights and bargaining into the bedroom and the kitchen and introduced public forms and norms of discourse where reciprocity, sacrifice, and gift giving had hitherto prevailed. (Illouz, 2008, p. 130)

Neoliberal intimacy has little tolerance for the forms of suffering and sacrifice, much less dependency, that disinterested love inevitably entails: "Romantic suffering is no longer the sign of selfless devotion or of an elevated soul; such love—based on self-sacrifice, fusion, and longing for absoluteness—is viewed as the symptom of an emotional dysfunction" (Illouz, 2010, p. 24). Illouz observes that many poor and working-class individuals manage to retain some notion of romantic love. This leaves us with an ironic twist of contemporary marital and interpersonal inequality. Poor and working-class people envision romantic love but do not have the resources to sustain marriage, while middle-class individuals have the resources for marriage but are losing their grasp on the idea of romantic love (Illouz, 2008, pp. 197–237; see also Illouz, 1997, pp. 220, 247–287).

Illouz's articulation of emotional capitalism offers a tragic example of how the neoliberalization of culture transforms human relationships. As I mentioned in the introduction to this chapter, neoliberal governmentality economizes human interactions even when the value at stake is not monetary. In effect, the individual subject becomes an entrepreneur of interpersonal relationships, managing them according to a logic of profit and loss. As many of the dating and social networking websites now illustrate so abundantly, the interpersonal world has become a highly competitive market. There will be winners, and there most certainly will be losers as well. This brings intense and even novel forms of suffering upon individuals, an issue that now demands our attention.

THE MARGINALIZATION AND CORRUPTION
OF PSYCHOLOGICAL SYSTEMS

It has been almost impossible to discuss neoliberal alterations of social institutions and interpersonal relationships without some reference to psychological effects, especially on what has traditionally been referred to as the self. Silva (2013) puts it succinctly: "The rise of neoliberalism in the economic sphere has prompted a radical re-envisioning of social relationships at the deepest level of the self" (p. 14). The "re-envisioning of social relationships" I have just explored—the alterations of social institutions and interpersonal relationships according to the governance of neoliberal capitalism—also alters the self "at the deepest level." This is because such institutions and relationships give rise to and shape the self. The question now, as before, is how do these alterations both *marginalize* and *corrupt* the self? I suggest that the marginalization of the self appears as a *reduction*, whereas the corruption of the self involves a *reinvention* that conceives the notion of the "authentic self" according to the therapeutic ethos of "emotional capitalism" (Illouz, 2007, 2008).

The reduction of self that occurs under neoliberal governance follows from and accompanies the reductions of institutions and interpersonal relationships. Referring to the erosion of self-sustaining institutions and relationships, Bauman (2004a) observes:

> All this is worrying, indeed frightening news. The blows strike right into the heart of the human mode of being-in-the-world. After all, the hard core of identity—the answer to the question "Who am I?" and even more importantly the continuing credibility of whatever answer might have been given to that question—cannot be formed unless in reference to the bonds connecting the self to other people and the assumption that such bonds are reliable and stable over time. We need relationships, and we need relationships in which we count for something, relationships to which we can refer to define ourselves. (p. 68)

Bauman concludes that, without such sustenance, the "postmodern" self of late capitalism has become fragmented, dispersed, fragile, and discontinuous, or, in his preferred term, "liquid." Individuals are left to construct a self by their own efforts, using whatever shards are left lying around. Yet, he admits, residents of the global market culture may not find a grounded, "cohesive" self to be very appealing:

> Fitting bits and pieces together into a consistent and cohesive totality called "identity" does not seem to be the main worry of our contemporaries .... Perhaps this is not their worry at all. A *cohesive*, firmly riveted and solidly constructed identity would be a burden, a constraint, a limitation on the freedom to choose. It would portend an incapacity to unlock the door when the next opportunity knocks. To cut a long story short, it would be a recipe for *inflexibility*. (2004a, p. 53, emphases in original)

As a matter of fact, as I have noted elsewhere (Rogers-Vaughn, 2012), many now regard an *incohesive* self, or "multiple, discontinuous, fluid self," as something to be celebrated as liberating. Furthermore, the difficulties involved in equating the cohesive self with a substance that hovers above history and social context, or understood within the project of the Enlightenment as a bounded, masterful agency residing inside the individual's skin—a view now rightly understood as exemplifying European domination—has led a skeptical strand of poststructuralism to discard the notion of self altogether. Rose (1998), for example, insists:

> Indeed the very idea, the very possibility of a theory of a discrete and enveloped body inhabited and animated by its own soul—*the* subject, *the* self, *the* individual, *the* person—is part of what is to be explained, the very horizon of thought that one can hope to see beyond. (p. 172, emphases in original)

One problem of reducing, much less discarding, the self is that we are left without the ability to mount an opposition to domination. Many theorists now regard this as an intentional agenda of neoliberal governance. Such a reduced self, argues Dufour (2003/2008), is unable to resist the will of the market. Couldry (2010) concludes that the poststructuralist dismissal of the self makes such a theory complicit with neoliberal hegemony. Boltanski and Chiapello (1999/2007), expert analysts of "the new spirit of capitalism," find this erosion of self to be disconcerting: "But if it is no longer acceptable to believe in the possibility of a more 'authentic' life at a remove from capitalism ... then what is there to halt the process of commodification?" (p. 466). This recognition leads a number of current liberation theologians, reorienting their critique to focus upon contemporary capitalism, to bring a renewed attention to the self or "subject." Sung (2011), for example, summarizing recent developments in liberation thought, states: "liberation is no longer considered solely or principally about the construction of a new society, but it is also about the concept of the subject" (p. 51).

We may see the celebration of a fragmented self as yet another way neoliberalization has co-opted postmodern theories, and thus reproduces another rather orthodox binary. Psychoanalyst Lynne Layton (2004) summarizes my own experiences in psychotherapeutic relationships: "Here, I want to discuss and critique celebrations of fragmentation. In postmodern work that lauds indeterminacy, fragmentation is essentialized, universalized, and celebrated in a way that seems not to acknowledge what it feels like to experience it" (p. 124). The notion of an enduring self-structure, or core self, does not have to conform to the vision of the masterful, bounded self of the Enlightenment, a vision that may actually have more in common with the rational-choice, self-interested subject of neoliberalism than with the reflexive subjectivities of embedded individuals. Layton concludes:

> An error of postmodern theories is their assumption that the experience of a core self precludes the possibility that one experience this self as evolving and changing in its interactions with the world and with others. A core self is constructed and not necessarily stagnant; nor is it necessarily narcissistic. (p. 136)

A structured self assumes a sense of history, belonging, and the ability to narrate one's experience. None of these require rigidity, stasis, or isolated singularity. And, as I have indicated, this is the only sort of self that is capable of a form of desire that can resist the ever-evolving ways that neoliberalization marginalizes the self.

The *corruption* of the neoliberalized self occurs as it attempts to resolve the dilemma posed by Bauman a few paragraphs back. How does one manage to remain flexible in adapting to the conditions of a world where institutions and relationships that sustain the self have waned, while also creating a coherent personal narrative that enables one to cope with these very conditions? The answer lies in Illouz's concept of "emotional capitalism," or what Silva calls the "mood economy." After interviewing young people born after the neoliberal transformation, often referred to a "millennials," Silva (2013) observes that, for these individuals, "legitimacy and self-worth are purchased not with traditional currencies such as work or marriage or class solidarity but instead through the ability to organize their emotions into a narrative of self-transformation" (p. 18). The result is a "therapeutic self" nurtured by the ever-present institutions of psychotherapy and self-help:

Inwardly directed and preoccupied with its own psychic and emotional growth, the therapeutic self has become a crucial cultural resource for ascribing meaning and order to one's life amid the flux and uncertainty of a flexible economy and a post-traditional social world. (p. 19)

The defining feature of the therapeutic self is a narrative of personal suffering. Illouz (2007) describes this "suffering self" as "an identity organized and defined by its psychic lacks and deficiencies, which is incorporated back into the market through incessant injunctions to self-change and self-realization" (p. 109). The narratives of such a self highlight the overcoming of personal trauma, dysfunctional families and relationships, addictions, depression, and so on, which are discussed through the discourse of disease and pathology. Other people appear in these narratives, more or less, as either obstacles to or facilitators of "recovery." Such narratives have become so normative, and supported by the therapy and self-help industries as well as the larger structures of contemporary capitalism, that I am in agreement with Illouz's skepticism regarding the claims by Philip Rieff, Robert Bellah, Christopher Lash, Philip Cushman, Eli Zaretsky, and others, "to the effect that the therapeutic ethos deinstitutionalizes the self" (p. 61). What these theorists likely mean is that this self is separated from *traditional* institutions. The structures of neoliberalism, however—in accordance with its "roll-out" processes—are highly institutionalized, and these structures help to maintain the therapeutic self, leading Illouz (2007) to conclude: "rarely has a cultural form been so institutionalized" (p. 61).

Does this mean that all attempts to empathize with personal suffering, or that all efforts to care for others that go under the designation "therapy," are misguided and complicit with neoliberal agendas? I think not. But any adequate response depends on additional specificity about what has been "corrupted" whenever the self is transmuted into the "therapeutic self." On the surface, how could any caring person be opposed to supporting another's sense of self, advocating authenticity, or empathizing with personal suffering? And yet, in the move from "embedded individualism" to "disembedded individualism" I described in the introduction to this chapter, *the meanings of all three of these terms—self, authenticity, suffering—have been radically altered.* The "self" now refers to an entity that can be communicated in rational terms, clothed with one or more of the many manufactured identities produced by the market, and is isolated from social and interpersonal obligations that are experienced as limitations on personal freedom. It is responsible for its own achievements and failures, which can be neither attributed to the support of others nor blamed on the intrusion of others. Here the notion of self is collapsed into identity, and identity, as Dardot and Laval (2009/2013) assert, "has become a consumable product" (p. 293). "Authenticity" now means being true to one's feelings, which are things unto themselves, are believed to arise solely from some deep interior well that is divorced from connections with others, cannot be questioned as to validity or accuracy, and must be communicated in a rational, linguistic, and unambiguous fashion.

The way suffering has been transmuted deserves particular scrutiny, especially by pastoral theologians, whose discipline is defined by the focus on "what hurts" as both revelatory and deserving of care. Under neoliberal governance, suffering, like the economy, has been *privatized* and *deregulated*. The privatization of suffering means that it is now "one's own" pain. It arises from one's own individual history and personal life story. The individual "owns" her suffering just as the capitalist owns his property, a condition Wendy Brown has called "wounded attachments" (1995, pp. 52–76). It is not believed to be shared with others, or thought to be one's participation in the suffering of a larger group or of humanity generally. It is a suffering that is de-historicized in any collective sense, deprived of a past and lacking hope for a future in which it may be redeemed. This is a suffering that completely defines the self. The deregulation of suffering requires the sufferer to manage their own pain and to be responsible for getting whatever assistance they may need. Prior to neoliberalism, sufferers might have looked to their communities or religious congregations for help in "regulating" their suffering. In better or "good enough" communities, this regulation would not come in the form of rigid control, but as a normalizing of their suffering or, alternatively, a radicalizing of suffering as a striving toward justice. The redemptive community thus offered sufferers an interpretation of their suffering in light of the community's tradition, a ritualizing of their pain, and other active supports.

I am tempted also to suggest that within neoliberal cultures, the only forms of suffering recognized as worthy of attention are *dysregulated* and generally *disembodied*. This becomes apparent when one asks about what forms of suffering simply do not come into view. The sufferings of the "therapeutic self" tend to be limited to "psychic pain," forms of distress that can be addressed by psychological techniques and management, or, in other words, those that can be "fixed" or at least "treated" so as to restore one's ability to compete in the market. I have discussed such "technologies of care" elsewhere (Rogers-Vaughn, 2013a, 2013b).

This leaves out a vast array of sufferings that have to do with embodiment or social injustice. What about suffering that arises from the intractable limitations of the material self, such as irreversible physical injury, permanent disability, incurable disease, and death? And what about grief, that universal suffering that attends death? Are we to regard it as something to be cured or treated as well? How about suffering that originates in social oppression and injustice, such as racism, sexism, or heterosexism, which ostensibly require *political* as well as therapeutic responses? What about suffering that attends war and violence, or even natural disasters? Are we to assume such sufferings are simply to be eliminated or tamed by the psychological techniques intended to manage trauma? Finally, what about the sufferings of untold millions of human beings subjected to inhumane working conditions, or crushed by grinding poverty, many of whom are malnourished or even dying of hunger? This is also a grim reminder of how the lens of the "suffering self" tends to ignore issues of class struggle. The sufferings of the poor or working-class individual are placed beside those of the wealthy person as if they are the same entity and require identical responses.

Ultimately, the privatized and deregulated sufferings of the therapeutic self must be placed into the context of neoliberal society—a culture based on competition in which every individual is an entrepreneur who must manage and promote his or her self as an *enterprise* (Dardot & Laval, 2009/2013, pp. 260–275). This corrupted self, a self in which soul is reduced, is what Dardot and Laval refer to as "the 'entrepreneurial subject' or 'neo-liberal subject,' or, more simply, the *neo-subject*" (pp. 259–260, emphasis in original). Such an individual is constantly exhorted to "be oneself" and to "flourish." In the words of Dardot and Laval:

> The self's new norm certainly consists in flourishing. To succeed, you must know yourself and love yourself. Hence the stress on the magical expression "self-esteem," key to all success. But these paradoxical statements about the injunction to be oneself and love oneself as one is are inscribed in a discourse that sets legitimate desire in order. *Management is an iron discourse in a velvet vocabulary.* (p. 274, emphasis added)

But there is a catch. A reduced and corrupted self is deprived of what is required to genuinely be a self. This results in a situation Dufour (2003/2008) calls hysterology:

> To employ hysterology is basically to postulate something that does not yet exist in order to derive authority for engaging in action. This is the situation in which the democratic subject finds herself, placed as she is under the constraint "Be yourself". She postulates something that does not yet exist (herself) in order to trigger the action through which she must produce herself as a subject. Now, given that this support is bound to be shaky, not to say non-existent, the act either fails by getting always deferred, or is accomplished but puts the subject in the situation of seeing herself perform an act she cannot believe in. The subject then feels herself to be an imposter. (pp. 70–71)

The "neo-subject" is, in other words, set up for failure. Her life is characterized by constant risk (Beck, 1986/1992; Brown, 2015, pp. 37–38; Dardot & Laval, 2009/2013, pp. 275–278). Furthermore, the privatization of suffering entails that this precarious self is solely responsible for his failures. Citing Ulrich Beck's work, Dardot and Laval (2009/2013) conclude:

> We are witnessing a radical individualization that leads to all forms of social crisis being perceived as individual crises and all inequalities being made the responsibility of individuals. The established machinery transforms external causes into personal responsibilities and "problems of the system are lessened politically and transformed into personal failure." (p. 277)

The individual's resignation to this privatization of risk and suffering is enforced, in turn, not only by a colonization of the mind but by the proliferation of debt. As thoroughly demonstrated by Lazzarato (2012), the global submission to a de-territorialized "Great Creditor" assures that we are transformed into debtors who cannot afford to resist (see also Žižek, 2015, pp. 48–57).

Dufour (2003/2008) and Ehrenberg (1998/2010), among others, observe that this emphasis on individual responsibility results in widespread depression as the characteristic form of personal suffering in the present age. Elsewhere (Rogers-Vaughn, 2014) I have summarized the evidence for a global increase in the incidence of depression during the period of neoliberal expansion. Indeed, Ann Cvetkovich (2012) argues that depression is how neoliberalism *feels*: "Depression … is thus a way to describe neoliberalism and globalization … in affective terms" (p. 11). Ehrenberg ties this directly to the internalization of risk and responsibility: "Depression presents itself as an *illness of responsibility* in which the dominant feeling is that of failure. The depressed individual is unable to measure up; he is tired of having to become himself" (p. 4, emphasis in original). It is perhaps telling that "major depression" did not exist as a free-standing psychiatric diagnosis until neoliberalism rose to political prominence, in 1980 (Rogers-Vaughn, 2014). The privatization of suffering thus underlies the current global pandemic of depression, and explains observations about the changes in my clients I shared at the beginning of this book.

Depression is today accompanied by a global increase of addiction. Ehrenberg (1998/2010) asserts: "Depression and addiction are the two sides of the sovereign individual." He concludes, in the same place: "As addictive explosion reflects depressive implosion, so the drug-taker's search for sensation reflects the depressed person's lack of feelings" (p. 232). I would simply add that addiction may, in many cases, function to anesthetize suffering, not only through the use of substances, but in the form of "process addictions"—compulsive eating, spending, sexual activity, video-gaming, work, exercise, and so on. Furthermore, as Cushman (1995) notes, addictive disorders are stimulated in a market-based society that emphasizes consumption and subjective intensity as the answer to feelings of powerlessness (pp. 276, 342–343). "Marketing," Dardot and Laval (2009/2013) contend, "is an incessant, ubiquitous *incitement-to-enjoy*" (p. 287, emphasis in original). Finally, Alexander (2008) points to evidence that addiction arises as an attempt to adapt to circumstances of "psychosocial dislocation," and that neoliberalization has contributed to the global dismantling of communities and solidarities that ground "psychosocial integration" (Part 1), and thus has funded "the globalization of addiction."

This last observation brings us full circle, back to the discussion of the erosion of social processes that began this chapter, as well as to the main concern of this book—the care of souls. I have suggested that soul designates the activity or capacity that holds individuals in relation with self, others, the world, and the Transcendent. It is, moreover, the form of communion that makes it possible to even exist as an individual subject. As Dardot and Laval (2009/2013) inquire: "How are subjects who owe no one anything to be held together?" (p. 291). Thus Alexander (2008) acknowledges that "soul," despite its theological baggage, "has a way of doggedly creeping back into the conversation." He then quotes Karl Polanyi: "The discovery of the individual soul is the discovery of community ... Each is implied by the other" (p. 58). The lesson of this chapter, in agreement with Wendy Brown (2015), is that "soulfulness" is one of the values that neoliberalism "threaten[s] to extinguish" (p. 111). Given the evidence that neoliberalization undermines soul, how can those of us who are charged with the care of souls, whether from religious commitment or not, afford to avert our gaze?

NOTES

1. The website for the GSS is available at http://www3.norc.org/GSS+Website/ (last accessed January 25, 2014).
2. http://www.bgsu.edu/arts-and-sciences/ncfmr.html. I should note here that these studies are limited to heterosexual, or male–female, marriages. There is not yet enough longitudinal data on same-sex marriage to determine if the same patterns would appear.

REFERENCES

Alexander, B. K. (2008). *The globalization of addiction: A study in poverty of the spirit*. New York, NY: Oxford University Press.

Ammerman, N. T. (2013). Spiritual but not religious? Beyond binary choices in the study of religion. *Journal for the Scientific Study of Religion, 52*(2), 258–278.

Bass, D. B. (2012). *Christianity after religion: The end of church and the birth of a new spiritual awakening*. New York, NY: HarperOne.

Bauman, Z. (2001). *The individualized society*. Cambridge: Polity.

Bauman, Z. (2003). *Liquid love: On the frailty of human bonds*. Cambridge: Polity Press.

Bauman, Z. (2004a). *Identity: Conversations with Benedetto Vecchi*. Cambridge: Polity Press.

Bauman, Z. (2004b). *Wasted lives: Modernity and its outcasts*. Cambridge: Polity Press.

Beck, U. (1986/1992). *Risk society: Towards a new modernity*. London: Sage Publications.

Benjamin, W. (1921/1996). Capitalism as religion. In M. Bullock & M. W. Jennings (Eds.), *Walter Benjamin: Selected writings, volume 1, 1913-1926* (pp. 288–291). Cambridge, MA: Belknap Press of Harvard University Press.

Berger, P. L. (1999). The desecularization of the world: A global overview. In P. L. Berger (Ed.), *The desecularization of the world: Resurgent religion and world politics* (pp. 1–18). Washington, DC: Ethics and Public Policy Center; and Grand Rapids, MI: William B. Eerdmans Publishing Company.

Berger, P. L. (2014). *The many altars of modernity: Toward a paradigm for religion in a pluralist age*. Boston, MA: Walter de Gruyter.

Bindley, K. (2013, March 13). Religion among Americans hits low point, as more people say they have no religious affiliation: Report. *The Huffington Post*.

Retrieved August 10, 2015, from http://www.huffingtonpost.com/2013/03/13/religion-america-decline-low-no-affiliation-report_n_2867626.html

Boltanski, L, & Chiapello, E. (1999/2007). *The new spirit of capitalism* (Gregory Elliott, Trans.). London: Verso.

Bourdieu, P. (1998, December 8). The essence of neoliberalism. *Le Monde diplomatique* [English edition]. Retrieved August 16, 2015, from http://monde-diplo.com/1998/12/08bourdieu/

Bowen, M. (1978). *Family therapy in clinical practice*. New York, NY: Jason Aronson.

Braedley, S., & Luxton, M. (2010). Competing philosophies: Neoliberalism and challenges of everyday life. In S. Braedley & M. Luxton (Eds.), *Neoliberalism and everyday life* (pp. 3–21). Montreal, QC: McGill-Queen's University Press.

Brown, W. (1995). *States of injury: Power and freedom in late modernity*. Princeton, NJ: Princeton University Press.

Brown, W. (2006). *Regulating aversion: Tolerance in the age of identity and empire*. Princeton, NJ: Princeton University Press.

Brown, W. (2015). *Undoing the demos: Neoliberalism's stealth revolution*. Brooklyn, NY: Zone Books.

Carbone, J., & Cahn, N. (2014). *Marriage markets: How inequality is remaking the American family*. New York, NY: Oxford University Press.

Carrette, J., & King, R. (2005). *Selling spirituality: The silent takeover of religion*. New York, NY: Routledge.

Centeno, M. A., & Cohen, J. N. (2012). The arc of neoliberalism. *Annual Review of Sociology, 38*, 317–340.

Connell, R. (2010). Understanding neoliberalism. In S. Braedley & M. Luxton (Eds.), *Neoliberalism and everyday life* (pp. 22–36). Montreal, QC: McGill-Queen's University Press.

Connolly, W. E. (2008). *Capitalism and Christianity, American style*. Durham, NC: Duke University Press.

Connolly, W. E. (2013). *The fragility of things: Self-organizing processes, neoliberal fantasies, and democratic activism*. Durham, NC: Duke University Press.

Corse, S., & Silva, J. M. (2013, August 9). *Intimate inequalities: Love and work in a post-industrial landscape*. Paper presented at the American Sociological Association, New York, NY. Retrieved August 17, 2015, from https://convention2.allacademic.com/one/asa/asa/

Couldry, N. (2010). *Why voice matters: Culture and politics after neoliberalism*. London: Sage Publications.

Cox, H. (1999, March). The market as God: Living in the new dispensation. *The Atlantic, 283*(3). Retrieved September 6, 2015, from http://www.theatlantic.com/magazine/archive/1999/03/the-market-asgod/306397/

Cruz, J. (2012). *Marriage: More than a century of change*. National Center for Family & Marriage Research. Retrieved August 17, 2015, from http://www.

bgsu.edu/content/dam/BGSU/college-of-arts-and-sciences/NCFMR/documents/FP/FP-13-13.pdf

Cushman, P. (1995). *Constructing the self, constructing America: A cultural history of psychotherapy*. Reading, MA: Addison-Wesley Publishing Company.

Cvetkovich, A. (2012). *Depression: A public feeling*. Durham, NC: Duke University Press.

Dardot, P., & Laval, C. (2009/2013). *The new way of the world: On neo-liberal society* (Gregory Elliott, Trans.). London: Verso.

Davies, W. (2014). *The limits of neoliberalism: Authority, sovereignty and the logic of competition*. London: SAGE Publications.

Dean, J. (2009). *Democracy and other neoliberal fantasies: Communicative capitalism and left politics*. Durham, NC: Duke University Press.

DuFour, D.-R. (2003/2008). *The art of shrinking heads: On the new servitude of the liberated in the age of total capitalism* (David Macey, Trans.). Cambridge: Polity Press.

Duggan, L. (2003). *The twilight of equality? Neoliberalism, cultural politics, and the attack on democracy*. Boston, MA: Beacon Press.

Eagleton, T. (2014). *Culture and the death of God*. New Haven, CT: Yale University Press.

Ehrenberg, A. (1998/2010). *The weariness of the self: Diagnosing the history of depression in the contemporary age* (Enrico Caouette, Jacob Homel, David Homel, & Don Winkler, Trans.). Montreal, QC: McGill-Queens University Press.

Elliott, A., & Lemert, C. (2009). *The new individualism: The emotional costs of globalization* (Rev. ed.). London: Routledge.

Farley, E. (1990). *Good and evil: Interpreting a human condition*. Minneapolis, MN: Fortress Press.

Fraser, N. (2007). Transnationalizing the public sphere: On the legitimacy and efficacy of public opinion in a post-Westphalian world. *Theory, Culture & Society, 24*(4), 7–30.

Goodchild, P. (2009). *Theology of money*. Durham, NC: Duke University Press.

Gould, E. D., & Paserman, M. D. (2003). Waiting for Mr. Right: Rising inequality and declining marriage rates. *Journal of Urban Economics, 53*(2), 257–281.

Graeber, D. (2015). *The utopia of rules: On technology, stupidity, and the secret joys of bureaucracy*. Brooklyn, NY: Melville House Publishing.

Greenstone, M., & Looney, A. (2012, February 3). *The marriage gap: The impact of economic and technological change on marriage rates*. The Hamilton Project. Retrieved August 17, 2015, from http://www.brookings.edu/blogs/jobs/posts/2012/02/03-jobs-greenstone-looney

Harvey, D. (2005). *A brief history of neoliberalism*. Oxford: Oxford University Press.

Hout, M., & Fischer, C. S. (2002). Why more Americans have no religious preference: Politics and generations. *American Sociological Review, 67*(2), 165–190.

Hout, M., & Fischer, C. S. (2014). Explaining why more Americans have no religious preference: Political backlash and generational succession, 1987-2012. *Sociological Science, 1,* 423–447.

Hout, M., Fischer, C. S., & Chaves, M. A. (2013, March). *More Americans have no religious preference: Key findings from the 2012 General Social Survey,* Institute for the Study of Societal Issues, University of California, Berkeley, CA. Retrieved August 10, 2015 from http://sociology.berkeley.edu/sites/default/files/faculty/fischer/Hout%20et%20al_No%20Relig%20Pref%202012_Release%20Mar%202013.pdf

Illouz, E. (1997). *Consuming the romantic utopia: Love and the cultural contradictions of capitalism.* Berkeley, CA: University of California Press.

Illouz, E. (2007). *Cold intimacies: The making of emotional capitalism.* Cambridge: Polity Press.

Illouz, E. (2008). *Saving the modern soul: Therapy, emotions, and the culture of self-help.* Berkeley, CA: University of California Press.

Illouz, E. (2010). Love and its discontents: Irony, reason, romance. *The Hedgehog Review, 12*(1), 18–32.

Johann, R. O. (1966). *The meaning of love: An essay towards a metaphysics of intersubjectivity.* Glen Rock, NJ: Paulist Press.

Jones, D. S. (2012). *Masters of the universe: Hayek, Friedman, and the birth of neoliberal politics.* Princeton, NJ: Princeton University Press.

Lane, R. E. (2000). *The loss of happiness in market democracies.* New Haven, CT: Yale University Press.

Lash, N. (1996). *The beginning and the end of 'religion'.* Cambridge: Cambridge University Press.

Layton, L. (2004). *Who's that girl? Who's that boy? Clinical practice meets postmodern gender theory.* Hillsdale, NJ: The Analytic Press.

Lazzarato, M. (2012). *The making of indebted man* (Joshua D. Jordan, Trans.). Los Angeles, CA: Semiotext(e).

Loy, D. R. (1997). The religion of the market. *Journal of the American Academy of Religion, 65*(2), 275–290.

Miller-McLemore, B. J. (1996). The living human web: Pastoral theology at the turn of the century. In J. Stevenson-Moessner (Ed.), *Through the eyes of women: Insights for pastoral care* (pp. 9–26). Minneapolis, MN: Fortress Press.

Nelson, R. H. (2001). *Economics as religion: From Samuelson to Chicago and beyond.* University Park, PA: The Pennsylvania State University Press.

Organization for Economic Co-operation and Development. (2014). SF3.1: Marriage and divorce rates. Paris, France: OECD Publishing. Retrieved August 18, 2015, from http://www.oecd.org/els/family/SF3_1_Marriage_and_divorce_rate_Jan2014.pdf

Peck, J. (2010). *Constructions of neoliberal reason.* Oxford: Oxford University Press.

Peltz, R. (2006). The manic society. In L. Layton, N. C. Hollander, & S. Gutwill (Eds.), *Psychoanalysis, class and politics: Encounters in the clinical setting* (pp. 65–80). London: Routledge.

Pizzigati, S. (2014, February 15). America's miserable economy may be ruining your love life: New research shows our growing economic divide is destroying romance in America. *Salon.* Retrieved August 17, 2015, from http://www.salon.com/2014/02/16/americas_miserable_economy_may_be_ruining_your_love_life_partner/

Putnam, R. D. (2000). *Bowling alone: The collapse and revival of American community.* New York, NY: Simon & Schuster.

Rieger, J. (2009). *No rising tide: Theology, economics, and the future.* Minneapolis, MN: Fortress Press.

Rogers-Vaughn, B. (2012). The social trifecta of human misery and problematical constructions of the self: Implications for formation and supervision. *Reflective Practice: Formation and Supervision in Ministry, 32,* 206–223.

Rogers-Vaughn, B. (2013a). Best practices in pastoral counseling: Is theology necessary? *The Journal of Pastoral Theology, 23*(1), 1–24.

Rogers-Vaughn, B. (2013b). Pastoral counseling in the neoliberal age: Hello best practices, goodbye theology. *Sacred Spaces, 5,* 5-45. Retrieved July 31, 2014, from http://www.aapc.org/media/127298/2_rogers_vaughn.pdf

Rogers-Vaughn, B. (2014). Blessed are those who mourn: Depression as political resistance. *Pastoral Psychology, 63*(4), 503–522.

Rose, N. (1998). *Inventing ourselves: Psychology, power, and personhood.* Cambridge: Cambridge University Press.

Rustin, M. (1991). *The good society and the inner world: Psychoanalysis, politics and culture.* London: Verso.

Silva, J. M. (2013). *Coming up short: Working-class adulthood in an age of uncertainty.* New York, NY: Oxford University Press.

Smith, J. K. A. (2014). *How (not) to be secular: Reading Charles Taylor.* Grand Rapids, MI: William B. Eerdmans Publishing Company.

Sung, J. M. (2011). *The subject, capitalism, and religion: Horizons of hope in complex societies.* New York, NY: Palgrave Macmillan.

Taylor, C. (2007). *A secular age.* Cambridge, MA: The Belknap Press of Harvard University Press.

Tillich, P. (1957). *Dynamics of faith.* New York, NY: Harper & Row.

Vaughn, K. I. (1992). Theologians and economic philosophy: The case of Paul Tillich and Protestant socialism. *History of Political Economy, 24*(1), 1–29.

Webster, D. (2012). *Dispirited: How contemporary spirituality makes us stupid, selfish and unhappy.* Winchester: Zero Books.

Yip, F. C.-W. (2010). *Capitalism as religion? A study of Paul Tillich's interpretation of modernity.* Cambridge, MA: Harvard Theological Studies.

Žižek, S. (2015). *Trouble in paradise: From the end of history to the end of capitalism.* Brooklyn, NY: Melville House Publishing.

CHAPTER 4

Neoliberalism as a Paradigm for Human Affliction: Third-Order Suffering as the New Normal

Dedicated readers, who have made it this far, may have concluded that enough has been said about the relationship between neoliberal capitalism and human suffering. After all, in the preceding chapter, I traced how neoliberalization alters the fabric of every society it touches from top to bottom, from the dismantling of social institutions that create meaning and belonging to the hollowing out of intimate relationships to the fragmentation of the individual self. I even briefly alluded to how, at the level of individual experience, today's actually existing capitalism modifies suffering through its characteristic processes of privatization and deregulation. It may now come as some surprise that I consider that analysis as operating through a relatively narrow lens, focusing as it does on the alteration of institutions and on the micropolitics of everyday life. What remains to be explored is how contemporary capitalism exacerbates the sufferings of entire populations of people; how it alters our general attitudes toward suffering and appraisals of its significance; how it shapes the ways we attend to, ignore, or legitimate suffering; and especially how it is creating a new order of suffering that is transforming already existing types of suffering such that their present forms are more difficult to recognize and address.

© The Author(s) 2016
B. Rogers-Vaughn, *Caring for Souls in a Neoliberal Age*,
DOI 10.1057/978-1-137-55339-3_4

A More Efficient Regime for the Global
Production of Suffering and Death

I should begin by acknowledging that the benefits of historical capitalism, even prior to the neoliberal revolution, have come at the cost of unimaginable human suffering. With regard to the history of the United States, great fortunes were amassed during the nineteenth century, during a time when "cotton was king," which catapulted this country into the political and economic prominence it enjoys to this day. This history has been meticulously documented by Edward Baptist in *The Half Has Never Been Told: Slavery and the Making of American Capitalism* (2014) and placed into global perspective by Sven Beckert in *Empire of Cotton: A New History of Global Capitalism* (2014). In 1802, Baptist observes, cotton represented just 14 % of exports from the United States, but by 1820 accounted for 42 % (p. 83). He later concludes: "By the 1840s, the United States had grown into both an empire and a world economic power—the second greatest industrial economy, in fact, in the world—all built on the back of cotton" (p. 413). And cotton, in turn, was built upon the backs of slaves: "Stories about industrialization emphasize white immigrants and clever inventors, but they leave out cotton fields and slave labor" (Baptist, p. xviii). This rapid capitalist expansion would have been impossible without a highly lucrative, efficient, and professional slave industry, which required the trading of black bodies as literal commodities on an open market. By 1860, the almost 4 million slaves owned by US citizens were worth over 3 billion dollars—nearly 20 % of the total wealth held by all US citizens (Baptist, Table 7.1, p. 246). Thus at the very foundation of industrial capitalism, not just in the United States, but globally, was what Beckert (2014) calls "war capitalism." He describes war capitalism as a system that began to emerge globally during the sixteenth century, which operated as a way of "organizing production, trade, and consumption." He concludes: "Slavery, the expropriation of indigenous peoples, imperial expansion, armed trade, and the assertion of sovereignty over people and land by entrepreneurs were at its core" (p. xv). Later he notes:

> War capitalism had an unprecedented transformative potential. At the root of the emergence of the modern world of sustained economic growth, *it created unfathomable suffering*, but also a consequential transformation of the organization of economic space: A multipolar world increasingly became unipolar. (p. 38, emphasis added)

It may sound incredible, with this breadth and depth of suffering as a historical backdrop, to claim that the neoliberal phase of capitalism represents both an extension and radical transformation of war capitalism. And yet this appears, unfortunately, to be the case. A good portion of our disbelief may be due to the success neoliberal interests have had in marketing their ideology and practices as the spread of freedom and equal opportunity. We are prompted to believe that the era of barbarism and colonialism and its accompanying brutal institutions—such as slavery—are behind us. A prevailing optimistic spirit leads some to proclaim that we have arrived at "the end of history" (Fukuyama, 1992/2006). What has happened throughout the world since 1980, however, belies the celebratory rhetoric of "free market" enthusiasts. Parallel to a phenomenal increase in accumulated wealth and market innovations, human suffering has increased exponentially.

Summarizing the devastating effects of the new global economy, Saskia Sassen (2014) argues that the shift from conventional capitalism to neoliberalism is comparable to the shift from premodern societies to modern capitalism: "We can characterize the relationship of advanced to traditional capitalism in our current period as one marked by extraction and destruction, not unlike the relationship of traditional capitalism to precapitalist economies" (p. 10). The shift to the current global economy is marked, she asserts, by two developments. The first is the segregation of the world "into extreme zones for key economic operations" (p. 9). Manufacturing, clerical services, and other sorts of labor are outsourced to low-cost areas. Meanwhile, the network of "global cities," or metropoles, is enriched. The world is once again multipolar, but the many poles are culturally and economically homogenized. Second is the radical financialization of the global economy. While finance is not new, Sassen observes: "What is new and characteristic of our current era is the capacity of finance to develop enormously complex instruments that allow it to securitize the broadest-ever, historically speaking, range of entities and processes." The outcome is a sweeping restructuring of the global economy: "While traditional banking is about selling money that the bank has, finance is about selling something it does not have" (p. 9). The ideal example of such a complex instrument, she concludes, is the derivative. By 2005, she notes, the global value of outstanding derivatives was about $630 trillion, which "was fourteen times [the] global gross domestic product (GDP)" (p. 9).

To put what Sassen is saying more directly, finance is about the buying and selling of *debt*. The selling of what the bank "does not have" is unpaid debt. The bundling and selling of debt is therefore speculation upon a *future* asset. Lazzarato (2012) claims: "neoliberalism has, since its emergence, been founded on a logic of debt" (p. 25). "In neoliberalism," he notes, "what we reductively call 'finance' is indicative of the increasing force of the creditor-debtor relationship" (p. 23). He concludes: "Politically, the *debt economy* seems to be a more appropriate term than finance or financialized economy, not to mention financial capitalism" (p. 24, emphasis in original). While from the perspective of those who own debt this appears simply as credit or financial investment, in the experience of those who hold debt this has become a dominant form of exploitation. Robert Reich (2010), a former US Secretary of Labor, comments that personal debt in the United States "rose from 55 percent of household income in the 1960s to an unsustainable 138 percent by 2007" (p. 23). While this rate fell somewhat following the recession that began in 2008, in part due to foreclosures and defaults, the Federal Reserve reports that household debt is again steadily increasing.[1] Meanwhile, data on household debt from other countries demonstrate that this is a global problem.[2] Lazzarato contends that the global debt economy is producing a new type of human subject, which he calls "indebted man."

As both Lazzarato (2012, 2015) and Sassen (2014) observe, the debt economy reconfigures class struggle. In Sassen's words: "People as consumers and workers play a diminished role in the profits of a range of economic sectors" (p. 10). Compared to earlier versions of capitalism, which were systems of incorporation or inclusion—though such inclusion often meant exploitation and even slavery—Sassen maintains that contemporary capitalism is a global system of *expulsion*. In the current global economy, millions of human beings are needed for neither production nor consumption. These unfortunate souls have become a permanent underclass. The existence of an ever-expanding population of migrants, refugees, prisoners, asylum seekers, the perpetually unemployed, and other outcasts become what Bauman (2004) calls "the waste products of globalization" (p. 66). We may justifiably think of them as excretions of the global debt economy. Elsewhere Bauman (1997) describes this mass of human beings:

> Not needed as producers, useless as consumers—they are people which the 'economy', with its logic of needs-arousing and needs-gratifying, could very well do without. Their being around and claiming the right to survival is a

nuisance for the rest of us; their presence could no more be justified in terms of competitiveness, efficiency or any other criteria legitimized by the ruling economic reason. (p. 157)

The very existence of the expelled is a threat to the "natural order" of the neoliberal economy. Thus, as a dimension of the "roll-out" phases of neoliberalization, the contemporary security state manages this population through policing and confinement—either literally or by economic segregation into "low rent" districts—as well as by direct or indirect extermination.

Bauman (1997) asserts that these tactics are made more effective "through exorcizing the horror of death" (p. 159). Neoliberalization thus numbs us to its own brutality, even as it is becoming an increasingly efficient regime of death and destruction. He notes that this is achieved by dual strategies that appear contradictory but are actually complementary. First is "the strategy of hiding the death of those close to oneself from sight and chasing it away from the memory" (p. 159). Expressions of ordinary grief and mourning are considered inappropriate for public display and are increasingly becoming pathologized (Rogers-Vaughn, 2014). Media coverage of flag-draped caskets of soldiers slain during the Vietnam War is gone in the days of the "War on Terror." Not only are once familiar death and grief rendered invisible, so is the violence that accompanies the neoliberal preoccupation with "security." In her book *Economies of Abandonment*, anthropologist Elizabeth Povinelli (2011) observes:

> What Foucault did not discuss was that neoliberalism transformed an older liberal governance of life and death .... Any form of life that could not produce values according to market logic would not merely be allowed to die, but, in situations in which the security of the market ... seemed at stake, ferreted out and strangled. This way of killing is not commensurate with an older sovereign power Foucault so viscerally described in the opening of *Discipline and Punish*. There are not public spectacles of drawn and quartered bodies—or lynched bodies. Secret agreements are made to remove the body to be tortured far away from public sight and scrutiny. (p. 22)

What we have here is nothing less than the privatization of death and violence. This allows neoliberal social orders, through what William Davies (2015) calls "the happiness industry," to foster the illusion that life within their protection is one in which "human flourishing" and positive emotions predominate. But simultaneously, it also enables them to conceal and deny their own production of terror and death.

The second strategy for masking the horror of death is a peculiar type of mass anesthesia. Bauman (1997) continues:

> Death close to home is concealed, while death as a universal human predicament, the death of anonymous and 'generalized' others, is put blatantly on display, made into a never ending street spectacle that, no more a sacred or carnival event, is but one among many of life's paraphernalia. So banalized death is made too familiar to be noted and much too familiar to arouse high emotions .... Its horror is exorcised through its omnipresence, made absent through the excess of visibility, made negligible through being ubiquitous, silenced through deafening noise. (p. 159)

In the United States this soul-killing detachment is facilitated by a media-produced phenomenon Bageant (2007) calls the "American hologram." Within this virtual space working-class people, he observes:

> are bathed, hour after hour, in the televised imagery of the new corporate state, in which eagles scream gloriously above the wreckage of the World Trade Center, in which the enemy is smitten on foreign shores, in which thrilling cavalcades of heavily armed motorcycle police and marching SWAT teams appear larger than life. Ignorant and sated people are not chilled by such sights on their television screens. Far from it. (p. 256)

Thanks to the efficient "happiness industry" mediated through this hologram, Bageant deems these people "approximately happy." He concludes: "When happiness is based completely on the thinnest observable material conditions of life—a new truck in the driveway, an iPod in your pocket, the availability of round-the-clock entertainment—it's easy to be happy" (p. 264).

Meanwhile, with populations suitably inoculated to their own grief and to the deaths of strangers, neoliberal processes continue their extension and restructuring of war capitalism in the service of capital accumulation. Achille Mbembe (2003) calls the emerging product "necropolitics," a word that points to the power of death under this form of governance. This new form of colonialism does not typically attempt the annexation of entire countries or geographies. Occupation is limited to zones of extraction, as well as to enclaves of resistance for the sake of control and policing. Wars under this form of capitalism do not aim for "the conquest, acquisition, and takeover of a territory," but appear as nomad-like "hit-

and-run affairs" (p. 30). Mbembe quotes Zygmunt Bauman to describe the way military forces appear in such scenarios:

> They rest their superiority over the settled population on the speed of their own movement; their own ability to descend from nowhere without notice and vanish again without warning, their ability to travel light and not to bother with the kind of belongings which confine the mobility and maneuvering potential of the sedentary people. (as cited by Mbembe, p. 31)

Finally, the right to kill is curiously disconnected from, yet usually in the service of, state sovereignty. Mbembe observes that violence is often carried out not by standing armies but by mercenary organizations that are backed by sovereign states (most often, today, the United States). Mbembe, borrowing a term from Deleuze and Guattari, calls these "war machines." These constitute the postmodern (neoliberal) form of war: "Polymorphous and diffuse organizations, war machines are characterized by their capacity for metamorphosis. Their relation to space is mobile" (p. 32). He concludes:

> A war machine combines a plurality of functions. It has the features of a political organization and a mercantile company. It operates through capture and depredations and can even coin its own money. In order to fuel the extraction and export of natural resources located in the territory they control, war machines forge direct connections with transnational networks. (pp. 32–33)

In other words, war machines serve the interests of global markets. Meanwhile, the violence perpetrated by these groups appears on corporate-owned news coverage (if it appears at all) as a distant skirmish between rival insurgents that is unrelated to viewers' own governments or the prices of their favorite products on the shelves at Wal-Mart or on offer at Amazon or the Apple Store. Those who must live in these zones of extraction, however, are condemned to existence in "*death-worlds,* new and unique forms of social existence in which vast populations are subjected to conditions of life conferring upon them the status of *living dead*" (p. 40, emphases in original). What passes for life in these areas of the world is, in effect, the new face of slavery. But, unlike the slavery of the earlier industrial capitalism, this slavery is—even in this age of technology and the internet—virtually invisible.

It is clear, moreover, that this violence is *systemic*. This was, of course, true even under traditional forms of capitalism. Žižek (2008) asserts: "Therein resides the fundamental systemic violence of capitalism, much more uncanny than any direct pre-capitalist socio-ideological violence: this violence is no longer attributable to concrete individuals and their 'evil' intentions, but is purely 'objective,' systemic, anonymous" (pp. 12–13). Žižek then goes on to argue that this violence has become far more abstract under the contemporary version of capitalism, with its reliance on financialization and extreme debt production. In its present neoliberal form, capitalism imposes violence even when military force is not utilized. The global evidence is now abundant. For example, in the mid-1990s, the United States and the European Union, catering to the demands of international agricultural businesses, insisted that the WTO, the IMF, and the World Bank adopt policies that allowed North American and European governments to continue providing heavy subsidies to their own farmers, while requiring governments in other parts of the world to reduce farm subsidies. These policies were implemented. The result? In just one country—India—about 216,500 farmers committed suicide between 1997 and 2009 (Leech, 2012, pp. 55–56). Why? Leech (2012) summarizes: "The common denominator is that all of the farmers who have committed suicide were deep in debt. In fact, the number of Indian peasant households in debt doubled between 1991 and 2001 from 26 per cent to 48.6 per cent" (p. 56).

Similar events have occurred globally. In 1994, the NAFTA was passed by its partner countries—the United States, Canada, and Mexico. Technically, the agreement allowed all three countries to subsidize agriculture. However, because Mexico was bound by the international limitations on farm subsidies mentioned in the preceding paragraph, in addition to the same limitations imposed by loans it received directly from the United States, it could not do so. Consequently, US corporations flooded Mexico with food that sold for less than that of Mexican farmers. Between 1997 and 2005, Leech (2012) documents, "Mexican producers of corn, wheat, rice, cotton and soybeans have lost more than $1 billion a year in earnings under NAFTA" (p. 46). Many peasant farmers became internal refugees, fleeing the countryside looking for work in the cities. Meanwhile, "under NAFTA's favourable investment conditions, U.S. and Canadian mining companies have displaced thousands of peasants and gained control over more than a million hectares of land in the state of Chiapas." The refugee crisis caused a glut of labor in the cities, which then held wages to an average of the equivalent of $1.74 per hour. Ironically, by 2003, many of those jobs had moved to other countries, especially China, "where the interests of capital were being better served through labour costs that were even lower than in Mexico" (p. 47). Conditions were even worse in some South American countries. In Colombia, which Leech calls "Latin America's neoliberal poster child," similar policies yielded 4 million internal refugees (p. 48).

Corporate-owned media respond to the global refugee crisis by using both methods for "exorcizing the horror of death" that Bauman outlines—either invisibilizing it or rendering it banal. But no refugee crisis is less visible than that in the world's wealthiest country, the United States, where refugees tend to be referred to simply as "the homeless" or the "very poor." In the United States neoliberal policies have also drastically increased this problem, most recently documented by Kathryn Edin and Luke Shaefer (2015). They note that, after several years of attacks beginning with Ronald Reagan's first presidential campaign, welfare as it had been known for 60 years ended with President Clinton's signing of the "welfare reform" bill in 1996. The new law replaced Aid to Families with Dependent Children (AFDC) with Temporary Assistance for Needy Families (TANF). It imposed time limits on aid, as well as stringent work requirements, whereas AFDC based aid solely upon documented need. This produced a dramatic reduction in public welfare. In 1994, welfare served 14.2 million people. By the fall of 2014, only 3.8 million were served. Edin and Shaefer observe: "Just 27 percent of poor families with children participate. There are more avid postage stamp collectors in the United States than welfare recipients" (p. 7). Welfare is so far off the public mind, they note, that even many who meet the criteria for TANF do not bother to apply, mistakenly believing that welfare no longer exists in any form. Welfare, the authors flatly conclude, is practically dead. This contributes to levels of poverty not seen in the United States since the Great Depression. To measure this, Shaefer did not use the official poverty line in the United States, which equals $16.50 per person per day. He did not even use the official line for "deep poverty"—the equivalent of $8.30 per person per day. Instead, he used the World Bank's metric for global poverty—$2 per person per day. This is a level of poverty "so deep that most Americans don't believe it exists in this country" (p. xiii). At this level, survival is grueling work. Edin conducted extensive field work and discovered people scavenging in garbage for recyclables to convert to cash (which nets only about $60 per month at best), selling their blood plasma, and (though outright prostitution was unusual) trading sex for necessities. As of 2011, 1.5 million households in the United States, including about 3 million children, were surviving on $2 per person per day—more than double the number before Clinton signed the "welfare reform" act in 1996 (p. xvii).

Despite the mounting global refugee crisis and increasing poverty, neoliberal rationality has no trouble explaining such suffering. One now familiar method is the discourse of scarcity, especially applied to populations outside the United States. Due to population growth, some argue, there is just not enough to go around. Thus people can only be expected to compete for whatever resources they can get. This discourse is easily debunked and has been repeatedly rebuffed in the research literature on world poverty. The actual reason today happens to be the increase in global inequality that has accompanied neoliberal expansion. For example, Leech (2012), citing data supplied by the United Nations Development Program, states:

> Europeans spent $11 billion a year on ice cream, $2 billion more than the amount required to provide safe drinking water and adequate sanitation for everyone in the [global] South. And the $17 billion that Americans and Europeans spend annually on pet food would easily have provided basic health care for everyone in the [global] South. (p. 82)

Leech concludes: "Such a degree of global inequality is not simply an unintended consequence of capitalism; it is an essential component of the global capitalist system." There is profit to be made supplying ice cream and pet food to Americans and Europeans, and none to be made offering water, sanitation, and health care to the Global South (p. 82).

Another explanation that dominates neoliberal discourse, especially directed toward domestic populations, is that poverty and other social problems are due to the bad decisions of individuals. Thus social problems are attributed to individual morality. The poor are simply lazy, unambitious, unfit, irrational, malingerers, or criminals. As Hamann (2009) notes: "The neoliberal approach to dealing with growing poverty, unemployment, and homelessness is not simply to ignore it, but to impose punitive judgments through the moralizing effects of its political rationality" (p. 45). Thus, as Wacquant shows in *Punishing the Poor* (2009), the prison system has been re-purposed to control social insecurity rather than simply criminal insecurity. This illuminates why, in the United States, the prison population has skyrocketed over the past three decades, at the same time that crime rates have remained steady and even declined in recent years. Meanwhile, what is left of welfare and other public services is made contingent on good behavior and a modicum of employment, serving as yet another effective method of social control. As Soss, Fording, and Schram demonstrate in *Disciplining the Poor* (2011), this not only manages social insecurity but also serves the interests of capital:

> Welfare programs for the unemployed have been redesigned to mimic the pressures and incentives of low-wage labor markets and to bolster these pressures with state authority.... The adults who participate in welfare programs today are not positioned outside the market; they are actively pressed into accepting the worst jobs at the worst wages. (p. 7)

In other words, the poor are actively conscripted to do essential jobs no one else will do on terms no one else would accept. The origins of such problems are neither scarcity nor personal morality. As Reid-Henry (2015) has recently documented, the origins are ultimately political and will require political solutions.

To summarize, neoliberalization is a more efficient regime for the global production of suffering and death, in both its rationality and its practices. The increase in suffering that has occurred in the transition from conventional capitalism to neoliberal capitalism is comparable to what transpired in the move from precapitalist societies to capitalism in earlier times. Moreover, the marginalizations and corruptions detailed in Chap. 3—of social, interpersonal, and psychological systems—reappear in the marginalization and corruption of suffering itself. Wherever suffering threatens to offer a foundation for human solidarity, it is invisibilized and suppressed. At the same time, the sufferings that are placed on display are made to serve the interests of today's actually existing capitalism.

There is, therefore, both a continuity with past forms of suffering and the production of new forms of suffering. It is critical that we grasp these continuities and transformations in order to both understand and resist a global form of governance that many researchers and scholars now identify as nothing less than genocidal. Samir Amin (2011) concludes, regarding today's capitalism: "the logic of the system is no longer able to ensure the simple survival of humanity. Capitalism is becoming barbaric and leads directly to genocide" (p. 106). This is not merely rhetoric. Hamann (2009) notes that the World Food Summit, in 1996, pledged to cut world hunger in half within 20 years. But in just over half that time, the number of hungry people in the world had *increased* by 18 million, "with an average of six million children dying of hunger each year" (p. 45). Leech (2012) refers to contemporary capitalism as "a structural genocide." Buttressing his argument with documented case studies from Mexico, South America, India, and Sub-Saharan Africa, he calculates that the practices of today's capitalism accounts for at least 10 million additional deaths *per year* globally (pp. 149–150). Given the preceding figures from world hunger alone, this figure is likely conservative. This level of death and suffering equals or exceeds the most infamous genocides in recorded history. Moreover, if today's version of capitalism is the primary culprit in the degradation of the environment, as Naomi Klein claims in *This Changes Everything: Capitalism vs. The Climate* (2014), then neoliberalism could become the only hegemony responsible for the possible extinction of humanity and life on the planet as we know it. The stakes have never been this high.

Now, if we pull back from these more extreme manifestations of suffering, as terrifyingly real as they may be, still other regions of suffering open up for investigation. These include one I have already mentioned—the reconfiguration of class struggle by a global debt economy—as well as transformations of already existing social injustices such as sexism and racism. In the remainder of this chapter, I will first pursue the general implications of paradigm theory for suffering under neoliberal governance. I will explore the emergence of a new order of suffering that has become normalized under the neoliberal paradigm, as well as identify how this new order may be altering already existing forms of suffering. Then, in the next chapter, I will review, as examples, the transformations of sexism, racism, and class conflict as they become entangled with this new order of suffering.

Neoliberalism as a Paradigm for Suffering

In his now famous book *The Structure of Scientific Revolutions*, Thomas Kuhn (1962/2012) developed a theory for how change occurs in science. The notion of paradigm change has become popularized and permeates culture, leading many scholars to complain about its overuse and possible misapplications when employed as a general theory of social change. I do not intend to enter these debates here. Rather, I will use a couple of ideas embedded in Kuhn's theory as pedagogical devices to interrogate neoliberalization with regard to suffering. Kuhn asserted that paradigm change in science yields theories or insights that are genuinely novel. He also demonstrated that, when such a transition occurs, prior data or theories persist in the new system, but are understood from a new perspective, or are rearranged and mean something different within the new paradigm. I use these notions to raise two questions. First, have new forms of suffering appeared with the advent of neoliberalization? Second, how has neoliberalization transformed already existing types of suffering?

The new forms of domination that appear in neoliberal capitalism have, I believe, been identified by Dany-Robert Dufour in his book *The Art of Shrinking Heads* (2003/2008). He refers to these forms of domination by the rather unwieldy terms deinstitutionalization, desymbolization, and desubjectivation. I will refer to these collectively as "the three Ds." In Dufour's thought, these processes are somewhat distinct, yet are entangled and reinforce one another. They have appeared, he argues, with neoliberalism, or what he calls "total capitalism." He contends that former types of domination worked through institutions, which Foucault called "disciplinary societies." Referring to the upheavals of the 1960s, Dufour maintains that something novel began to occur:

> The highly committed militant actions of the day did not take into account that the institutions they were targeting were the very apparatuses that the most aggressive fraction of capitalism wished to destroy. It no longer wanted to assert itself by placing disciplinary controls on life; it wanted a completely new form of domination, and the events of the 1960s ... hastened its introduction. (p. 157)

Dufour ties this destruction of institutions to desubjectivation or the reduction and fragmentation of the human subject. Without transcendental values provided by cultural institutions, the individual has no way to be grounded or even to think critically. There is little left but the market. He concludes of total capitalism: "It is destroying institutions ... in such a way as to produce individuals who are supple, insecure, mobile and open to all the market's modes and variations" (p. 157). Dufour clearly suggests here that genuine individuality depends upon embeddedness in cultural institutions. In my view, this does not imply social determinism. Rather, individuals exist as individuals, as I have stated before, in their capacity to improvise upon what is given by the sociocultural surround. What is also apparent here is the entanglement between institutions and subjectivity. The erosion of institutions must also include a reduction in subjectivity. Finally, Dufour argues that these are novel developments in human history, and that they necessarily imply novel forms of suffering that are consequent upon the new forms of domination. Prior to neoliberalism, domination was exercised by means of the disciplinary powers of institutions. Today domination occurs through the suppression of these institutions. Prior to neoliberalism, domination required replacing a particular type of subject with a new form of subject. Today it occurs through the fragmentation and dispersal of the subject altogether.

These themes are by now familiar to the reader, for I have discussed them in the preceding chapter as the erosion of social systems (collectives) and psychological systems (the self or subject) that occurs due to the neoliberalization of culture. The remaining novel form of suffering Dufour identifies is the effect of desymbolization. Before moving to what he intends by this term, however, I must pause to clarify and develop Dufour's claims. I believe what I have to say here is consistent with Dufour's theory rather than simply an overturning of it. However, Dufour often articulates his position on these novel forms of suffering in a way that appears overextended. For example, it is surely the case that the imperial conquests that have occurred during human history inevitably included the dismantling and/or co-optation of indigenous institutions. These same sociocultural displacements also produced psychological disturbances similar to what Dufour describes as the fragmented and dispersed subject, as the works of theorists such as Frantz Fanon (1952/1967, 1963/2004) have shown. Indeed, Alexander (2008) refers to this phenomenon as "psychosocial dislocation," and uses historical case studies to portray how this appears when indigenous societies are disrupted. Moreover, clinicians and relief workers are familiar with the psychological states Dufour describes, as they arise in virtually all instances of severe trauma. Traumatized individuals experience fragmentation and feel "unreal," even disembodied. They also, in anticipation of our consideration of desymbolization, are rendered mute. They are unable to articulate, narrate, or "make sense of" what is happening to them. Given all this, how can Dufour possibly claim the sorts of sufferings he describes have not existed before in history?

The answer has to do with Kuhn's description of paradigms. A paradigm describes what has become "normal," routine or status quo. The experiences Dufour describes have existed before, but only (to use Kuhn's term) as "anomalies." That is, they have occurred as *crises*, transitional conditions between states of relative stability. What Dufour is suggesting,

I believe, is that under neoliberal capitalism, these conditions have become paradigmatic, or *normal*. Alexander (2008) points toward this difference:

Whereas individual people can become dislocated by misfortunes in any society, including tribal, feudal, and socialist ones, and whereas the downfall of any society produces mass dislocation, *only free-market society produces mass dislocation as part of its normal functioning even during periods of prosperity*. Along with dazzling benefits in innovation and productivity, globalisation of free-market society has produced an unprecedented, worldwide collapse of psychosocial integration. (p. 60, emphasis added)

Alexander concludes: "To the degree that Western civilization approximates a free-market society, dislocation is not the pathological state of a few but the general condition" (p. 61). The challenge, then, is to imagine the new order of suffering corresponding to this "general condition."

This theme has been repeated and elaborated by a number of theorists across disciplines. Eric Cazdyn (2012), for example, engages critical theory, philosophy, and psychoanalysis to describe what he calls "the new chronic." He observes: "crisis is not what happens when capitalism goes wrong, but when it goes right .... The point is that crisis is built right into the system of capitalism—not only when it busts, but when it booms" (p. 2). Cazdyn proceeds to place "the new chronic," along with its associated phenomena—"the global abyss" and "the living dead"—into the context of late capitalism. Inspired by his own ongoing struggle with leukemia, Cazdyn uses his experience as an analogy for what he perceives as the new normal in a neoliberal world:

We have entered something like a new chronic mode, a mode of time that cares little for terminality or acuteness. Every level of society is stabilized on an antiretroviral cocktail. Every person is safe, like a diabetic on insulin. A solid remission, yes, but always with the droning threat of relapse—of collapse, if not catastrophe. (p. 13)

Likewise, as I noted in the introduction, several psychoanalysts have asserted that similar conditions they see in their patients are attributable to the "traumatogenic environment" imposed under contemporary capitalism (Layton, Hollander, & Gutwill, 2006, pp. 1–5). Žižek (2011) openly wonders what we are to take the word "trauma" to mean in a neoliberal order, where it now refers to the ordinary state of affairs rather than the exception. A similar point is made by Catherine Malabou (2012) in her discussion of "destructive plasticity." In my estimation, all of these theories are deeply resonant with my explication of the erosions of social, interpersonal, and psychological systems outlined in Chap. 3. And all support Dufour's thesis that the forms of suffering generated by deinstitutionalization, desubjectivation, and desymbolization are novel in the sense that they constitute a new normal, thus a new paradigm for suffering.

Which brings us now to desymbolization. What does Dufour mean by this? Dufour (2003/2008) summarizes: "Desymbolization refers to a process designed to rid symbolic exchanges of that which is in excess of them and which at the same time institutes them: their foundations" (p. 160). Analogous to the erosions of collectives, interpersonal relationships and psychological spaces I discussed in the last chapter, this process hollows out communication such that words and images become fleeting signifiers rather than symbols. Communication is rendered trite, ironic, and pedestrian. It lacks a "transcendent sphere of principles and ideals" ordinarily provided by culture, which is "a repository of moral principles, aesthetic canons, models of truth, and so on" (p. 160). Thus robbed of their depth, language and images no longer embody values that have the ability to resist those of the market. There are no longer, claims Dufour, "soteriological narratives," either of religions, nation states, or those for the liberation of workers, that retain enough credibility and cohesion to oppose the market (pp. 44–51). Neoliberalism has eroded the foundations of such narratives.

A similar claim has been made, in theology, by Edward Farley (1996). In *Deep Symbols*, Farley concerns himself with "the global turmoil of late capitalism," which he implicitly equates with postmodernity (p. 1). Farley, like Dufour, appeals to the novelty he sees in the erosion of deep symbols:

> What appears to be new in postmodern societies is not a displacement of old symbols for new ones but a weakening if not elimination of all words of power. All deep symbols now appear to be imperiled by postmodern discourses, societal traits, and sociologies of knowledge. (pp. 13–14)

In this new order, observes Farley, "all language takes place in quotation marks" (p.14). He continues:

> But with the loss of the words of power, quaintness applies to all such terms: thus "tradition," "duty," "conscience," "truth," "salvation," "sin," "God."

These too need the quotation marks that indicate we are aware that they do not quite work anymore and are not quite to be taken seriously. (p. 15)

He concludes, "I suspect the term 'theology' is about to join that list of quaint terms we no longer use" (p. 14).

Finally, Couldry (2010) provides a bridge between this erosion of deep symbols and the general ability to narrate our everyday lives. Couldry asserts that neoliberalism undermines this ability, which he calls "voice." In his estimation, neoliberalism is a "voice-denying rationality" (p. 10). Voice, he contends, is socially grounded. Like both Dufour and Farley, Couldry argues that voice depends upon functioning communities and traditions. "Voice," he argues, "is not the practice of individuals in isolation" (p. 7). Furthermore, voice is materially grounded. As such, voice is implicated in material inequality:

> If, through an unequal distribution of narrative resources, the materials from which some people must build an account of themselves are *not* theirs to adapt or control, then this represents a deep denial of voice, a deep form of oppression. This is the oppression W. B. Dubois described as 'double consciousness', a 'sense of always looking at oneself through the eyes of others.' (p. 9, emphasis in original)

Thus, although everyone in neoliberalized societies may suffer a reduction of voice, this will be exacerbated by the extreme material inequality in these societies. Moreover, loss of voice will be unequally distributed, with those with fewer material resources being the more severely affected. The inability to narrate one's life, then, participates in the oppressions occurring at the intersections between class, race, gender, sexuality, and other loci of social injustice. This will become more apparent in the following chapter.

THIRD-ORDER SUFFERING

In everyday life under the neoliberal paradigm, the somewhat distinct forms of suffering produced by deinstitutionalization, desubjectivation, and desymbolization—the three Ds—are deeply entangled. Collectively they yield what I identify as a new *order* of suffering, a category corresponding to what Cazdyn (2012) calls "the new chronic." I wish to be explicit about what this means for the care of souls. Under previous historical paradigms, there were two orders of suffering. The first comprised forms of suffering that are simply given in the human condition—death, grief, separation, illness, disability, natural calamities, conflict, physical pain, and so on. In previous ages, people dealing with first-order suffering generally did so from within collectives that accompanied them in their distress, with a more-or-less durable and cohesive sense of self, and with cultural narratives and liturgies that helped "make sense" of what they were enduring. Second-order suffering is distress produced by human evil, whether individual or collective, direct or indirect. Examples include malicious acts of individuals (murder, violence, theft, fraud, deception, etc.) as well as collective actions—war, group violence, enslavement, oppressive working conditions, and injustices focused upon identities (racism, sexism, heterosexism, ethnic- or religion-based discrimination, etc.). This also comprises oppression emanating from Foucault's "disciplinary societies." Here, significantly, the source of suffering is readily identifiable, even if, in the case of disciplinary control, it is rather impersonal—as in "the state," "the corporation," or "the church." And there is a palpable potential, if not the actuality, of forming collectives for resistance. There are, as well, narrative resources at hand for articulating such resistance. I am proposing, in this book, that heretofore the theories and practices of pastoral care, as well as other forms of soul care, have been directed toward these two orders of suffering. We have not yet, in my estimation, developed theories and practices adequate for addressing "the new chronic."

True to the character of paradigm change, *third order suffering*—the new normal for human distress appearing under neoliberalism—is not easy to articulate, perhaps impossible to articulate, in the terms of first- and second-order suffering. Without strong, vibrant collectives to support them, individuals are more-or-less left to their own devices to deal with distress. We might describe them as in a state of spiritual homelessness. These unfortunate souls are abandoned, left to interpret their sufferings as signs of personal failure. They are not guilty. They are ashamed. They do not have adequate narrative resources at hand to understand, to "make sense of," their sufferings. They are left simply with market-generated narratives of "personal recovery" (Illouz, 2008; Silva, 2013), which, like insulin for the diabetic, are perpetually fragile in the face of what they are up against. Such narratives are window-dressing, a veneer of order imposed over what once would have been a durable sense of self. The terms used to describe first- and second-order suffering now fail them, largely because the source of their sufferings are no longer easily identified. Their oppressors, for example, no longer have faces, even the impersonal "faces" of the state, the corporation, or the church. Yet to say the oppressor is some abstract "evil" seems not to capture the thing.[3] Their options are either to look within, blaming their sufferings on themselves, or to stare into the fog. Most people today take the first option. The primary symptomologies for this option, as I noted in Chap. 3, are either profound but diffuse depressions or polymorphous and fluid addictions (fitting adaptations to a commodity-driven world), as both Ehrenberg (1998/2010) and Dufour (2003/2008) have asserted. An apparent symptom for the second option is a violent striking out into the fog, literally in a blind rage. Dufour argues that this is the only conceivable explanation for the random mass shootings that have appeared since the advent of neoliberalism. This sort of violence, he observes, is new (2003/2008, pp. 79–80, 167). It may also be a dimension of some organized acts of terror. We are told, for example, that typical recruits to Islamic State in Iraq and the Levant (ISIL) are disaffected young people from Western countries whose motives seem not to be clearly either religious or political.

Unlike Kuhn's scientific revolutions, however, paradigm changes in culture do not require leaving preceding paradigms behind. *In the case of suffering, third order suffering does not simply replace first or second order suffering. Rather, it arises alongside them. The three orders coexist and interpenetrate. They too are entangled.* People arriving at my psychotherapy office do not come clearly labeled as one, two, or three. They present as messy mash-ups of the three orders. Because we have no language adequate for third-order suffering, however, they almost always articulate their "presenting problem" in first- or second-order language: "my mother died," "my spouse left me," "we are having marriage troubles," "I'm having panic attacks," "my boss is harassing me because I'm black." They may say "I'm depressed" or "I have an addiction," but they usually understand these referents in objective, market-friendly terms, as having either simply moral or organic causes. Because first- and second-order suffering have not disappeared, the theories and practices we have developed to address them will persist and continue to have relevance.

That being said, the neoliberalization of culture means that third-order suffering is increasingly pervasive. *More importantly, it is transforming both the appearance and the lived experience of first and second order suffering.* In the language of Chap. 3, it is both marginalizing and corrupting these forms of suffering. Marginalization, as I have indicated, appears as insidious sorts of denial. Corruption points to the ways already existing forms of suffering are transformed under the new paradigm. Unmoored subjects, deprived of adequate collective support, with only a fragile and amorphous sense of self, and without a sufficient way to narrate their distress, will experience death, grief, separation, loneliness, depression, anxiety, and so on, in a profoundly different way. Furthermore, under the new chronic, these will no longer be experienced as transitory crises or trauma, but as an ongoing way of being. Similarly, acts of violence and oppression—including sexism, racism, and other types of social injustice—will assume new, mutated forms. It is my judgment that the primary challenge for pastoral care, psychotherapy, social activism, and other approaches to caring for souls today is not the effort to fix discrete personal problems or even to redress specific injustices. It is, rather, to aid people, individually and collectively, in finding their footing—to articulate the deep meanings that ground their lives and to strengthen healthy collectives and social movements that hold some residue of transcendental values. These constitute the fundamental resources for addressing whatever ongoing crises people may be enduring under the new chronic.

From the standpoint of theory formation, as I noted in the introduction, this entails a reorientation of pastoral theology and other theories concerned with caring for souls. Theories regarding care for first- and second-order suffering, such as the particular subtypes mentioned in the preceding paragraph, will be reconceived to address the transmutations occurring due to their entanglements with third-order suffering. Of course, I have insufficient time and space to accomplish all this here. I will, however, offer three instances to demonstrate how this might be approached. Because they have such a prominent place in processes of neoliberalization, in the following chapter, I will discuss the transformations of sexism, racism, and class struggle under neoliberal governance.

Notes

1. The Federal Reserve reported, in April of 2015, that household debt had been increasing for seven consecutive quarters by the end of 2014: http://www.federalreserve.gov/econresdata/notes/feds-notes/2015/deleveraging-and-recent-trends-in-household-debt-20150406.html (Accessed on 06 December 2015).

2. OECD (2015), Household debt (indicator). doi: 10.1787/f03b6469-en (Accessed on 06 December 2015).

3. The theologian Paul Tillich has suggested a better term for the anonymous power of capitalism is "the demonic." See Yip, Francis Ching-Wah, (2010), *Capitalism as Religion? A Study of Paul Tillich's Interpretation of Modernity*, Cambridge, MA: Harvard Theological Studies (pp. 31–53).

REFERENCES

Alexander, B. K. (2008). *The globalization of addiction: A study in poverty of the spirit*. New York, NY: Oxford University Press.

Amin, S. (2011). *Ending the crisis of capitalism or ending capitalism?* (Victoria Bawtree, Trans.). Cape Town, ZA: Pambazuka Press.

Bageant, J. (2007). *Deer hunting with Jesus: Dispatches from America's class war*. New York, NY: Crown Publishers.

Baptist, E. E. (2014). *The half has never been told: Slavery and the making of American capitalism*. New York, NY: Basic Books.

Bauman, Z. (1997). *Postmodernity and its discontents*. Cambridge: Polity Press.

Bauman, Z. (2004). *Wasted lives: Modernity and its outcasts*. Cambridge: Polity Press.

Beckert, S. (2014). *Empire of cotton: A new history of global capitalism*. New York, NY: Alfred A. Knopf.

Cazdyn, E. (2012). *The already dead: The new time of politics, culture, and illness*. Durham, NC: Duke University Press.

Couldry, N. (2010). *Why voice matters: Culture and politics after neoliberalism*. London: Sage Publications.

Davies, W. (2015). *The happiness industry: How the government and big business sold us well-being*. London: Verso.

DuFour, D.-R. (2003/2008). *The art of shrinking heads: On the new servitude of the liberated in the age of total capitalism* (David Macey, Trans.). Cambridge: Polity Press.

Edin, K. J., & Shaefer, H. L. (2015). *$2.00 a day: Living on almost nothing in America*. New York, NY: Houghton Mifflin Harcourt.

Ehrenberg, A. (1998/2010). *The weariness of the self: Diagnosing the history of depression in the contemporary age* (Enrico Caouette, Jacob Homel, David Homel, & Don Winkler, Trans.). Montreal, QC: McGill-Queens University Press.

Fanon, F. (1952/1967). *Black skin white masks: The experiences of a black man in a white world* (Charles L. Markmann, Trans.). New York, NY: Grove Press.

Fanon, F. (1963/2004). *The wretched of the earth* (Richard Philcox, Trans.). New York, NY: Grove Press.

Farley, E. (1996). *Deep symbols: Their postmodern effacement and reclamation*. Valley Forge, PA: Trinity Press International.

Fukuyama, F. (1992/2006). *The end of history and the last man.* New York, NY: Free Press.

Hamann, T. H. (2009). Neoliberalism, governmentality, and ethics. *Foucault Studies, 6,* 37–59.

Illouz, E. (2008). *Saving the modern soul: Therapy, emotions, and the culture of self-help.* Berkeley, CA: University of California Press.

Klein, N. (2014). *This changes everything: Capitalism vs. the climate.* New York, NY: Simon & Schuster.

Kuhn, T. S. (1962/2012). *The structure of scientific revolutions* (4th ed.). Chicago, IL: University of Chicago Press.

Layton, L., Hollander, N. C., & Gutwill, S. (2006). Introduction. In L. Layton, N. C. Hollander, & S. Gutwill (Eds.), *Psychoanalysis, class and politics: Encounters in the clinical setting* (pp. 1–10). London: Routledge.

Lazzarato, M. (2012). *The making of indebted man* (Joshua D. Jordan, Trans.). Los Angeles, CA: Semiotext(e).

Lazzarato, M. (2015). *Governing by debt* (Joshua D. Jordan, Trans.). South Pasadena, CA: Semiotext(e).

Leech, G. (2012). *Capitalism: A structural genocide.* London: Zed Books.

Malabou, C. (2012). *Ontology of the accident: An essay on destructive plasticity* (Carolyn Shread, Trans.). Cambridge: Polity Press.

Mbembe, A. (2003). Necropolitics. (Libby Meintjes, Trans.). *Public Culture, 15*(1), 11–40.

Povinelli, E. A. (2011). *Economies of abandonment: Social belonging and endurance in late liberalism.* Durham, NC: Duke University Press.

Reich, R. B. (2010). *Aftershock: The next economy and America's future.* New York, NY: Alfred A. Knopf.

Reid-Henry, S. (2015). *The political origins of inequality: Why a more equal world is better for us all.* Chicago, IL: University of Chicago Press.

Rogers-Vaughn, B. (2014). Blessed are those who mourn: Depression as political resistance. *Pastoral Psychology, 63*(4), 503–522.

Sassen, S. (2014). *Expulsions: Brutality and complexity in the global economy.* Cambridge, MA: Belknap Press.

Silva, J. M. (2013). *Coming up short: Working-class adulthood in an age of uncertainty.* New York, NY: Oxford University Press.

Soss, J., Fording, R. C., & Schram, S. F. (2011). *Disciplining the poor: Neoliberal paternalism and the persistent power of race.* Chicago, IL: University of Chicago Press.

Wacquant, L. (2009). *Punishing the poor: The neoliberal government of social insecurity.* Durham, NC: Duke University Press.

Yip, F. C.-W. (2010). *Capitalism as religion? A study of Paul Tillich's interpretation of modernity.* Cambridge, MA: Harvard Theological Studies.

Žižek, S. (2008). *Violence: Six sideways reflections.* New York, NY: Picador.

Žižek, S. (2011). *Living in the end times.* London: Verso.

CHAPTER 5

Muting and Mutating Suffering: Sexism, Racism, and Class Struggle

A common theme among critics of neoliberalism is the assertion that neoliberalism is an intrinsically sexist and racist project, and yet that it buries this fact beneath prolific claims to being a meritocracy that proclaims "equal opportunity" while publicly embracing "diversity" and "multiculturalism." It is surely telling that even among the most right-wing ideologues currently on the political scene in the USA, no one openly confesses to being a racist or sexist. On the contrary, these words are used as epithets to hurl at opponents on the left and the right alike. The USA has even elected its first black President. Does this mean we have embarked upon a "post-racial" and "post-patriarchal" age? Far from it. Welcome to the world's first non-sexist patriarchy and its first non-racist white supremacy!

In the introduction to her book *The Twilight of Equality?*, Lisa Duggan (2003) asserts that, from its inception,

> neoliberalism has assembled its projects and interests from the field of issues saturated with race, with gender, with sex, with religion, with ethnicity, and nationality .... In order to facilitate the flow of money up the economic hierarchy, neoliberal politicians have constructed complex and shifting alliances, issue by issue and location by location—always in contexts shaped by the meanings and effects of race, gender, sexuality, and other markers of difference. (p. xvi)

Likewise, Henry Giroux (2005) concludes:

© The Author(s) 2016
B. Rogers-Vaughn, *Caring for Souls in a Neoliberal Age*,
DOI 10.1057/978-1-137-55339-3_5

> Under the aggressive politics and culture of neoliberalism, society is increasingly mobilized for the production of violence against the poor, immigrants, dissenters, and others marginalized because of their age, gender, race, ethnicity, and color. (p. 12)

At the same time, neoliberal forms of rationality actively promote equality, diversity, inclusion, and multiculturalism. Michaels (2006) observes: "A society free not only of racism but of sexism and of heterosexism is a neoliberal utopia where all the irrelevant grounds for inequality (your identity) have been eliminated and whatever inequalities are left are therefore legitimated" (p. 75). Similarly, Reed (2009) insists that such reasoning is critical for the advancement of neoliberalization. According to this logic, the "removal of 'artificial' impediments to its functioning like race and gender will make it even more efficient and just" (para. 21).

How can all of these assertions be true? What we have here is another of the incongruities of contemporary capitalism. To understand what is going on here let us consider, in turn, how neoliberalism appears as a patriarchal system that mutes and mutates sexism, and also as a white supremacist system that accomplishes the same with racism. Following these deliberations, I will examine how neoliberalization is also muting and mutating class conflict. In the language of the preceding chapter, what is at stake is an examination of how third-order suffering is altering these dimensions of injustice. Finally, I will close this chapter with some implications for interpreting intersectionality theory.

Gender-Blind Patriarchy

Does neoliberal capitalism, as actually practiced, constitute a patriarchal system? A number of feminist critical theorists (Braedley & Luxton, 2010; Connell, 2005; Duggan, 2003; Fraser, 2013a) are asserting that neoliberalism represents a global imposition of dominant masculinity. These scholars argue that the gender dynamic within contemporary capitalism has remained hidden. Connell (2010) concludes:

> There is an embedded masculinity politics in the neoliberal project. With a few exceptions, neoliberal leadership is composed of men. Its treasured figure, "the entrepreneur," is culturally coded masculine. Its assault on the welfare state redistributes income from women to men and imposes more unpaid work on women as carers for the young, the old, and the sick. Its

attack on "political correctness" and its rollback of affirmative action specifically undermine the gains of feminism. In such ways, neoliberalism from the 1980s on offered middle-class men an indirect but effective solution to the delegitimation of patriarchy and the threat of real gender equality. (pp. 33–34)

Connell points to the heart of the matter, which concerns the place of women in the system of production within advanced capitalism, as well as their lack of power in the system. There is no lack of evidence for her statement. Sarah Jaffe (2013) documents that, in the USA, "women make up just under half of the national workforce, but about 60 percent of the minimum-wage workforce and 73 percent of tipped workers" (para. 2). Moreover, in the long-term "recovery" following the recession that began in 2008, women recovered only 12 % of jobs lost, while men regained 63 %. Jaffe concludes: "Women may be overrepresented in the growing sectors of the economy, but those sectors pay poverty wages" (para. 6).

Perhaps the most telling evidence concerns women's lack of power in this system. In his definitive work on "political powerlessness" in the USA, Stephanopoulos (2015) uses the huge dataset assembled by Gilens for his book *Affluence and Influence* (2012) and adds extensive empirical studies of his own to answer the question of who does and does not have influence over political decisions. Stephanopoulos confirms that the difference between male and female power was the largest of any two groups he compared. He concludes: "Despite their large population share and the range of laws protecting them from discrimination, women continue to be alarmingly powerless relative to men" (p. 1598).

Finally, as Braedley and Luxton (2010) note, this is not peculiar to the USA. The advent of neoliberalism, they document, "has resulted in a global decline in women's positions and material well-being" (p. 13). In addition, this does not appear to be simply a by-product of neoliberal ideology and practice. Rather, it is intrinsic to the system: "Indeed, neoliberalism was developed in part to counter the equality demands of feminist, anti-racist, and anti-imperialist activists, as well as the socialist demands to end class exploitation" (p. 12). In the words of geographer Phil Hubbard (2004), neoliberal policies

are not just about the re-centralisation and accumulation of corporate capital, but are also about the re-inscription of patriarchal relations in the urban landscape. Indeed, I want to argue that the neoliberal city serves the interests of both capital and the phallus, with neoliberal policy reliant on the cultivation of a political economy that is, at one and the same time, a sexual economy. (p. 666)

In short, neoliberalism is an intentional re-institution of patriarchy. But, I hasten to add, this is not a type of patriarchy we have seen before. The novelty of this patriarchal system appears when we ask how it can claim to promote equality. The answer requires an understanding of how it mutes and mutates sexism. When I say that neoliberalism "mutes" sexism, I am referring to how it preemptively silences voices that would otherwise claim they are being oppressed because of their gender. It accomplishes this by removing substantive meaning from the word "equality," reducing it to "equal opportunity." In other words, it redefines equality in terms of the market. This ties equality to the isolated, competitive individualism I discussed in Chap. 3, along with its emphasis on the entrepreneurial self. This necessarily marginalizes claims of gender inequality, largely because women no longer have a collective voice as women. Instead, women are rendered, along with everyone else, as isolated individuals competing on equal terms with other individuals. Sexism, we might say, has thus been *privatized.* This occurs in multiple ways. Duggan (2003) notes: "The specific neoliberal spin on this cultural project was the removal of explicitly racist, misogynist language and images, and the substitution of the language and values of *privatization* and *personal responsibility*" (p. 16, emphases in original). In one sense, then, privatization entails a flat denial of any systemic, structural sexism. This does not mean, however, that neoliberal powers deny sexism exists at all. Rather, sexism is now attributed only to the actions and attitudes of *individual* misogynists, who are then maligned or censured. The answer to sexism, then, is no longer social justice, but subjecting wayward individuals to rehab or mandatory "diversity training." At any rate, governments, corporations, and other institutions are absolved of any responsibility other than the management of these wayward sexists. As the preceding quote by Connell indicates, sexism is also *deregulated.* As part of the "roll back" phase of neoliberalism discussed in Chap. 2, affirmative action is eroded and, since structural sexism is said not to exist, attention to "political correctness" is ridiculed.

Meanwhile, during the "roll out" phase, sexism is covertly (i.e. shorn of sexist language or misogynistic behavior) re-regulated. This is accomplished under the rationality of personal responsibility. Duggan (2003) notes that an apt example is the "welfare reform" act I mentioned in the previous chapter, passed by the US Congress in 1996 and signed by President Clinton. Tellingly, the title of this act was "The Personal Responsibility and Work Opportunity Reconciliation Act" (PRWORA). As I noted before, one effect of this legislation was to move people off welfare rolls and into a poverty-wage labor market. These were disproportionally women. A less obvious effect was how the PRWORA encouraged the "role of marriage as a coercive tool of the privatization of social costs." To make up for the dismantling of the social safety net, women were induced to rely on their wage-earning spouses and stay home to care for dependent children and aging adults. Women were also urged to undertake volunteer work in the community, much of which amounted to "unpaid labor underpinning the privatized social safety net" (p. 17). All this conjures up the writings of the socialist feminists of the 1970s, who analyzed the role of the nuclear family for both production and reproduction in capitalist societies. This is exhibited by a collection of essays published under the title *Capitalist Patriarchy and the Case for Socialist Feminism* (Eisenstein, 1979). In her editorial introduction, Eisenstein forcefully concludes: "If the other side of production is consumption, the other side of capitalism is patriarchy" (p. 29).

In a way analogous to processes I have already discussed, concerns about sexism are not only marginalized, but corrupted. This has to do with the way feminism has been co-opted by neoliberalization. The broad acceptance of "equal opportunity" in the place of substantive equality is just one feature of this corruption. Sarah Jaffe (2013, 2014), criticizing what she calls "neoliberal feminism" or "trickle-down feminism," complains that as the plight of working women has worsened, "I watched feminist writers seem to give a collective shrug" (2013, para. 5). Mourning her sense that feminism has largely been reduced to exhorting women to "lean in" and to a focus on "breaking through the glass ceiling," Jaffe (2014) concludes: "Neoliberal feminism is a feminism that ignores class as a determining issue in women's lives" (p. 7). Similarly, feminist critical theorist Nancy Fraser (2013a) has traced streams of second-wave feminism that unwittingly entered into collusion with the rise of neoliberalism. In a column written for *The Guardian*, Fraser (2013b) records the result: "The state-managed capitalism of the postwar era has given way to a new form of capitalism—'disorganized,' globalising, neoliberal. Second-wave feminism emerged as a critique of the first but has become the handmaiden of the second" (para. 3). Fraser calls for a new turn in feminism that returns to "large scale social theory" and a critique of contemporary capitalism (2013a, pp. 227–241). This is also a feature of Lisa Duggan's work (2003), which I have been citing. And of course this focus has never left the thought of black feminist theorists such as bell hooks and Angela Davis, to whom I will return when I discuss intersectionality.

If the muting of sexism is achieved by the marginalization of radical feminism, its mutation is completed by this co-optation of feminism. The result is a domination by the gender-blind patriarchy of today's actually existing capitalism. The foregoing discussion points to the current entanglement between second-order and third-order suffering. Both the erosion of collectives (deinstitutionalization) and loss of a public language to even speak of *structural* sexism (desymbolization) are implicit in this exploration. If we add these to an accelerating lack of self-cohesion (desubjectivation), it becomes apparent how the suffering of women and those impacted by their distress has been transformed under this new paradigm. Women, especially younger women born since the neoliberal revolution, are increasingly unable to articulate the sources of their distress. Consequently, they are typically accepting the neoliberal insistence that their travails have nothing to do with being women and everything to do with their own personal failures. Silva (2013), in her groundbreaking field interviews with working-class millennials, concludes with a statement that is inflected by all of the "three Ds":

> In the end, by rejecting solidarity with others, insisting that they are individuals who can define their own identities and futures, and hardening themselves against social institutions and the government, working-class men and women willingly embrace neoliberalism as the commonsense solution to the problems of bewilderment and betrayal that plague their coming of age journeys. (p. 84)

Throughout her book, *none* of the young women she interviews insinuate that their struggles might have anything to do with being a woman, or that they are in any way living in "a man's world," or that they could or should unite with other women to fight inequality. Furthermore, the men and women alike embrace ideals of virile masculinity. One of Silva's interviewees asks, "What are you going to do *as my man?*"—a question that summarizes the representative attitude of heterosexual women toward potential partners (p. 63. emphasis in original). While the men delay commitment because they cannot fulfill traditional male obligations of earning power, the women do not see this as a problem of economic inequality.

Rather, they see it as "pure selfishness," and insist on waiting for a man who can compete and provide. Consequently, they delay marriage or do not marry at all. This is an excellent example of what Kelly Oliver (2004), following Fanon, calls "the colonization of psychic space."

ANTIRACIST WHITE SUPREMACY

Baran and Sweezy (1966) observe that neither Marx nor Engels fully anticipated the transmutation of capitalism as it would appear under "monopoly capitalism." Writing during the height of the Civil Rights Movement in the USA, they begin a chapter on "race relations" as follows:

> The race problem in the United States was not created by monopoly capitalism. It was inherited from the slave system of the Old South. However, the nature of the problem has undergone a transformation during the monopoly capitalist period; and in a world in which the colored races are shaking off the bonds of oppression, it is apparent to everyone that the future of the United States will be deeply, and perhaps decisively, influenced by the further development of relations between the races inside the country. (p. 249)

The transformation to which the authors refer is the urbanization of black populations under monopoly capitalism, and their broad subjection to a "subproletariat" status. As the preceding statement suggests, they also firmly believed that the global rebellion by colonized people, coupled with the Civil Rights Movement in the USA, pointed to a better future for "the colored races," both at home and abroad. But if Marx and Engels had not foreseen the development of monopoly capitalism, neither did Baran and Sweezy anticipate the alterations to "race relations" that would soon occur under what Barry Lynn (2010) and others would call "the new monopoly capitalism."

Just as neoliberalization has responded to the real threats of substantive equality that emerged in the 1960s by reinscribing patriarchy, it has simultaneously reinstituted white supremacy. In parallel with theorists of gender, a number of critical race theorists have borne witness to this development. David Theo Goldberg (2009) concludes: "Neoliberalism ... can be read as a response to this concern about the impending impotence of whiteness" p. 337). Dana-Ain Davis (2007) argues that neoliberalism is a system in which "the reproduction of white privilege is generated in the absence of blatant racism" (p. 354). She asserts: "White status is the unmarked success of neoliberalism" (p. 356). Henry Giroux (2008) maintains that under neoliberal rationality and practice, a "new racism" has emerged. Unlike the old racism, this form is hidden, denied, and thus more difficu to oppose (pp. 60–83). Geographers Roberts and Mahtani (2010), more over, show that this holds true in their own country (Canada), and tha neoliberalization does not simply produce racist consequences, but is a *intrinsically* racial process.

Again, as was the case with sexism, empirical evidence is not difficult t find. Indeed, so much evidence exists that recounting it would be ove whelming. I will mention a few examples. A study by the Pew Researc Center, released in December, 2014, demonstrates that wealth inequalit has increased along racial lines.[1] In 1983, at the beginning of the neolit eral revolution, white households in the USA held eight times the wealt of black households. By 2013, this had increased to 13 times. The averag white household in 2013 had a net worth of $141,900. For black house holds, it was $11,000. As mentioned previously, incarceration under th neoliberal state is used to enforce social security rather than simply crim nal security. This means the number of people imprisoned in the USA ha skyrocketed, from a total of about 320,000 in 1978 to about 1.5 *millio* in 2013. This increase has been divided along racial lines. In 2013, th incarceration rate for black males was six times greater than white male whereas black females were twice as likely to be imprisoned than whit females. Most astounding is that, as of December 31, 2013, almost 3 of all black males in the country were in prison.[2] This has famously le Michelle Alexander (2012) to refer to mass incarceration in the USA a "the new Jim Crow."

In addition, Stephanopoulos's authoritative research (2015) on "politi cal powerlessness" in the USA shows that blacks are "relatively powerles at both the federal and state levels." He concludes: "Sadly, decades afte the struggles of the civil rights era, blacks continue to require heightene judicial protection" (p. 1598). Finally, Goldberg (2009) demonstrate that neoliberalization is a racializing process globally, not only in the US but also in Western and Northern Europe, South Africa, Latin America and in Israel and Palestine.

As with sexism, this is racism that, true to neoliberal formation, ha been both privatized and deregulated. Any type of systemic or structura racism is vigorously denied. Privatized racism is reduced to the behavior of individual "bad apples." As Goldberg (2009) states: "The individualiza tion of wrongdoing, its localization as personal and so private preferenc expression, erases institutional racisms precisely as conceptual possibility" (pp. 362–363). Importantly, this does not entail state neutrality with regard to racism. Ironically, the state is now in the position to *protect* at least some racist actions: "Rather, the state is restructured to support the privatizing of race and the protection of racially driven exclusions in the private sphere where they are off-limits to state intervention" (p. 337). The result? "Race is rendered accordingly before, beneath, or beyond the law" (p. 363). This provides a striking example of the entanglement of second-order racism with third-order (deinstitutionalized) racism. In this discourse, the state is no longer the chief instrument of direct racist activities. Instead, acts of racism are relegated to the private sphere, including non-governmental collectives, where they are now frequently given room to run amuck.

The privatization of race leads directly to its deregulation. In Goldberg's (2009) words: "Racisms denuded of their conceptual referents in the final analysis are racisms deregulated" (p. 344). Racial deregulation in the USA is apparent in the broad erosion of affirmative action and in the Supreme Court's 2013 evisceration of the Voting Rights Act (Shelby County vs. Holder). It is also at work in the aforementioned dismantling of the social welfare system, which has disproportionately impacted blacks and other minorities. Meanwhile, while race has been deregulated through the "roll back" processes of neoliberalization discussed in previous chapters of this book, it has been simultaneously re-regulated as part of its "roll out" processes. As mentioned in Chap. 2, this includes aggressive policing and surveillance to manage "unruly populations." While these populations are invariably poor, they are racially articulated by neoliberal discourse as a cover for its more general agenda of increased inequality (Gilens, 1996). As Parenti (2015) summarizes, "among the important things criminal justice does is regulate, absorb, terrorize, and disorganize the poor. At the same time it promulgates politically useful racism" (para. 59). One consequence is the disproportional imprisonment of blacks I have just noted. Another is the epidemic in the USA of killings of unarmed blacks by police officers, which is currently being highlighted by the Black Lives Matter movement.

In short, neoliberalism is a systemic re-institution of white supremacy. But again, as is the case with sexism, this is not a type of white supremacy we have seen before. Like sexism, racism has been both muted and mutated. In an amazing reversal, it carries out a program of white privilege under the banner of "antiracism." How has this happened? Goldberg (2009) contends that this new form of antiracism is best referred to as "antiracialism," which is a denial that the term "race" denotes anything of significance. It no longer even exists as a category to which one can appeal. He declares this to be a "born again racism," concluding: "Born again racism is racism without race, racism gone private, racism without the categories to name it as such" (p. 23). Incredibly, racism is now a term applied to people who "play the race card," or, in other words, attempt to give voice to those who continue to suffer because of the color of their skin. Racism is reduced simply to *invoking* race as a category of analysis or critique (p. 360). This, then, is an extreme form of desymbolization. Advocates who attempt to talk about race-based oppression are rendered mute. Worse than that, they are derided as "the real racists."

If such desymbolization mutes racism by eroding the discourse for naming it, it mutates racism as well, yielding a new form referred to by many as "colorblind racism." Once again, we are back to how neoliberalization both marginalizes and corrupts already existing forms of suffering. Colorblind racism is a mutation, or corruption, of an already existing form of racism. It is, in effect, a corruption of a corruption. To be more precise, it is a third-order form of suffering that now appears alongside, and entangled with, second-order racism. Giroux (2008) observes that the older forms of racist practices and ideologies, what I am calling second-order racism, have not disappeared. Rather, "they have been transformed, mutated, and recycled and have taken on new and in many instances more covert modes of expression" (p. 60). Omi and Winant (2014) argue that colorblindness is "racial neoliberalism," and that not only does it obscure the idea of race (desymbolization) but it also marginalizes the Black Movement of the 1960s, with its focus on "demands for economic redistribution and political inclusion" (p. 18). In other words, it works to dissolve (deinstitutionalize) the collectives and solidarities that were the heart of that movement. Pastoral theologian Cedric Johnson (2016b) refers to this attack upon the Black Movement as "dismantling a freedom movement" (pp. 30–34).

But this points primarily to the conservative or right-wing form. There is also a liberal or progressive version. While some feminist theorists have explored how neoliberalism has co-opted feminism, a number of critical race theorists have investigated neoliberalized varieties of the progressive impetus toward racial equality. What these versions share is the aforementioned transformation of substantive equality into "equal opportunity." Thus, in his W.E.B. Dubois Lectures at Harvard, Paul Gilroy (2010) laments how a stream of progressivism equates racial justice simply with inclusion, or "pursuing the expansion of African American access to capitalism's bounty" (p. 5). This type of progressivism is also susceptible to reproducing Duggan's (2003) economics/culture split, which I discussed in Chap. 2. In the racialized variation, as narrated by Giroux (2008), "race becomes a matter of taste, lifestyle, or heritage but has nothing to do with politics, legal rights, educational access, or economic opportunities." He concludes: "color-blindness deletes the relationship between racial differences and power" (p. 69). To paraphrase what Jaffe (2014) said with regard to sexism, cited previously, neoliberal antiracism is an antiracism that ignores class as a determining issue in black lives. In a statement paraphrasing the work of Walter Benn Michaels (2006), political scientist Adolph Reed, Jr. (2013), criticizes the neoliberal ideal of a just society that ignores class:

> society would be just if 1 percent of the population controlled 90 percent of the resources, provided that blacks and other nonwhites, women, and lesbian, gay, bisexual, and transgender (LGBT) people were represented among the 1 percent in roughly similar proportion as their incidence in the general population. (p. 54)

Neoliberal antiracism, and the form of identity politics that accompanies it, Reed (2009, 2013) concludes, is a vision of racial equality that separates race from class. The upshot of his view is that, although we can well imagine a classless society in which racism persists, in actually existing societies, it is impossible to address racism without also addressing class struggle.

Finally, the desymbolizing and deinstitutionalizing trajectories of third-order racism coalesce in its characteristic desubjectivation. The desubjectivation of blacks under neoliberal governance has been superbly described by Cedric Johnson (2016b). He deftly explores how many African Americans experience "racialized neoliberal society" as "a loss of hope that results in a numbing detachment from others and a destructive disposition toward one's self and the world" (p. 57). The various discourses and power relationships of the neoliberal age, Johnson argues, "produce new forms of black subjectivity even as older forms persist" (p. 58). Johnson is pointing, I believe, to the co-existence and entanglements of what I am calling second- and third-order suffering. On the one hand, the *subjectivation* of second-order suffering persists. This appears, for example, in Johnson's investigation of Fanon's notion of black subjects "turning white," which occurred under the pressures of traditional capitalism and continues today (pp. 71–73). Here one form of subjectivity is supplanted by another, alien and alienating one. On the other hand, in a chapter aptly titled "Forgetting to Remember" (pp. 77–99), Johnson refers to neoliberal society as a "traumatogenic environment," and uses trauma theory to explore the particular effects of neoliberal culture upon black subjects. After delineating specific neoliberal practices that traumatize black subjects, he describes states of hyperarousal; intrusive thoughts, affects and behaviors; and a general numbing and frozen animation that today typify many black individuals. In my estimation, Johnson, in this chapter, is pointing to features of the *desubjectivation* of black lives in the neoliberal age. Rather than one subjectivity being supplanted by another, such as blackness by whiteness, subjectivity is reduced, fragmented or dispersed altogether. This constitutes a racialized version of what Cazdyn (2012) calls "the new chronic," which I have previously discussed. Moreover, Johnson also offers a preliminary exploration of how the new (third-order) forms of black subjectivity become entangled with the old (second-order) forms (pp. 93–95).

Silva (2013), as I noted in the preceding discussion of third-order sexism, demonstrates that the shunning of solidarity and the acceptance of the discourse of personal responsibility is just as relevant to the new racism. Her interviews with working-class millennials abundantly illustrate their general elision of race as a category of domination and subjection. Just as the women she interviews seem largely unaware that they live in a man's world, many of the black individuals seem strangely unaware that they live in a white man's world. To the degree they are aware, this appears to bear little significance to their acceptance of responsibility for their own struggles or failures. Silva characterizes the responses of young blacks as conflicted: "they both recognize the systematic force of racism but also resist seeing themselves as it victims" (p. 106). Wanda, a 25-year-old restaurant server who is black, criticizes her parents for their inability to beat their addictions and improve their financial standing (pp. 10–12). She concludes: "*I feel like it's their fault that they don't have nothing.*" She believes, furthermore, that it is up to her to manage her own feelings and behaviors in order not to end up like them: "If my *mentality* were different, then most definitely I would just be stuck" (p. 12, emphases in original). Many of the blacks Silva interviews mentioned experiences of racism, and yet held themselves as individually responsible for overcoming such challenges. Julian, a 27-year-old black man, admits race remains an issue, but confesses: "at the end of the day looking in the mirror, I know where all my shortcomings come from. *From the things that I either did not do or I did and I just happened to fail at them*" (p. 106, emphasis in original). Silva discovered a pervasive acceptance of the neoliberal ideology of meritocracy among her respondents, regardless of how they identified racially: "Thus, disdain for minorities who cannot pull themselves up by their bootstraps prevails among both white and black respondents" (p. 107). Finally, Silva observes that working-class young people have largely given up on collective life and solidarity. She notes that "their everyday experiences of humiliation and betrayal" teach them "that they can depend on others only at great cost" (p. 109). Silva concludes:

> Through this process, they become acquiescing neoliberal subjects, rejecting all kinds of government intervention, and affirmative action in particular, as antithetical, and thereby offensive, to their lived experiences. In this way, potential communities of solidarity are broken apart by the strain of insecurity and risk. (p. 109)

Taken altogether, Silva's field work among working-class young people in the USA provides ample evidence for the dissolution of collectives (deinstitutionalization), the loss of a credible way to narrate life with any depth and durability (desymbolization), and a fragmentation of identity or sense of self (desubjectivation) that is occurring in this population. As I have already stated, this is important prognostically, given that this is the first generation born subsequent to the neoliberal revolution. Her work also documents how third-order suffering is transforming both sexism and racism in everyday life.

Another implication of Silva's findings, one which she does not fully explore, is that there is very little *class consciousness* among this population. Indeed, the young people Silva interviews appear even less aware of themselves as distinctively "working class" than they do of themselves as gendered or raced. This is a crucial matter because, as noted in the preceding discussions, otherwise progressive narratives concerning inclusivity and diversity that separate gender and race from class are vulnerable to being co-opted by neoliberal agendas. This indicates the critical importance of what is usually referred to as intersectionality theory. Before leaving considerations of how the neoliberal paradigm transforms the particular sufferings of sexism and racism, therefore, I must consider how theorizing third-order suffering might influence how we understand both class struggle and intersectionality.

THE NEOLIBERAL AVERSION TO INTERSECTIONALITY

The theories dubbed by the term "intersectionality" offer us a profoun wisdom we dare not distort or misunderstand. Neoliberal material interest would seduce us away from this wisdom by substituting a bland "diver sity," "inclusivity," or "multiculturalism." Such terms appear liberal an progressive, but are not radical. They support rather than challenge a nec liberal status quo. It should give us pause to consider, for example, tha "diversity training" was first promoted within the cultures of very larg corporations. The goal here is to get workers to recognize and appreciat those who are marked as different—by race, gender, religion, sexual orien tation, ethnicity, and so on—so that they "get along" and thus the mecha nisms of production run smoothly and efficiently. It also reduces cost by minimizing the risk of expensive lawsuits. Typically, racism, sexism heterosexism, religious discrimination, and so forth are only nominall treated as matters of social injustice. Finally, neoliberal-friendly diversit serves capitalist agendas of consumption. "Martin Luther King's vision o a beloved community," concludes bell hooks (2000), "gets translated int a multicultural multiethnic shopping spree. Commitment to consumptio above all else unifies diverse races and classes" (p. 82).

Among many progressives within the academy, this stand-in for inter sectionality appears in what Wendy Brown (1995) calls "the multicultural ist mantra, 'race, class, gender, sexuality'." Regarding the invocation o this mantra, Brown argues, "class is invariably named but rarely theorize or developed" (p. 61). This is significant, for, as I stated in the conclusio of the preceding section, progressive narratives concerning inclusivity an diversity that separate gender and race from class are vulnerable to bein co-opted by neoliberal agendas.

Theorists committed to intersectionality must remain vigilant to avoi being pulled into such prevailing understandings of diversity. Contrary t both conservative and liberal forms of multiculturalism, intersectionalit theorists who attend to the historical roots of this type of analysis continu to emphasize the importance of class. Among pastoral theologians, Nanc Ramsay (2014) has recently been emphasizing the magnitude of intersec tionality theory for an adequate understanding of suffering and care. Sh rightly observes that, from its emergence among black feminists in th 1970s, this sort of theorizing has argued that the oppressions circulatin around identities are not simply about the lack of respect for cultural dif ference but also about how *power* unevenly circulates through society. Thi means that racism and sexism, for example, cannot be understood apar from class. Thus bell hooks (2000) asserts: "It is impossible to talk meaningfully about ending racism without talking about class" (p. 7). Likewise, Joy James (1998), introducing a collection of works by Angela Davis, summarizes: "Davis felt that black liberation was unobtainable apart from an international workers' movement against capitalism, imperialism, and racism." She concludes: "Her understanding [was] that a mass liberation struggle needed to be class-based in order to confront the racist foundations of capitalism" (p. 8). A detailed consideration of class persists in other contemporary intersectionality theorists. Margaret Andersen and Patricia Hill Collins (2007), in their introduction to *Race, Gender, & Class: An Anthology*, carefully distinguish their "matrix of domination model," with its laser focus on power differentials, from the "difference model" that tends to govern current discourse (pp. 5–12).

However, intersectionality theory does not always preserve the sustained critique of capitalism that characterized the work of 1970s radical feminists (a critique that does, in fact, persist in both hooks and Davis). These women were almost invariably socialists, and relied on sophisticated Marxist analyses of class, coupled with attention to how the power dynamics around race, gender, and sexuality are imbricated in, and thus alter and amend, Marx's understanding of class struggle (see Eisenstein, 1979). This is nowhere more evident than in the statement issued by The Combahee River Collective, a solidarity of black feminist lesbians, in 1977 (Eisenstein, pp. 362–372). These women insisted:

> We realize that the liberation of all oppressed peoples necessitates the destruction of the political-economic systems of capitalism and imperialism as well as patriarchy. We are socialists because we believe the work must be organized for the collective benefit of those who do the work and create the products and not for the profit of the bosses.... We need to articulate the real class situation of persons who are not merely raceless, sexless workers, but for whom racial and sexual oppression are significant determinants in their working/economic lives. Although we are in essential agreement with Marx's theory as it applied to the very specific economic relationships he analyzed, we know that this analysis must be extended further in order for us to understand our specific economic situation as black women. (p. 366)

Angela Davis (1983), however, finds traces of this approach in Marx himself. At the conclusion of an essay on "Class and Race in the Early Women's Rights Campaign," she quotes Marx approvingly: "labor in a white skin can never be free as long as labor in a black skin is branded" (p. 69).

CLASS STRUGGLE AND THIRD-ORDER SUFFERING

I am largely in agreement with the approach of these early black feminists, although I remain undecided about whether an end to the suffering produced by advanced capitalism absolutely requires the complete extermination of capitalism in any form. Leaving that question aside, what I must now ask is how third-order suffering transforms class struggle, and how this in turn might inform our perspective on intersectionality theory.

In my view, even the most sophisticated contemporary analyses of class remain generally tied to depictions of second-order suffering. These explorations largely continue to see class as connected to established institutions, such as traditional production facilities and labor unions; look to some type of shared narratives concerning work; and, at the level of individual subjectivity as well as group identity, depend on a more-or-less reliable consciousness of class. I am not opposed to these analyses, nor do I regard them as outdated. As I have argued, the appearance of third-order suffering does not entail the complete disappearance of second-order suffering, with which it is now entangled. Furthermore, the rightward drift of politics in the USA has yielded a situation in which even conventional class analysis appears radical. In the words of theologian Joerg Rieger (2013), "In the rare cases when class is addressed, especially in the United States, it is connected to notions of poverty, social stratification, or income differentials, which are insufficient at best and misleading at worse" (p. 1). Even the work of social scientist Robert Putnum, with whose work I opened this book, is limited to this unsatisfactory view of class.

Rieger (2013) asserts that class is a *relational* term. It only has meaning as a description of the relationships *between* classes (pp. 3–5). This returns us to Marx's analysis of class struggle. It is not just that the rich are rich, for example, and the poor are poor. Rather, the poor are poor because the rich control the means of production and use their political clout to rig the game in their own favor. As Michael Zweig (2012) insists, class is more about power than it is cultural distinctions or even money. Moreover, class is best understood as referring to one's place and function in the capitalist system of production. To be in the working class means having little power over the conditions and consequences of one's labor. All this is congruent with class as understood by the 1970s feminists. A recovery of this second-order understanding of class oppression gets us much further than we now stand.

So, how is class being transformed by neoliberalization? The reader will not be surprised that I will now claim, in parallel to the discussion of racism and sexism, that class is being profoundly altered by the three Ds—deinstitutionalization, desymbolization, and desubjectivation (Dufour, 2003/2008). Thus, as in the cases of racism and sexism, we can now perceive an emerging version of class oppression that accords with third-order suffering. If the new sexism assumes the form of a gender-blind patriarchy, and the new racism takes the form of an antiracist white supremacy, class oppression now appears as the de-classification of capitalism. The workplace collectives and labor narratives that once funded a durable sense of self for workers have suffered marginalization and corruption. Class consciousness is being steadily displaced by class unconsciousness. If we compare the era of exaggerated inequality that existed in the USA early in the twentieth century with the pronounced inequality of today, the early twenty-first century, large-scale evidence for the difference between second-order and third-order class-based suffering appears. Steve Fraser (2015) calls these "the first Gilded Age" and "the second Gilded Age." The first Gilded Age was characterized by wide social unrest. Workers went on strike en masse, often involving violent conflict with their bosses and employers, as well as with police, mercenary soldiers, and even the US military. The Communist Party and various socialist organizations were gaining public acceptance. Theologians will remember this as the era of the Social Gospel Movement (Carter, 2015). Many religious leaders were growing critical of capitalism. By contrast, the incredible level of inequality today is met by compliance and widespread silence. Fraser thus calls this "the age of acquiescence." This does not mean labor organizations and voices are entirely absent. They have, however, been marginalized, almost to the point of political insignificance. My own father, a devoted union member during the 1970s and 1980s, is now a critic of unions and accuses them of contributing to the problems of workers and society. This attitude toward labor unions is now broadly apparent in US politics. Another sign of decreasing awareness of class-based oppression is the growing lack of protection for workers. Adolph Reed, Jr. (2013) observes:

> Legal remedies can be sought for injustices understood as discrimination on the basis of race, gender, or other familiar categories of invidious ascription; no such recourse exists for injustices generated through capitalism's logic of production and reproduction without mediation through one of those ascriptive categories. (p. 54)

A thorough discussion of third-order suffering in relation to class would require a book of its own. Here I will simply point to a few features. Under second-order class-based oppression, workers generally know from where their suffering comes—demeaning supervisors, unfair company policies, hazardous working conditions, depressed wages, and so on. Under neo-liberal governance, this is less true for large segments of the population. Increasing numbers of workers have become entrepreneurs out of neces-sity, engaging in what has become widely known as the "gig economy," or "on-demand economy."[3] Who are these workers to hold liable for their distress, except the abstract and faceless "economy," when they experience hardship? But traditional employees often fare no better. If they do not make a living wage, or garner a wage that seems unfair, they may simply be told they are being paid what "the market" dictates as the going rate. Meanwhile, virtually all workers strive under the neoliberal ideology of meritocracy. They are encouraged to see themselves as self-managers. If they lose their jobs, suffer demotions, or are underemployed, they typi-cally blame themselves for what is experienced as a personal failure. This theme appears throughout Silva's (2013) extensive interviews with 100 working-class young people. She initiates the conclusion of her study as follows: "The power of the postwar working class who had battled big business and won was decimated by the neoliberal turn of the 1970s, leav-ing the militancy that once fueled their collective movement *nowhere to spread but inward*" (p. 144, emphasis added).

Silva (2013) notes that her conclusions are inspired by Sennett's and Cobb's *The Hidden Injuries of Class* (1972/1993), a book which basi-cally argues that class conflict cannot be fully appreciated without detailed attention to its *psychological* effects. Silva updates this argument by observ-ing that, under neoliberalism, "risks are increasingly redistributed away from the state and onto the individual" (p. 145). She therefore reorients Sennett's and Cobb's line of reasoning to "the hidden injuries of risk" (pp. 144–157), which brings to mind the plight of laborers Guy Standing (2014) calls "the precariat," a term he creates to describe the precari-ous state of workers in an on-demand, entrepreneurial, project-oriented, part-time economy. It is a mistake to assume the precariat refers only to the poor or even simply the working class. Many professionals today fall into this group. For example, I am a highly educated professional. However, I do not hold a full-time job. Rather, I am self-employed in my part-time psychotherapy practice, which does not offer a guaranteed income, ben-efits, or paid time off. In addition, I hold another part-time job teaching at a major university. While I am grateful to receive a number of benefits from the university, including health insurance, this does not include paid time off, the security of tenure, or eligibility for research grants or sabbaticals. Finally, I work another part-time job—research and writing—for which I am essentially unpaid. None of this is a complaint. I am generally well paid and have far more control over my work than the average laborer. But this does serve to illustrate that, under neoliberalism, there are far fewer differences between "middle-class" professionals and the "working class" than in former times. This leads Wysong, Perrucci, and Wright (2014) to claim that, in the USA, neoliberal policies have yielded a "*new class system*" in which prior distinctions between "middle class" and "working class" make little sense (p. 2, emphasis in original). These researchers demonstrate that we now live in a polarized and rigid two-class system in which the vast majority of residents, including most professionals and most of the professoriate, form the "new working class" (pp. 31–42). This new class structure is, moreover, tied to "the new economy," characterized by "acute and chronic crises" (pp. 56–59). Life in the new working class becomes precarious for everyone. We are all enshrouded by risk, even when we earn living wages or better. This means that third-order suffering, what Cazdyn (2012) calls "the new chronic," stealthily encroaches upon our daily lives. It hangs like a specter over our existence. Falling over the edge of the economic precipice is not the only potential cause of trauma; we are chronically traumatized because we must constantly *fear* that fall. We know that the next economic crisis, if not personal life crisis, may put us over the brink.

Second-order class suffering, the naked oppression experienced within the Weberian "iron cage" constructed by capitalist institutions, has metastasized into an infinite variety of third-order isolated confinements that we voluntarily inhabit. In this novel labor environment, according to Dardot and Laval (2009/2013), "everyone is enjoined to construct their own individual little 'iron cage'" (p. 262). The sufferings of these isolated workers—fragmentation, demoralization, depression, addiction, depersonalization, hyperstimulation, and so on (pp. 288–298)—are indistinguishable from the markers of chronic trauma. These are the symptoms not of subjectivation but of desubjectivation. Marx's famous dictum, "all that is solid melts into air," now applies to subjectivity. These symptoms of a vaporized self, Dardot and Laval assert, have a common root: "they can all be related to the erosion of the institutional frameworks and symbolic structures in which subjects found their place and identity" (p. 288). What I have called the "three Ds," in other words, now occupy the space of labor. They are the new faces of precarity.

The desubjectivation occurring in the neoliberal workplace has been highlighted by Boltanski and Chiapello (1999/2007) in *The New Spirit of Capitalism*. They note that in this sort of labor, one's very self becomes the means of production. The worker must behave such that the customer or employer is convinced that she is *really sincere* in her carefully performed demeanor. This has been extensively researched by Bunting (2005) in her book, *Willing Slaves*. After interviewing hundreds of human service workers, Bunting describes this unique psychological exploitation. She calls this "emotional labor." Where muscle strength is uppermost for laborers in manual forms of work, "its modern-day equivalent is emotional empathy and the ability to strike up a rapport with another human being *quickly*" (p. 61, emphasis in original). Corporations, she observes, have learned that "empathy has become big business" and that "empathy makes money," because customers are far more likely to return to stores and service providers, and even pay a premium, for receiving "a certain kind of interaction" (pp. 61, 66–67). Bunting cites one consultant firm who was hired to conduct "empathy audits" for any company that "wants its employees to sound warmer or more natural" (pp. 66–67). A human resources manager for a retail giant boasts that his employees are exhorted and trained to provide "miles of smiles" and adds: "It's got to be a *real* smile" (p. 103, emphasis in original). This practice not only oppresses workers, who are denied the spontaneous response of self-expression because they must follow a corporate script, but it commodifies human relationships. Bunting concludes:

> There is a world of difference between the waitress who chooses to smile, quip with her customers and be good-natured, and the one whose behavior has been minutely prescribed by a training manual. The former has some autonomy over her own feelings; the latter has been forced to open up more aspects of herself to commodification. (p. 71)

The end result for laborers can be disastrous: "Employees are left to manage the dilemmas of authenticity, integrity and their sense of their own natural, spontaneous personality, which all spill into their private lives" (p. 72). Our thoughts, interpersonal desires, and even our feelings belong to the work rather than to ourselves. More importantly, the repetition of pseudo-authenticity blurs the boundary between the "real self" and the "virtual self." We may, ultimately, lose our grip on what it means to even be a self.

Finally, desubjectivation relative to class is not confined to what happens at the workplace. Third-order class-based suffering also arises from the alteration of subjectivity by the debt economy. It has become quite fashionable to draw a firm distinction between the "real economy," the market of material labor, consumption, and exchange; and the "virtual economy," or the finance industry, which creates profit through the speculative trading of esoteric instruments based on debt. This suggests that the debt economy is not quite real, or that it is ultimately reducible to the more conventional terms of material labor and exchange. There are problems with this nomenclature. First, how is the finance industry, which now accounts for the vast majority of capital in global circulation, not in any way a real economy? Second, while money as debt may, as Goodchild (2009) argues, have a "spectral quality," the oppression it governs is quite real. Goodchild contends that in today's economy, all money is essentially debt and concludes: "The value of money is still paid for in flesh and blood" (p. 236). However, the distinction between the material economy and the debt economy is helpful if, following Lazzarato (2012), we reframe the difference as that between money as *"revenue"* and money as *"capital"* (p. 74, emphases in original). As revenue, "money is a means of payment" for already existing goods and services. It facilitates a system of material exchange. As capital, however, "money functions as a financing structure" (p. 74). Here money serves as an extension of credit—the investors' term for debt-creation. As credit/debt, money "has the possibility of choosing and deciding on future production and commodities and, therefore, on the relations of power and subjection underlying them" (p. 74). Lazzarato concludes: "Money-revenue simply reproduces power relations, the division of labor, and the established functions and roles. Money as capital, on the other hand, has the ability to reconfigure those relations" (p. 74).

This is critical, for it means that credit/debt has the potential for altering the class structure and dynamics of any society. And this is exactly what has happened, Lazzarato (2012) asserts, under neoliberalism. While debt has existed since the beginning of civilization, prior to neoliberalism indebtedness amounted to a temporal crisis. It was assumed that a debt would, at least potentially, be redeemed and the debtor/creditor power imbalance dissolved. Lazzarato calls this "finite debt." Neoliberalism, on the other hand, made debt creation central to its program from the beginning. A feature of its expansion of economic inequality is the creation of "infinite debt," debt that effectively is never repaid (pp. 77–88). This holds true not only for individuals and households but sovereign states as well. Even those too poor to afford credit are pulled into the repayment of public debt through regressive taxation (p. 32). This condition of perpetual indebtedness, in my view, is a way to understand "the new chronic" (Cazdyn, 2012) in economic terms. Here debt is no longer occasional or transitional, but *normative*. It is, in other words, another marker of third-order suffering. And, under neoliberalism, debt now defines the global economy. Its reach is universal. Debt, concludes Lazzarato, "is a universal power relation, since everyone is included within it" (p. 32).

Moreover, according to Lazzarato (2012), debt as normative now defines class structure: "Debt constitutes the most deterritorialized and the most general power relation through which the neoliberal power bloc institutes its class struggle" (p. 89). In a more recent work, Lazzarato (2015) argues that, under neoliberalism, "class division no longer depends on the opposition between capitalists and wage-earners but on that between debtors and creditors" (p. 66). This may paint the matter too starkly. As I have been arguing, third-order suffering has not replaced second-order suffering, but exists alongside and is entangled with second-order suffering. Nonetheless, I do believe Lazzarato is describing a transformation of class struggle that is occurring. His argument that we now have essentially two classes—creditors and debtors—may represent a way to articulate the two-tiered class structure described by Wysong, Perrucci, and Wright (2014) in strictly financial terms.

This transformation of class struggle subtly alters the nature of labor. As debtors, we do not just create profit for the investor class—the new "owners"—when we are in the workplace. We are creating surplus value even in our sleep and with every breath we take. We are not simply employed. We are owned. We do not simply access the means of production; we have *become* the means of production. Debt, which by definition is an asymmetrical power relation, is internalized. Thus labor, Lazzarato observes, "becomes indistinguishable from 'work on the self'" (2012, p. 33). Lazzarato points to a prescient essay Marx wrote as a young man: "Comments on James Mill" (pp. 54–61). Credit, Marx (1844/2005) argues here, does not simply exploit material labor. It captures the individual's very existence:

> Within the credit relationship, it is not the case that money is transcended in man, but that man himself is turned into *money*, or money is *incorporated* in him. *Human individuality*, human *morality* itself, has become both an

object of commerce and the *material* in which money exists. Instead of money, or paper, it is my own personal existence, my flesh and blood, my social virtue and importance, which constitutes the material, corporeal form of the *spirit of money*. Credit no longer resolves the value of money into money but into human flesh and the human heart. (p. 215, emphases in original)

In this essay, Marx clearly states that credit focuses upon the morality of the debtor. Her being is defined by solvency or insolvency, a judgment she implicitly accepts. The permanence and universality of debt under neo-liberalism makes this moral status virtually ontological, or at least experienced as such. Lazzarato (2015) concludes: "Debtors interiorize power relations instead of externalizing and combatting them. They feel ashamed and guilty" (p. 70).

What this suggests is that we consider debt to be a form of *moral injury*. As such, the creditor–debtor relationship epitomizes the entanglement between second- and third-order suffering. Debt begins as a colonization of the psyche, reorienting the soul around solvency and repayment. In this sense, it is a subjectivation, a re-forming of the subject, and thus an instance of second-order suffering. Once planted into the soul, however, it acts as a cancer, consuming its own host. Experts on moral injury, such as Brock and Lettini (2012), describe their tormented subjects as souls who have taken on an unpayable moral debt. Their sense of self begins to dissolve, as they identify their very being as the source of injustice. Just so, under the extreme conditions of contemporary capitalism, subjectivation as a debtor leads inexorably to desubjectivation, to third-order suffering. Common outcomes, as mentioned before, include increasing rates of depression, addiction, and suicide.

INTERSECTIONALITY AS A POST-CAPITALIST THEORY: THE INTER-RELATIONALITY OF SUFFERING

In light of the foregoing discussions of the neoliberal alterations of sexism, racism, and class conflict, I propose that we understand intersectionality theory as a post-capitalist project. This is not a stretch, given its origin among 1970s feminists who were themselves quite critical of capitalism. This requires, however, careful attention to the radical impulse within intersectionality theory and a dedicated precision regarding terminology. Otherwise, as I have already noted, it can quite easily be co-opted by neoliberal versions of diversity and multiculturalism. I will make no effort to be exhaustive in this concluding section. Rather, I draw upon prior sections of this chapter to suggest, in summary fashion, five features of an intersectionality theory that help to preserve its post-capitalist spirit. In brief, a post-capitalist intersectionality theory: (a) is primarily concerned with understanding the social generation of suffering rather than individual identity formation; (b) emphasizes a material grounding in actual human relationships rather than intersections between abstract categories of difference; (c) refuses to ontologize or prioritize the differences that appear in relationships; (d) strives to establish solidarities rather than dwelling solely upon the recognition of difference; and (e) works toward an increase in consciousness that addresses both second- and third-order suffering.

As for the first point, I have the impression that intersectionality theory, despite its original countercultural impetus, is often read superficially as first and foremost a discourse about identity formation and cultural difference. The isolated individualism of neoliberal rationality, furthermore, tends to interpret identity as simply a matter of personal choice or individual formation. The combination of these two moves robs intersectionality theory of its radical critique. This can have unfortunate real-life consequences. For example, psychologists Grzanka and Miles (2016), after studying the literature and training videos for "LGBT Affirmative Therapy," conclude that this psychotherapy training program reconceives intersectionality simply as a matter of "multiple identities." They argue that this is an instance of the "multicultural turn" in psychology, elements of which "are actually consonant with neoliberal transformations of social and institutional life that foremost function to *incorporate* difference, rather than to redirect and reconfigure the ways power and material resources are unfairly distributed" (emphasis in original).[4] They conclude that, while this form of therapy should not be seen as "fundamentally neoliberal," it is co-opted by a neoliberal agenda that ignores structural inequalities and shifts responsibility onto individual agents. The result, as we will see in the next chapter, is that individuals may blame themselves and remain unaware of the social–material origins of their distress.

The overriding concern of intersectionality, however, is not identity but the suffering arising from systemic oppression. It is a theory about the social genesis of suffering more than it is an identity theory. In her overview of intersectionality theory, pastoral theologian Nancy Ramsay (2014) observes that social justice is "the normative goal in intersectionality"

p. 456). This means that, while it may indeed shed light on questions regarding identity, its main concern is social well-being. The statement of the Combahee River Collective (1977/1979), for example, focuses on social systems of oppression. The intersections the authors envision are not between identities as such. In the initial paragraph, they note that their analyses and practices are "based upon the fact that *the major systems of oppression are interlocking*" (p. 362, my emphasis). The spirit of this document is preserved in bell hooks's (2004) recurrent description of contemporary oppressions as emanating from "imperialist white-supremacist capitalist patriarchy" (p. 17).[5] Unlike many of the lists common in the intersectionality literature—race, class, gender, sexuality, and so on—the culprits here are *systems* rather than identity categories. Furthermore, the concern here is laser-focused on *suffering*.

Oppression is accomplished, however, by both configuring identities and manipulating the power dynamics circulating around and through them. The black feminists who wrote the Combahee River Collective statement believed that, while racism, sexism, and heterosexism cannot be reduced to class conflict, neither can the oppressions around these identities be understood without comprehending their place in capitalist systems of production. For our purposes here, it is critical to remember that neoliberal rationality is perfectly capable of co-opting intersectional discourse, primarily by reemploying the economics/culture divide I have previously discussed in this book. This has become evident during the 2016 presidential campaigns in the USA, in which the problems of racism and sexism are often discussed without reference to class struggle. As Denvir (2016) has observed, such injustices "cease to be intersectional the moment they are abstracted from political economy" (para. 7).

Speaking of abstraction, those who espouse a post-capitalist intersectionality, which is to say, a version of this theory that retains its historical origins, will have reservations about this designation. This brings us to the second feature of a post-capitalist intersectionality. The term "intersectionality" is highly conceptual and immaterial. On its face, it appears to conjure up a mental exercise in which abstract categories of difference, rather than actual people, are interrelated. Worse yet, it could be taken to imply—contrary to its original principles—that these are categories of essential difference that are first separate, with the challenge being how to theorize their points of contact. In addition to leaving aside considerations of class, this is precisely what neoliberalized forms of intersectionality tend to do. The neoliberal imagination conceives societies as aggregates of distinctive and separate-but-equal individuals. The intellectual problem is then how to explain the ways these individual building blocks intersect.

Perhaps, then, we need a better word for theorizing the sufferings emerging around social differences. It is generally accepted that the term intersectionality first appeared in a paper by the legal scholar Kimberle Crenshaw (1989). Thus neither the term "intersectionality" nor any of its derivatives appears in the statement of the Combahee River Collective (1977/1979). Rather, the document consistently refers to human *relationships*. Markers of difference (identities) are understood as entangled in the dynamics of everyday relationships, not only between individuals but also between individuals and social systems, as well as between collectives. Womanist theologian and ethicist emilie townes (personal communication, January 19, 2016) suggests that a better term might be *inter-relationality*. In my view, this means that the differences suffusing actual relationships, and the sufferings that often originate in them, are embedded in the materiality of relationships. They appear as we relate in concrete ways—eating together, living together, working together—including the ways we collaborate within and among collectives, as well as how we construct the economics and policies of social life. From this perspective, identities are always formed in relationships. They may be healthy or unhealthy, just or unjust, or combinations thereof. But they are never simply "personal choices." Thus Ramsay (2014) observes: "Intersectional approaches to identity clearly link individual and social dimensions to any experience of identity. Identity is socially and historically constructed" (p. 456). The sociologist Zygmunt Bauman (2004) adds that identity "cannot be formed unless in reference to the bonds connecting the self to other people and the assumption that such bonds are reliable and stable over time" (p. 68). In more just relationships and societies, individuals have enough liberty to improvise upon what is given to them, and identities remain flexible. In less just societies, identities are simply imposed and rigid.

I have been claiming that neoliberal transformations of sexism and racism refer to identity categories that are shorn of class. This may be a good place to comment on the connection, within an inter-relational perspective, between class and other identities. In a previous publication I have argued that class is not an identity (Rogers-Vaughn, 2015). I must now repent of that opinion. At the time, I was focused on the difference between class and identity as this term is understood within neoliberal identity politics. Inter-relationality, however, gives us a way to understand identity, and even identity politics, from outside neoliberal discourse.

Class, of course, has to be amenable to identification. Otherwise there could be no "class consciousness," as well as forms of solidarity and social movements founded upon it. I still claim, however, that class is "a different kind of difference." As theologian Joerg Rieger (2013) has noted, to talk about inclusion or diversity with regard to class, as we might with gender and race, makes little sense (p. 199). For instance, applying affirmative action to gender and race leads to a more equitable society. If applied to class differences, however, "it would mean the end of capitalism" (p. 202). What I wish to add here is that the economic and political power differentials indicated by the term class are not simply the basis for a potential identity. More importantly, class power manifests the capacity to *generate* and *reconfigure* identities, including those attributed to sex, gender, and race. For example, the ability to have an identity, much less multiple identities, as well as the degree of agency to improvise upon identity varies with class power. Bauman (2004) summarizes this capacity:

> At one pole of the emergent global hierarchy are those who can compose and decompose their identities more or less at will, drawing from the uncommonly large, planet-wide pool of offers. At the other pole are crowded those whose access to identity choice has been barred, people who are given no say in deciding their preferences and who in the end are burdened with identities enforced and imposed *by others*; identities which they themselves resent but are not allowed to shed and cannot manage to get rid of. (p. 38, emphasis in original)

Although I reject the notion of identity as a personal choice, I am reinterpreting Bauman's position with reference to the relative capacity to improvise upon what is given. Most of us, says Bauman, "are suspended uneasily between those two poles," and must tolerate a level of anxiety surrounding the precariousness of our identities (p. 38). Finally, Bauman notes: "there is a lower space than low—a space underneath the bottom" (p. 39). In this space dwell those whom he calls the "underclass," those whom Sassen (2014) calls "the expelled." These inhabitants have no identities at all, even those that may be oppressive:

> The meaning of the 'underclass identity' is an *absence of identity*; the effacement or denial of individuality, of 'face'—that object of ethical duty and moral care. You are cast outside the social space in which identities are sought, chosen, constructed, evaluated, confirmed or refuted. (Bauman, 2004, p. 39, emphasis in original)

Bauman is pointing here to desubjectivation in its most extreme form, and thus to what I am calling third-order suffering. While desubjectivation appears in other classes, in the underclass it is pervasive and near-absolute. But what I wish to emphasize here is that class has a dual meaning. It is both a potential identity and a power that generates and configures other identities.

Thirdly, a post-capitalist intersectionality, or inter-relationality, refuses to ontologize or prioritize the differences that appear in human relationships. It is clear to most people, I think, that class is not ontological. It is not, in other words, given or natural. The ideal of social mobility—shared in the USA by political conservatives and liberals alike—assumes that one may be born into one class but ascend (or descend) into another. This is one thing that distinguishes capitalism, which divides society into classes, from pre-capitalist feudal societies, which divided the populace into rigid caste systems. What is often missed is that race and gender have no more ontological status than class. Scientific efforts to identify essential differences according to race and gender, beyond somatic variations such as sexual anatomy, skin pigmentation, eye color, body morphology, and hair texture have either come up empty or confirmed cultural stereotypes (e.g. Fields & Fields, 2014; Fine, 2010). Reed (2013) concludes that such efforts are "nothing more than narrow upper-class prejudices parading about as science" (p. 51). Theories emphasizing inter-relationality eschew assertions of essential difference and seek instead to identify ways that a hegemony utilizes asserted differences to serve its interests and agendas. The focus here is on how dominant powers create, configure, and utilize identities to accomplish political and material agendas. Regarding designations of race, Victor Anderson (1999) has been a pioneer in asserting that "blackness" is not ontological. Similarly, Fields and Fields (2014) argue that racism does not emerge because there are races. Rather, practices of racism create the notion of race through a process the authors call "racecraft." As Harry Chang (Liem & Montague, 1985) claimed during the 1970s, racialization is a type of reification: "Money seeks gold to objectify itself—gold does not cry out to be money" (p. 39). The upshot of all this, according to Reed, is that race and gender are "ascriptive differences" utilized by systems of domination: "Ideologies of ascriptive difference help to stabilize a social order by legitimizing its hierarchies of wealth, power, and privilege, including its social division of labor, as the natural order of things" (p. 49).

This is not an argument for a "class first" approach. While gender and race, like class, are created and configured within matrices of domination, the consequent sexism and racism are quite real and take up lives of their own. *Moreover, gender, race and class are always already entangled.* It would be futile to attempt to prioritize them, even in concrete instances of oppression. For this reason, the statement of the Combahee River Collective (1977/1979) asserts that "race, sex, and class are simultaneous factors in oppression" (p. 371). It is tempting to think that each may assume priority, depending on contextual circumstances. Even bell hooks (Lowens, 2012), in a recent interview, observes that theories of intersectionality "allow us to focus on what is most important at a given point in time. ...Like right now, for many Americans, class is being foregrounded like never before because of the economic situation" (para. 19). I fear that such declarations may be slippery slopes that function to maintain antagonistic divisions within the progressive left. Furthermore, such a position does not attend to how, in everyday life, the oppressions circulating around these identities are *directly*, rather than inversely, proportional. It just does not seem to be the case that, with the increasing economic inequality under neoliberalism, class concerns move to the foreground, while sexism and racism recede. Rather, they all rise together and in tandem. It is true that rampant inequality has intensified class conflict and made it more visible. However, sexism has also increased under these conditions, with disproportional numbers of women pressured into low-paid and unpaid work, and with discrimination and violence against women accelerating (Braedley & Luxton, 2010; Connell, 2010). Likewise, growing economic inequality has been accompanied by suppressed income for blacks and by more frequent and egregious acts of violence and exploitation toward people of color (Giroux, 2010; Goldberg, 2009). It is surely no coincidence that this period, in the USA, has been marked by massive incarceration of blacks and an escalation in killings of unarmed blacks by law enforcement officials. As a parent, I fear for the future of my two biracial sons, now eight years of age, who will likely experience oppression at the hands of dominant neoliberal powers unless substantial changes occur. The point is that economic and social exclusion and exploitation go together. We simply can no longer afford a "class first" or "race first" or "gender first" approach to political action.

This brings us to a fourth dimension of a post-capitalist inter-relationality. While the statement of the Combahee River Collective (1977/1979) may be interpreted as laying out the significance of identity politics, it is not the same identity politics that have become so familiar in neoliberal societies. Neoliberal identity politics have effectively balkanized what was once "the public." Society breaks up into a multitude of identity groups, each more or less insulated from the others and in competition with them. This sort of fractiousness is absent in the statement of the Combahee River Collective. While clear about their own identity and interests, these women look for ways to collaborate with others, especially for political action. They stress, for example: "Although we are feminists and lesbians, we feel solidarity with progressive black men and do not advocate the fractionalization that white women who are separatists demand" (p. 365). After noting a number of examples, they emphasize that they "continue to do political work in coalition with other groups" (p. 371). This underscores that a post-capitalist inter-relationality presses through the recognition of difference in search of *solidarity*. If the problems of class exploitation, sexism, and racism arise together, then they must be addressed together. Pastoral theologian Cedric Johnson (2016a) observes:

> Social exclusion and labor exploitation are different problems, but they are never disconnected under capitalism. And both processes work to the advantage of capital. Segmented labor markets, ethnic rivalry, racism, sexism, xenophobia, and informalization all work against solidarity. (para. 77)

Any approach that gives primacy to a particular identity, much less attributing ontological status to it, necessarily undermines solidarity and political action. Johnson singles out "liberal antiracist discourse," which separates race from class and prioritizes racism, as an example:

> Liberal antiracist discourse further isolates the conditions of the most excluded segments of workers, separating their experiences from those of other workers, and their labor from the broader processes at work, instead of emphasizing the empirical and potential unity of the laboring classes. (para. 78)

This aids and abets the "divide and conquer" strategy that financial elites have historically used to divide working people against each other.

Finally, a post-capitalist inter-relationality strives toward the increase of consciousness, particularly with regard to the social origins of suffering. Even with regard to second-order suffering, consciousness-raising is often critical. This is because the complex machinations of institutions and social systems tend to occur, as Marx often noted, "behind the backs" of the people. With third-order suffering—which arises from the synergy of deinstitutionalization, desymbolization, and desubjectivation—the increase of consciousness is even more important. As I discussed in previous sections, neoliberal rationality denies and thus renders sexism, racism, and class conflict invisible. Furthermore, by undertaking the "Three Ds," neoliberalization erodes a sense of belonging, a common language for naming the suffering, and any durable agency. This yields the most profound unconsciousness imaginable, including, ultimately, a lack of awareness of going-on-being. How is the language of inter-relationality to make any sense for people in such a condition? Where are its referents now? We are reduced here to a voiceless and nameless suffering. So that is where we must begin. William Davies (2015) speaks, I believe, to this situation: "Rather than seek to alter our feelings, now would be a good time to take what we've turned inwards, and attempt to direct it back out again" (p. 11). Part of the wisdom of inter-relationality is that nothing can "make sense" outside of relationships. Especially when we no longer know who we are, and our suffering has no name, we need others who will be present to bear witness. We can only direct our suffering back out when we can direct it to others, even when this means, initially, sitting in silence together. There is no hope unless we can begin with at least this seed of solidarity. This does not mean "psychotherapy for everybody." Rising from such a deep unconsciousness occurs best in groups, and perhaps even in movements, where "deep calls unto deep." After many years of activism, Angela Davis (2016) confesses:

> I don't know whether I would have survived had not movements survived, had not communities of resistance, communities of struggle. So whatever I'm doing I always feel myself directly connected to those communities and I think that this is an era where we have to encourage that sense of community particularly at a time when neoliberalism attempts to force people to think of themselves only in individual terms and not in collective terms. It is in collectivities that we find reservoirs of hope and optimism. (p. 49)

So, to undo the spell of neoliberalism, we must "play the record in reverse." That means finding paths, however meager, back to solidarity. And this brings us to the next chapter, in which I must respond to the inevitable question: "Where do we go from here?"

NOTES

1. http://www.pewresearch.org/fact-tank/2014/12/12/racia wealth-gaps-great-recession/#comments (Accessed 05 Januar 2016).
2. All statistics on incarceration are from a September 2014 report t the US Department of Justice, titled "Prisoners in 2013," availab at http://www.bjs.gov/content/pub/pdf/p13.pdf (Accessed 0 January 2016).
3. Katy Steinmetz, "Exclusive: See How Big the Gig Economy Real Is," *Time*, January 6, 2016, available at http://time.com/4169532 sharing-economy-poll/ (Accessed January 31, 2016).
4. At the time of this writing, this article was only available online an had not been paginated, thus page numbers are not yet available fo citations within this article.
5. While I am using a particular citation here, variations of this phras appear throughout hooks's writings and interviews.

REFERENCES

Alexander, M. (2012). *The new Jim Crow: Mass incarceration in the age of colo blindness* (Rev. ed.). New York, NY: The New Press.

Andersen, M. L., & Collins, P. H. (Eds.). (2007). *Race, class, & gender: An anth ogy* (6th ed.). Belmont, CA: Thomson Wadsworth.

Anderson, V. (1999). *Beyond ontological blackness: An essay on African America religious and cultural criticism*. New York, NY: Continuum.

Baran, P. A., & Sweezy, P. M. (1966). *Monopoly capital: An essay on the America economic and social order*. New York, NY: Modern Reader Paperbacks.

Bauman, Z. (2004). *Identity: Conversations with Benedetto Vecchi*. Cambridg Polity Press.

Boltanski, L, & Chiapello, E. (1999/2007). *The new spirit of capitalism* (Gregor Elliott, Trans.). London: Verso.

Braedley, S., & Luxton, M. (2010). Competing philosophies: Neoliberalism an challenges of everyday life. In S. Braedley & M. Luxton (Eds.), *Neoliberalis and everyday life* (pp. 3–21). Montreal, QC: McGill-Queen's University Pres

Brock, R. N., & Lettini, G. (2012). *Soul repair: Recovering from moral injury aft war*. Boston, MA: Beacon Press.

Brown, W. (1995). *States of injury: Power and freedom in late modernity*. Princeto NJ: Princeton University Press.

Bunting, M. (2005). *Willing slaves: How the overwork culture is ruling our live* London: Harper Perennial.

Carter, H. W. (2015). *Union made: Working people and the rise of social Christianity in Chicago.* New York, NY: Oxford University Press.

Cazdyn, E. (2012). *The already dead: The new time of politics, culture, and illness.* Durham, NC: Duke University Press.

Combahee River Collective. (1977/1979). The Combahee River Collective: A black feminist statement. In Z. R. Eisenstein (Ed.), *Capitalist patriarchy and the case for socialist feminism* (pp. 362–372). New York, NY: Monthly Review Press.

Connell, R. (2010). Understanding neoliberalism. In S. Braedley & M. Luxton (Eds.), *Neoliberalism and everyday life* (pp. 22–36). Montreal, QC: McGill-Queen's University Press.

Connell, R. W. (2005). *Masculinities* (2nd ed.). Berkeley, CA: University of California Press.

Crenshaw, K. (1989). Demarginalizing the intersection of race and sex: A black feminist critique of antidiscrimination doctrine, feminist theory and antiracist politics. *The University of Chicago Legal Forum,* 139–167.

Dardot, P., & Laval, C. (2009/2013). *The new way of the world: On neo-liberal society* (Gregory Elliott, Trans.). London: Verso.

Davies, W. (2015). *The happiness industry: How the government and big business sold us well-being.* London, UK: Verso.

Davis, A. Y. (1983). *Women, race & class.* New York, NY: Vintage Books.

Davis, A. Y. (2016). In F. Barat (Ed.), *Freedom is a constant struggle: Ferguson, Palestine, and the foundations of a movement.* Chicago, IL: Haymarket Books.

Davis, D.-A. (2007). Narrating the mute: Racializing and racism in a neoliberal moment. *Souls: A Critical Journal of Black Politics, Culture, and Society, 9*(4), 346–360.

Denvir, D. (2016, February 19). Hillary Clinton's cynical race appeals: The revenge of neoliberal identity politics. *Salon.* Retrieved February 20, 2016, from http://www.salon.com/2016/02/19/hillary_clintons_cynical_raceappeals_the_revenge_of_neoliberal_identity_politics/

DuFour, D.-R. (2003/2008). *The art of shrinking heads: On the new servitude of the liberated in the age of total capitalism* (David Macey, Trans.). Cambridge: Polity Press.

Duggan, L. (2003). *The twilight of equality? Neoliberalism, cultural politics, and the attack on democracy.* Boston, MA: Beacon Press.

Eisenstein, Z. R. (Ed.). (1979). *Capitalist patriarchy and the case for socialist feminism.* New York, NY: Monthly Review Press.

Fields, K. E., & Fields, B. J. (2014). *Racecraft: The soul of inequality in American life.* London: Verso.

Fine, C. (2010). *Delusions of gender: How our minds, society, and neurosexism create difference.* New York, NY: W. W. Norton & Company.

Fraser, N. (2013a). *Fortunes of feminism: From state-managed capitalism to neoliberal crisis*. London: Verso.

Fraser, N. (2013b, October 13). How feminism became capitalism's handmaiden—And how to reclaim it. *The Guardian*. Retrieved February 28, 2016, from   http://www.theguardian.com/commentisfree/2013/oct/14/feminism-capitalist-handmaiden-neoliberal

Fraser, S. (2015). *The age of acquiescence: The life and death of American resistance to organized wealth and power*. New York, NY: Little, Brown and Company.

Gilens, M. (1996). "Race coding" and white opposition to welfare. *The American Political Science Review, 90*(3), 593–604.

Gilens, M. (2012). *Affluence & influence: Economic inequality and political power in America*. Princeton, NJ: Princeton University Press and the Russell Sage Foundation.

Gilroy, P. (2010). *Darker than blue: On the moral economies of Black Atlantic culture*. Cambridge, MA: The Belknap Press of Harvard University Press.

Giroux, H. A. (2005). The terror of neoliberalism: Rethinking the significance of cultural politics. *College Literature, 32*(1), 1–19.

Giroux, H. A. (2008). *Against the terror of neoliberalism: Politics beyond the age of greed*. Boulder, CO: Paradigm Publishers.

Giroux, S. S. (2010). Sade's revenge: Racial neoliberalism and the sovereignty of negation. *Patterns of Prejudice, 44*(1), 1–26.

Goldberg, D. T. (2009). *The threat of race: Reflections on racial neoliberalism*. Malden, MA: Wiley-Blackwell.

Goodchild, P. (2009). *Theology of money*. Durham, NC: Duke University Press.

Grzanka, P. R., & Miles, J. R. (2016). The problem with the phrase "intersecting identities": LGBT affirmative therapy, intersectionality, and neoliberalism. *Sexuality Research and Social Policy*. doi:10.1007/s13178-016-0240-2.

hooks, b. (2000). *Where we stand: Class matters*. New York, NY: Routledge.

hooks, b. (2004). *The will to change: Men, masculinity, and love*. New York, NY: Washington Square Press.

Hubbard, P. (2004). Revenge and injustice in the neoliberal city: Uncovering masculinist agendas. *Antipode, 36*(4), 665–686.

Jaffe, S. (2013). Trickle-down feminism. *Dissent*. Retrieved February 27, 2016, from https://www.dissentmagazine.org/article/trickle-down-feminism

Jaffe, S. (2014). Neoliberal feminists don't want women to organize. *The Public Eye*, 6–7. Retrieved February 28, 2016, from http://www.politicalresearch.org/wp-content/uploads/downloads/2014/10/Public-Eye-Magazine-Fall-2014.pdf

James, J. (Ed.). (1998). *The Angela Y. Davis reader*. Malden, MA: Blackwell Publishing.

Johnson, C. C. (2016a, February 3). An open letter to Ta-Nehisi Coates and the liberals who love him. *Jacobin*. Retrieved February 28, 2016, from https://

www.jacobinmag.com/2016/02/ta-nehisi-coates-case-for-reparations-bernie-sanders-racism/

Johnson, C. C. (2016b). *Race, religion, and resilience in the neoliberal age.* New York, NY: Palgrave Macmillan.

Lazzarato, M. (2012). *The making of indebted man* (Joshua D. Jordan, Trans.). Los Angeles, CA: Semiotext(e).

Lazzarato, M. (2015). *Governing by debt* (Joshua D. Jordan, Trans.). South Pasadena, CA: Semiotext(e).

Liem, P., & Montague, E. (Eds.). (1985). Toward a Marxist theory of racism: Two essays by Harry Chang. *Review of Radical Political Economics, 17*(3), 34–45.

Lowens, R. (2012). How do you practice intersectionalism? An interview with bell hooks. *Common Struggle.* Retrieved February 28, 2016, from http://commonstruggle.org/bellhooks

Lynn, B. C. (2010). *Cornered: The new monopoly capitalism and the economics of destruction.* Hoboken, NJ: Wiley.

Marx, K. (1844/2005). Comments on James Mill, élémens d'économie politique. In Karl Marx & Frederick Engels (Eds.), *Karl Marx, Frederick Engels: Collected Works, Volume 3: 1843-1844* (pp. 211–228) (Clemens Dutt, Trans.). New York, NY: International Publishers.

Michaels, W. B. (2006). *The trouble with diversity: How we learned to love identity and ignore inequality.* New York, NY: Holt Paperbacks.

Oliver, K. (2004). *The colonization of psychic space: A psychoanalytic social theory of oppression.* Minneapolis, MN: University of Minnesota Press.

Omi, M., & Winant, H. (2014, Fall). How colorblindness co-evolved with free-market thinking. *The Public Eye,* 16–18. Retrieved February 28, 2016, from http://www.politicalresearch.org/wp-content/uploads/downloads/2014/10/Public-Eye-Magazine-Fall-2014.pdf

Parenti, C. (2015, July 28). The making of the American police state. *Jacobin.* Retrieved January 18, 2016, from https://www.jacobinmag.com/2015/07/incarceration-capitalism-black-lives-matter/

Ramsay, N. J. (2014). Intersectionality: A model for addressing the complexity of oppression and privilege. *Pastoral Psychology, 63*(4), 453–469.

Reed, A., Jr. (2009). The limits of anti-racism. *Left Business Observer, 121.* Retrieved February 27, 2016, from http://www.leftbusinessobserver.com/Antiracism.html

Reed, A., Jr. (2013). Marx, race, and neoliberalism. *New Labor Forum, 22*(1), 49–57.

Rieger, J. (2013). Instigating class struggle? The study of class in religion and theology and some implications for gender, race, and ethnicity. In J. Rieger (Ed.), *Religion, theology, and class: Fresh engagements after long silence* (pp. 189–211). New York, NY: Palgrave Macmillan.

Roberts, D. J., & Mahtani, M. (2010). Neoliberalizing race, racing neoliberalism: Placing "race" in neoliberal discourses. *Antipode, 42*(2), 248–257.

Rogers-Vaughn, B. (2015). Powers and principalities: Initial reflections toward a post-capitalist pastoral theology. *Journal of Pastoral Theology, 25*(2), 71–92.

Sassen, S. (2014). *Expulsions: Brutality and complexity in the global economy.* Cambridge, MA: Belknap Press.

Sennett, R., & Cobb, J. (1972/1993). *The hidden injuries of class.* New York, NY: W. W. Norton & Company.

Silva, J. M. (2013). *Coming up short: Working-class adulthood in an age of uncertainty.* New York, NY: Oxford University Press.

Standing, G. (2014). *The precariat: The new dangerous class* (Rev. ed.). New York, NY: Bloomsbury Academic.

Stephanopoulos, N. O. (2015). Political powerlessness. *New York University Law Review, 90,* 1527–1608.

Wysong, E., Perrucci, R., & Wright, D. (2014). *The new class society: Goodbye American dream?* (4th ed.). Lanham, MD: Rowman & Littlefield Publishers.

Zweig, M. (2012). *The working class majority: America's best kept secret* (2nd ed.). Ithaca, NY: Cornell University Press.

CHAPTER 6

Beyond Self-Management: Re-Membering Soul

I concluded the previous chapter suggesting that any path forward from where we are today would require both increased consciousness and solidarity. While I believe this to be true, undertaking the analysis of neoliberalism I have conveyed in this book leaves me wary. The ubiquity, severity, and mystifying character of the suffering I have tried to describe in these pages makes me worry that any effort to propose a response, no matter how careful, may come across as blithe, naïve, or undeservedly optimistic. Indeed, I must confess that I have often wondered, while conducting the research for this project, how we can avoid, both individually and collectively, simply resigning ourselves to despair. Personally, learning more about the deep effects of global neoliberalization has done nothing to relieve my tendencies toward melancholy. The first time I taught a course titled "Pastoral Care and Global Capitalism," I found that my students, mostly individuals in their twenties, required little persuasion about the corrosive effects of contemporary capitalism. Perhaps dwelling too long on the analysis, we found ourselves skating along the edge of collective despair. Finally, their forbearance wearing thin, the students pleaded: "Yes, but what can we do?" Of course, there is no way around this question. My students expect a response, as do the people who come to me for pastoral psychotherapy, as do you, my persevering reader.

© The Author(s) 2016
B. Rogers-Vaughn, *Caring for Souls in a Neoliberal Age*,
DOI 10.1057/978-1-137-55339-3_6

So, in this chapter I will respond. But I will not be proposing specif "evidence-based" techniques for countering the effects of neoliberalisr There is no *Diagnostic and Statistical Manual of Neoliberal Disorde* coupled with sets of "best practices" for alleviating the particular di tresses they produce. I will not be designing a manualized plan for Ant Neoliberal Therapy (ANT), selling glossy ANT promotional packets, offering weekend certification programs in ANT. We simply cannot be neoliberalism at its own game, or on its own terms. We would be cru to offer individuals, couples, and families, already impossibly burden with the expectation to manage their problems for themselves, new ar improved methods for self-management. Even if this "worked," we w have only succeeded in helping people cope with the system as it is. W will have done nothing to change it. If anything, the system will hav become even more resilient than before.

Moreover, the belief that even the most intransigent problems can l solved by better techniques and technologies is sheer optimism, which one of those things neoliberalism does best. As I will assert later, in th postscripts, what we need instead is hope. Whereas optimism indicat a belief that things will turn out okay, hope remains embedded in vi ceral suffering. In the words of Gabriel Marcel (1951/1978), "The tru is that there can strictly speaking be no hope except when the tempt tion to despair exists" (p. 36). Equating optimism with belief in progres Christopher Lasch (1991) observes:

> The worst is always what the hopeful are prepared for. Their trust in life would not be worth much if it had not survived disappointments in the past, while the knowledge that the future holds further disappointments demonstrates the continuing need for hope. Believers in progress, on the other hand, though they like to think of themselves as the party of hope, actually have little need of hope, since they have history on their side. *But their lack of it incapacitates them for intelligent action.* Improvidence, the blind faith that things will somehow work out for the best, furnishes a poor substitute for the disposition to see things through even when they don't. (p. 81, emphasis added)

With the accumulating failures of neoliberalism becoming ever mor apparent, I believe we can conclude that things are not turning out for th best. If we are to respond intelligently and compassionately, we have t begin where we find ourselves. A neoliberal world is a place of profoun despair. This is our point of departure.

The texture and depth of this despair becomes more evident when we consider how third-order suffering characterizes the present age. While it is true that a lack of consciousness is not new, unconsciousness has never been as normative as it is today. Indeed, compared to third-order suffering, first- and second-order suffering are remarkably conscious forms of human misery. The advantage of these older forms of distress is that their enhanced awareness can fund both personal and social transformation. I venture that, historically, the capacity for change has been directly proportional to the breadth and intensity of first- and second-order suffering. Not only are people generally aware of such anguish, often excruciatingly so, they also tend to recognize its origins. When these sorts of suffering reach a critical level, personal and/or social transformation(s) are practically assured. The opposite seems to be the case with third-order suffering. Here the degree of distress is *inversely proportional* to the potential for change. Suffering that has been privatized, that has lost its voice and its grounding in a symbolic order, and has been dispersed by the fragmentation of self and soul, is unlikely to produce transformation in any human system—social, interpersonal, or psychological. Furthermore, the increasing entanglement of third-order suffering with first- and second-order suffering, as I have argued, alters these forms toward its own character. This further reduces the opportunities for resistance and change. With a bit of artistic license, we might portray this as zombie suffering. We are hollowed out and going to pieces, but hardly awake. The horror of this age is that we are not horrified.

What is the character of this slumber? In Chap. 4 I discussed Zygmunt Bauman's theory regarding how neoliberalization enacts a dual strategy to accomplish the denial and avoidance of death and suffering. If we associate these strategies with the character of third-order suffering, we can identify two levels of unconsciousness. At the first and most profound level, third-order suffering is suffering that is not aware of itself as suffering. Catherine Malabou (2012) identifies this as a feature of "destructive plasticity":

> What destructive plasticity invites us to consider is the suffering caused by an absence of suffering, in the emergence of a new form of being, a stranger to the one before. Pain that manifests as indifference to pain, impassivity, forgetting, the loss of symbolic reference points. (p. 18)

At this level, third-order suffering is reminiscent of Kierkegaard's (1849/1980) "despair that is ignorant of being despair." An individual under the spell of such "... is altogether secure in the power of despair"

(p. 44). Nothing can be done with suffering that remains so deeply unconscious. It cannot be addressed, resolved, repaired, or comforted. Nor can
it inspire change that would relieve any injustice or condition upon which
it might be founded. The first and necessary step to care for the weakened souls under such a spell is, perhaps counterintuitively, to help them
become aware of their distress. This must remain part of the conundrum
to be taken up in this chapter.

In the second level of unconsciousness there can be extreme suffering,
misery that is quite conscious, but with little to no awareness of its origins.
Suffering and the larger web of powers funding it have been de-linked. As
I have observed throughout this book, under neoliberal existence such
suffering usually manifests psychologically as intractable mood disorders
(indefinable depressions and paralyzing anxieties) and polymorphous
addictions. Because such suffering has been unlinked from its sources,
it appears senseless. It is mystified. Thus it cannot be fully addressed. It
can only be *managed*. As Cazdyn (2012) says of "the new chronic," a
feature of what I am calling third-order suffering: "Every level of society
is stabilized on an antiretroviral cocktail. Every person is safe, like a diabetic on insulin" (p. 13). Here the intent is no longer caring for souls,
but the administration of souls in a state of suspended animation. Cazdyn
summarizes:

> The new chronic mode in medicine, in which the utopian desire to cure
> is displaced by the practical need to manage and stabilize, if not preempt
> the disease altogether (practiced in fields as varied as oncology, HIV, and
> psychiatry), is also at work in politics and culture. I am highly skeptical of
> this mode. (p. 6)

I am suggesting that de-linking sufferings from the interlocking systems within which they originate inevitably reduces care to management.
This unlinking is intrinsic to the entrepreneurial individualism of neoliberal cultures. As I have observed in previous chapters, this means that
suffering originates inside individuals—in their bodies, in their psyches,
and perhaps, by extension, from within the small circle of their interpersonal intimates and associates. Within the current hegemony we lack
understanding of the ways in which these bodies, psyches, and proximal
circles are connected to systems outside themselves. Moreover, individuals
are responsible for their own distress, using whatever resources they can
access. This further reduces care to *self-management*.

In this chapter I am asserting that caring for souls requires us to escape these small boxes in which we simply help people manage their suffering. This is not just a logical conclusion, but also a moral imperative. Moving beyond these confines, moreover, will entail breaking the spell of both types of unconsciousness I have just mentioned. Simultaneously, as we shall see, getting beyond self-management involves the refusal to merely psychologize suffering. As Ian Parker (2007) has argued, modern psychologies have integrated capitalist notions of private property into their theories and practices (pp. 9–54). For example, we encourage people to "own" their feelings, thus reproducing the individualism and social relations of capitalism. This has become even more problematic living in the extreme conditions of capitalism's neoliberal manifestation. Caring for souls in the neoliberal age will thus oblige us to discover ways to assist people in disowning their feelings. In the words of William Davies (2015), which I have cited before but are worth repeating here: "Rather than seek to alter our feelings, now would be a good time to take what we've turned inwards, and attempt to direct it back out again" (p. 11). This dis-owning does not mean we no longer acknowledge our experience. Rather, we now recognize our emotions and other psychological phenomena as emerging from the entangled systems within which we exist. The spirit of this turning out is expressed in the words of an anonymous group of French intellectuals and activists who identify themselves as "The Invisible Committee" (2009): "We are not depressed; we're on strike. For those who refuse to manage themselves, 'depression' is not a state but a passage, a bowing out, a sidestep towards a *political* disaffiliation" (p. 34, emphasis in original). Depression, we might say, arises when we own as individuals what does not rightly belong to us. Here moods, emotions, and other psychological phenomena are no longer *sui generis*. They do not emerge spontaneously from an isolated and mysterious interior world. Rather, they are symptoms of the flow of power and interest through the social, political, and material systems within which we all live.

Finally, earlier in this book I identified soul as that activity or capacity that binds individuals with others, with society, with creation, and with the Eternal. In a profound sense soul *is* this fabric of connection. I will discuss soul in more detail in this chapter and in the postscripts. For now, it is sufficient to recognize that third-order suffering, in a way that distinguishes it from both first- and second-order suffering, entails the erosion of soul. The ruthless individualism of neoliberalization necessarily involves unprecedented fragmentation and isolation, as we have observed in previous chapters. Whereas in first- and second-order suffering the powers of soul may become misdirected, disoriented, or burdened, third-order suffering means that soul has consequently become *weakened*. Experientially, this appears in the twin unconsciousness I have just mentioned—suffering that is not aware of itself as suffering and suffering that is oblivious to its actual origins. Soul that has deteriorated to this extent is soul that has become dis-membered. *Caring for souls in the neoliberal age, therefore, will require us to move beyond self-management to the re-membering of soul.*

How might this re-membering be accomplished? As I have stated earlier, this cannot be reduced to flow charts or manualized techniques and procedures. I must also add that I am continuing to explore potential paths for moving forward, both in my theorizing and in pastoral psychotherapeutic practice. I do not have this all figured out. I request that the reader accept this chapter, and this book in its entirety, as an invitation to join in an ongoing conversation with me and others who are working in a similar vein. That being said, the situation of our world and its inhabitants is dire. We do not have the luxury to wait until we fully understand what must be done before acting. In fact, we are not likely to reach any adequate understandings without acting. I am therefore offering what remains of this chapter as a contribution to this conversation, from someone who continues to work both in the academy and in clinical practice.

I proceed in four moves. First, I will discuss caring for soul in terms of what some have called the new materialism, investigating an emerging approach to care in psychology and psychotherapy as a project that is congruent with this perspective. Second, I explore the dialectics of suffering, how suffering itself is an embryonic form of resistance, and the ground and motive for proliferating resistance and change. This will include a summary of a reorientation within psychoanalytic theory and practice that is currently underway as an example of this dialectic, particularly as it pertains to addressing the two types of unconsciousness I have mentioned. The conjoined dialectical materialism of these first two moves, I believe, serves as the critical reorientation and point of departure for soul-care in the present age. Third, I will provide clinical material from pastoral psychotherapy to illustrate this reorientation. Finally, I will summarize why psychotherapy is inadequate to the current challenge. I do not believe we can address neoliberalization and third-order suffering as a psychotherapy project. Far from it. I am simply beginning by looking for clues from within my own practice context. I do believe, however, that the close attention to suffering individuals afforded by this context can offer valu-

le insights that may prove useful in more encompassing forms of soul-
re, such as social justice movements, community activism, and certain
olitical efforts.

A Very Material Soul

stute readers may have noticed certain affinities between the methods I
ave used and the arguments I have advanced in this book and the history
f thought widely known as dialectical materialism. By materialism, of
ourse, I am not referring to ostentatious consumption or greed. Rather,
aterialism here denotes a manner of thinking and practice that gives
riority to bodies, the corporeal conditions for survival and well-being,
ctuality, and material relationships and processes. This tradition opposes
ny form of reflection that assigns primacy to ideas themselves—to men-
l constructs, pure thought, mind, rationality, discourses, disembodied
uls or essences, or assertions of a transcendent order detached from the
aterial world. Given that religion is often associated in the public imagi-
ation with spiritual or transcendent realities believed to lie beyond this
orld, readers may wonder how a Christian minister could be so taken
ith materiality. The answer may have something to do with my roots
the working class of southern Appalachia. I spent my formative years
ith my hands and feet in the soil. I earned my first wages at the age of
ven, picking cotton by hand under a hot August sun. I worked alongside
y maternal grandfather on his small farm near Dog Town, Alabama, as
e planted and harvested crops and tended to cows, chickens, and pigs.
overty, and the threat of poverty, was ever present. Many of the people
rrounding me were capable of deep reflection, but they rarely concerned
emselves with anything other than work, material sustenance, and the
re of family and neighbors. Even religion revolved around material life.
he rural Christian congregations of my youth, including Ruhama Baptist
hurch, where my grandfather served as pastor, were full of preaching and
nging about heaven. Yet I am bemused when I hear people refer to their
ith as "otherworldly." The images of this supposedly transcendent realm
ere inevitably material—resurrected but very real bodies, the sharing of
lestial banquets, reunions with loved ones, joyful gatherings by flowing
reams, and the wiping of tears from the eyes. This was an earthly paradise
st into the future. Eschatological visions were not immaterial. Rather,
ey sought to address the sufferings and injustices of the present world.
hese were people of the land. They often spoke proudly of themselves,
d their faith, as being "down to earth." Indeed, they were.

And so, regardless of any hopes about what might lie on the other sid of death, I have always known, as Appalachian folk would say, "dow deep in my bones," that religious faith has to do with how we live in rel tion to the land, to its creatures, with each other, and with the Etern we encounter always already there. This book is an extension and expa sion of this visceral sort of knowledge. Its original impulse emerges n from Marx, Freud, or Feuerbach, but from these humble people of tl earth. Here faith encompasses not only such proximal relationships of n upbringing, but also the more distal material relationships and process of economics, politics, and the continually evolving world. As may ha become obvious by now, I also understand soul as thoroughly material, the quite substantial fabric that weaves us all together and with all that i We are all entangled. This is the soul to which I refer whenever I speak caring for souls.

Referring to my previous work regarding depression (Rogers-Vaugh 2014), theologian Joerg Rieger (2016) finds that it "... exemplifies son of the implications of new materialist thinking even if it has not adopte that name ..." (p. 138). While I was not familiar with new materiali theory at that time, the imprint of this sort of analysis on my thinking now clear. Indeed, the method I have used from Chap. 4 forward is hea ily influenced by William Connolly, professor of political science at Johi Hopkins University, a leader in new materialist theorizing. In *The Fragili of Things* (2013), Connolly explores human economic and political activ ties, such as neoliberalism, as systems embedded in the various self-reg(lating open systems of the material cosmos. This entanglement—a ter I have shamelessly borrowed from Connolly and use liberally througl out this book—makes all things more fragile and unpredictable than the appear. Such thinking also appears in the work of Connolly's colleague Johns Hopkins University, Jane Bennett, especially in her book, *Vibra: Matter: A Political Ecology of Things* (2010). In theology new materiali thought is evident not only in the reflections of Rieger (2009, 2016 but also in the work of Catherine Keller (2003, 2015), particularly i her latest book, *Cloud of the Impossible: Negative Theology and Planeta: Entanglement*, in which she converses with Connolly and, like him, quite critical of neoliberal capitalism.

What makes these materialisms "new," as Rieger (2016) points out, their rejection not only of "crude idealism," but also of a "crude mat(rialism" that understands matter in a mechanical, deterministic, an reductionist way (pp. 135–136). Instead, the natural world, includin inanimate matter, is understood as consisting of innumerable interlocking systems, each manifesting its own agency, power, and creativity (pp. 143–144). What I have done, in this book, is to consider some implications of Connolly's exposition of the new materialism for human systems. Connolly is primarily concerned with the entanglements between large-scale human systems—neoliberalism and democratic activism—and between these systems and those of the natural world. I have focused, instead, on the entanglements between neoliberalism and three self-regulating but open and interlocking human systems—the social (institutions, collectives), interpersonal, and psychological. I believe I have done this in a fashion congruent with Connolly's approach. These entanglements, in turn, shed light on third-order suffering and its imbrications with first- and second-order suffering. Indeed, my understanding of third-order suffering is informed by descriptions offered by theorists who themselves manifest new materialist thought—Catherine Malabou's (2012) "destructive plasticity" and Eric Cazdyn's (2012) "the new chronic."

The new materialism not only helps describe the sufferings of the neoliberal age, but also simultaneously suggests a way to imagine responding to these sufferings. Unfortunately, the sources upon which pastoral theological reflection has historically drawn tend to be steeped in idealism. This is perhaps most apparent in a reliance on theological doctrines and religio-spiritual narratives whose connection to materiality is tangential at best. It also arises in the more recent dependence on some postmodern theories that prioritize discourse to the point that claims about actuality are regarded with suspicion. What I wish to focus upon now, however, is our utilization of modern psychology, which has arguably been our primary cognate discipline. While current psychological theories usually acknowledge physiological contributions to distress, they avoid crude materialism. After all, reducing mental or emotional conditions purely to chemical, neurological, or genetic causes would be the end of psychology as a discipline. On the other hand, psychology often has resorted to idealistic explanations for such problems. Cognitive psychology, for instance, which originated in the United States, locates the source of mental and emotional anguish in how individuals think, imagine, or perceive. Positive psychology is a type of cognitive psychology that attempts to adjust people's thought patterns toward optimism, confidence, and affirmation. Its methods, we are told, can yield happiness and flourishing under even the most challenging material circumstances (Greenberg, 2010). Even some psychoanalytic theories, which manifest a more complex assessment of mental states, portray a psyche filled with contents so reified that distress seems to emerge spontaneously from a relatively insulated interior world. Fortunately, many practicing psychotherapists do, to some degree, take into account the material circumstances of their patients. However, this is typically limited to factors that are immediately observable from the standpoint of the therapist and patient—physical illness and disability, employment status, interpersonal relationships, financial concerns, housing conditions, and so forth. What is missing is attention to the larger social-material systems that play a powerful role in configuring these more immediate circumstances, including the individual subjects themselves.

There have been, nonetheless, minority voices in psychology that have taken account of the broader material forces that configure proximate environments, individual subjects, and their sufferings. Jacoby (1983) has noted that many of the early psychoanalysts, particularly those circulating through the Berlin Institute, described themselves as socialists or Marxists. These analysts generally believed that neurotic suffering was shaped primarily by forces in the greater social and political environment. Otto Fenichel (1945), a leader within this circle, concluded:

> Neuroses do not occur out of biological necessity, like aging; nor are they purely biologically determined, like leukemia .... Neither are neuroses "influenced by social conditions" as tuberculosis is, where circumstances of residence and diet may decide the course of the illness. Neuroses are social diseases in a much stricter sense .... Neuroses are the outcome of unfavorable and socially determined educational measures, corresponding to a given and historically developed social milieu and necessary in this milieu. They cannot be changed without corresponding change in the milieu. (p. 586)

The precise content and dynamics of "the unconscious," according to these analysts, depended predominantly upon the historical and social context of the individual subject. This orientation continued in the United States among the so-called Neo-Freudians, including Erich Fromm, Karen Horney, and H.S. Sullivan, all of whom were quite critical of capitalism (Jacoby, 1983, pp. 105–111, 153–158). By the time of Fromm's death in 1980, as neoliberalism was on the rise, this strain within North American psychoanalysis had largely died out (Gold, 2002). Notable holdouts have included Joel Kovel (1981) and Paul Wachtel (1983). Only recently, as the problems with neoliberalism have become more apparent, have psychoanalysts in the United States been giving renewed attention to the social-material origins of suffering, and to capitalism in particular (Altman, 2015; Layton, Hollander, & Gutwill, 2006). However, psychology textbooks used in educational institutions within the United States rarely, if ever, mention such work.

Outside the United States, psychologies emphasizing the broader social and material context for distress have enjoyed more purchase. The pattern was set early by Frantz Fanon (1952/1967, 1963/2004), a psychoanalytically informed psychiatrist born in Martinique, who explored the impact of colonization on subject formation. In Latin America, Ignacio Martín-Baró (1994), a Jesuit priest who was killed by a Salvadoran death squad in 1989, founded a "liberation psychology" that not only grounded psychological distress in the material conditions of life, but also criticized the imbrications between modern psychology and political and economic oppression. Liberation psychologies have made some inroads in North American faculties (Watkins & Shulman, 2008). But, again, few psychology students or practitioners in the United States have ever heard about this movement.

Meanwhile, beyond the borders of the United States a rich dialogue between psychoanalysis and social theory has continued. Layton, Hollander, and Gutwill (2006) observe:

Interestingly, the United States has been unique in its isolation from the dialogue between critical social theory and psychoanalysis. Such interchange fared better in the United Kingdom, Continental Europe and Latin America .... In some countries, most notably France and Argentina, a left psychoanalysis emerged that was identified with revolutionary struggles against social as well as psychological repression. (p. 4)

Currently, the most generative instance of social materialism in psychological theory may be the critical psychology movement that has emerged within the United Kingdom, a loose association that includes a number of analysts but is not exclusively psychoanalytic. This psychology is "critical" in that it represents "... an attempt to problematize the place of psychological explanations in patterns of power and ideology" (Parker, 2015b, p. 6). Early contributions appeared in a collection of essays titled *Critical Psychiatry: The Politics of Mental Health*, edited by David Ingleby (1980a). Notable leaders in this movement have included Andrew Samuels (1993, 2001), David Smail (1997, 2001, 2005), Paul Moloney (2013), and Ian Parker (2007, 2015a, 2015b). The richness of conversation within this diverse movement is on display in a recent compilation edited by Del Loewenthal (2015), which includes transdisciplinary perspectives. Meanwhile, Jeremy Carrette (2007) has provocatively placed critical psychology into conversation with the study of religious experience. The impact of critical psychology in the United Kingdom has been considerable, even influencing the public position statements of the Division of Clinical Psychology within the British Psychological Society.[1]

Critical psychology offers an invaluable resource for theorizing responses to human suffering in the neoliberal age. Space does not permit a comprehensive survey. Instead, I will synopsize the approach of clinical psychologist David Smail, perhaps one of the most underappreciated representatives of this movement. Smail's argument is most lucid in his final book, *Power, Interest and Psychology: Elements of a Social Materialist Understanding of Distress* (2005). Smail contends that the everyday culture of contemporary capitalism is idealistic and is served by a prevailing psychology that is likewise idealistic:

> The modern consumer is in this way a pleasure-seeking idealist, dislocated from a real world, a real body and a real society. We must believe, among other things, that the earth's resources are infinite, that mind will triumph over matter and that there's no limit to what you can achieve if you really try. Psychology helps a lot in this enterprise. (p. iii)

Entire populations are absorbed in the spectral powers of imagery and narrative enchantment. Meanwhile, global elites control the reins of material interests: "Thieves sack the mansion undisturbed while its occupants remain sunk in their dreams" (p. 56). This idealism is coupled, in modern psychology, with individualism:

> Margaret Thatcher's much-cited view that 'There's no such thing as society, only individuals and their families,' finds an unacknowledged echo in almost all approaches to therapy, including those that continued throughout the second half of the twentieth century to wrap themselves in the mantle of 'science.' (p. 11)

This idealism-plus-individualism concoction, Smail maintains, serves the interests of capital. It is most apparent, he observes, in cognitive-behavioral therapies (CBT) and narrative therapies that privilege the power of discourse. Smail calls these therapeutic methods "magical voluntarism." He concludes: "With many 'postmodernist' approaches (e.g. 'narrative therapy') magical voluntarism reaches its apotheosis: the

orld is made of words, and if the story you find yourself in causes you
stress, tell yourself another one" (p. 7). These types of therapy, Smail
intends, exert power not because they are true, but because they are
eful: "... it *suits the interests* both of those who assert it and those who
sent to it" (p. 7, emphasis in original).
Unsurprisingly, Smail is also critical of any psychology that posits an
nterior world" divorced from society and the material world. This leads
m also to oppose psychoanalysis, which he seems to deem incapable of
nbracing his social-materialist viewpoint. Consider, however, the follow-
g comments by the psychoanalyst Joel Kovel (1981):

> It now struck me that what we study under the name of "psychology" ... is
> a kind of value extracted from a particular kind of labor. This labor includes
> as an essential component a praxis that forces people out of the ground
> of their participation in society, makes them, in other words, into discrete
> individuals, standing there, shivering and alone—and then studies their shiv-
> ers and their solitude, giving names like "self," "personality," and "mental
> apparatus" to the outcome. (p. 33)

This passage is so close to Smail's claims, he could have written it himself.
So much for the psychologies Smail rejects. What is his constructive
oposal? Despite the problems with psychology, he asserts, it must be
tained because: "Ultimately, our concern is with human subjectivity,
ith the experience of being a person, and in particular with the types
' suffering and pain that being a person can engender" (Smail, 2005,
iv). The decisive issue is not to dispose of psychology altogether, but
ask whose interest a particular psychological theory or therapy serves.
eoliberal interests, Smail notes, divide the world into winners and los-
s, "... the supermen versus the wimps." Further, this "ruthless world,"
hich denies common humanity with others, especially those less fortu-
ite, is not natural. It can be chosen or rejected. He flatly states: "This
ook is founded on just such a rejection. I'm siding with the wimps" (p.
. The test of any adequate psychology is not solely one of truth, but also
orality. Psychological theorizing and practice engages us in an ethical
1oice. It "... rests on a compassionate solidarity with others" (p. v).
irther, an ethical psychology dispenses with idealism and embraces
aleriality:

> The avoidable pain and suffering that forms the focus of our attention is not
> a 'mental' thing, but arises from our nature as embodied beings .... For we
> are bodies in a world: of course (and very importantly) in a physical world,

but also a socially structured, material space-time in which what we do to each other has enormous importance. (p. iv)

Inattention to material reality "… leads to an increasingly deplete environment, unbalanced society and tortured subjectivity." And a anguished subjectivity, in turn, "… is a function very largely of the fir two …" (p. 16).

Smail (2005) thus proposes a therapeutic approach that turns trad tional psychology "inside out." Human motivation arises not from driv emerging from within, but from *social interests*. Rather than being ". *pushed from within* by various urges and desires … they are *pulled fro without* by the social manipulation of … inescapable biological features e being human" (p. 35, emphases in original). Smail identifies this "soci manipulation" by the term *power*, which is divided into *proximal po ers*—those in the immediate environment of the individual, such as wor education, interpersonal relationships, and family—and *distal powers*, suc as economics, politics, ideology, and culture (pp. 26–39). Despite the fa that individuals tend only to be aware of the proximal powers in the lives, it is the distal powers, Smail asserts, that are most critical in shaj ing subjectivity and individual suffering. Although proximal powers serv to nuance and give specificity to subject formation, they are themselv formed by the far more potent distal powers. This reverses the meaning c "the unconscious": "Unconsciousness ceases to be a property of individi als, and becomes an external, social phenomenon. We are unconscio of what lies in the darkness beyond our power horizon—what we cann know or have been prevented from knowing" (p. 33). Thus the goal c therapy is no longer an "insight" that leaves individuals solely respor sible for their feelings and conduct, but an "outsight" that illuminates tl external, material causes of distress. This helps individuals to put "… tl extent of their own responsibility for their condition … into its prop perspective" (p. 32). "Free will" is limited to whatever the social mate rial environment allows to a particular individual in a specific place an time (p. 43). All power, in other words, derives from the material soci surround.

Smail leaves us with a clinical practice that is modest in its claims to tran formation, at least relative to conventional psychology. Psychotherapy her becomes "… a source of solidarity rather than a technology of 'change' (p. 80). Its benefits are condensed to four: (a) it *demystifies* individual su fering by linking it to its social material origins; (b) it *rescues subjectivi* from the prison of ideality; (c) it *rehabilitates character* by restoring solidarity and compassion; and (d) it *reinstates the environment*, rather than the individual or the therapeutic relationship, as the primary context for justice and care (pp. 80–86).

Smail (2005) delivers a powerful and important corrective for both the idealism and the individualism embedded in much of our pastoral theology and care, as well as in psychotherapy and caring for souls generally. He is especially useful for addressing the second type of unconsciousness in third-order suffering—the lack of awareness of the linkage between such suffering and the larger systems in which it originates. However, we still need more than Smail has to offer. First, while Smail's analysis is not rigidly deterministic—he does, for example, allow a small bit of agency to individuals—there is a risk here of collapsing the psychological into the social. This is most discernable in his ambivalence about subjectivity. While he insists psychology remains necessary because we must attend to subjectivity, he flatly rejects any sort of "interior, 'psychological' world" (p. 40). The problem seems to revolve around the meaning he attributes to the term "world," for otherwise he values an "inner" life. While denying it the status of "world," Smail celebrates "… a wonderful confusion of feeling and imagination, thinking, dreaming and memory that furnishes our personal idea of what it is to be human and to be alive. It constitutes our subjectivity" (p. 64). He then proceeds to refer to this as a "… wildly idiosyncratic *interior* which is to be found *within* each one of us …" (p. 64, my emphases). Moreover, Smail tends to get caught up in the very interior/exterior binary he so firmly rejects, as when he insists that unconsciousness is an "external, social phenomenon." The problem, it seems to me, is not whether there is an "interior" life (or even "world"), but that subjectivity cannot be isolated from the surrounding milieu— which is the value of Smail's overall claim. A better way to think of this, following Connolly's new materialist theorizing, is that the psychological subject is herself a self-regulating but open system that is entangled with other systems, both larger and smaller. Unconsciousness, for example, is now neither simply interior nor exterior, but exists within the entanglements between psychological systems and other human (and perhaps non-human) systems.

This relates to a second problem. While Smail (2005) values subjectivity, he has few means for describing its intricacies and idiosyncratic textures. His only resource, at least in this book, appears to be his training in a cognitive psychology he otherwise harshly criticizes. Thus subjective life is reduced largely to self-talk, or what he calls "commentary" (pp. 40–41). He manages to rescue such cognitions for his purposes, however, by understanding them as social constructions. Unfortunately, this renders the social materialist shaping of subjectivity to be a matter of imposition, portrayed in a series of schematics (pp. 27, 30–31, 33, 36, 38, 41). What is missing is a theory of individuality. There is no way to understand how a particular individual appropriates and improvises upon the social surround, in such a way as to distinguish him from other individuals. There is also no theory about human desire, even understood by way of entanglements, for recognizing how such improvisation might occur. And, because unconsciousness is posited only in relation to an exterior, we are left with no way to conceive of the first aspect of the twin unconsciousness of third-order suffering—the suffering that is not aware of itself as suffering—much less how this might be addressed. For this we must look elsewhere.

Finally, Smail (2005) tends to view suffering as a thing-unto-itself. Either it is existential, what I call first-order suffering, or it is the outcome of social oppression, what I call second-order suffering. In either case, there is no response except either stoic resignation or interpersonal comfort and empathy. For Smail, solidarity appears to be primarily a quality of interpersonal relationships. While he alludes to the necessity for political action, he seems suspicious of collective efforts to unite around a common suffering. He is especially leery of religion (pp. 80, 85, 95). What is also missing here, then, is an appreciation of the dialectical significance of suffering—of suffering as a nascent form of resistance. I believe these lacunae in Smail's social materialist approach may be filled in by recent developments in psychoanalytic theory and practice, to which I now turn.

INDIVIDUALITY: A WINDOW INTO THE DIALECTICS OF SOUL

One of my mentors, the pastoral theologian Liston Mills, was fond of saying: "Human beings are fundamentally recalcitrant. They don't change until they're miserable." In one simple statement he was pointing to an elemental human dialectic—the dynamic between the resistance to change and the motivation to change. Importantly, he located the impetus for change in human suffering. I am unwilling, however, to locate a clinging to the status quo in some sort of essential stubbornness. Instead, I propose that this dialectic is intrinsic to the life of soul. Up to this point it may seem that I understand soul as simply designating the entanglement of all things. As we shall see later on, this is not quite the case. Entanglement as such is ontology, just the way things occur. As Connolly (2013) makes clear, and as I have discussed in previous chapters, neoliberalism itself manifests its own peculiar entanglements. *Rather, soul is a way of existing within these entanglements—a way characterized by love, attachment, appreciation, wonder, longing.* Depending upon a particular material and historical context, soul may strive either to maintain relative stability or to resist. Soul may even endeavor to do both at once. Meanwhile, both the ontology of entanglement and the dialectics of soul assume individuality. Process thought, for example, contends that, without the individuality of actual occasions, we would have only a uniform and static sameness. Likewise, love depends on the presence "others," on those who stand out in all their particularity.

What I intend to accomplish in this section is to explore the individual human subject as she is formed and as she strives to establish and maintain her attachments in the context of a neoliberal society. The clinical situation provides an opportunity for such an investigation, which then serves as a window through which to view the dialectics of soul under these conditions. As Layton (2007) notes, concerning the particular vulnerabilities of neoliberal subjects, the clinic is now "... one of the few places left in the US where one has permission to express them without shame" (p. 152). Kovel (1981), summarizing the effects of capitalism upon human subjectivity, concludes: "Analysts see the negative underside of these elements of capitalist culture in the stillness of their offices" (p. 56). The point is to understand how the suffering we come to know in this context—as opposed simply to the therapeutic encounter itself—serves as a nascent ground for resisting the deleterious effects of neoliberalization in general, and third-order suffering in particular.

I know of no adequate substitute for conducting this assessment than psychoanalysis. This set of theories and practices, now over a century old, is the study of human subjectivity *par excellence*. For much of its history, psychoanalysis has been an aid to social conformity or adaptation, using reified ideas of psychic structure and content believed to be applicable in all times and places. It would be a mistake, however, to identify psychoanalysis with its conservative forms. In 1980, summing up the contributions to *Critical Psychiatry*, Ingleby (1980b) observed:

> Today ... it seems less and less plausible to regard psychoanalysis purely as an instrument of conformity ... it is nowadays hard to see how any significant

understanding of the social meaning of 'mental illness' could be achieved while turning a blind eye to psychoanalysis. (p. 10)

More recently, Parker (2015b) concludes: "It seems that there is some radical potential within psychoanalysis, a potential that we should not reject out of hand just because certain applications of psychoanalysis have been politically conservative" (p. 26). The key to this radical potential, of course, is that individual subjectivity must be historicized and contextualized. Fromm (1962/2010), for instance, has gone so far as to say: "If we could take an X ray of any individual in any given society, you would find the social history of the last five-hundred years at least in that individual" (p. 98). This includes not just conscious processes—affects, imaginations, perceptions, ideas, and so on—but unconsciousness as well. This presents two challenges. The first, as Kovel (1981, pp. 61–85) has argued, is to distinguish transhistorical characteristics of human desire from their circumstantial appearances. The second, related issue, is to account for the idiosyncratic ways people resist or adapt to their historical context such that individuality is preserved.

This brings us to the focal questions for this section. What is basic to human desire, and how does neoliberalization co-opt such desire in its molding of the subject? What dynamics within this desire might remain to resist such shaping? Finally, in light of the double unconsciousness of third-order suffering, how might we side with this resistance to liberatory effect? In response to these questions, I will draw here primarily upon Lynne Layton's explication of normative unconscious processes, supplemented with Christopher Bollas's description of normotic illness.

Like other representatives of what has come to be called the relational school of psychoanalysis, Layton does not locate what is transhistorical about human desire in innate, organically rooted drives, such as hunger, sex, or aggression. Rather, desire is first and foremost for human contact—love, approval, and recognition. Subject formation revolves around two types of relational experience: "… one in which we are treated as objects by the significant figures in our lives and one in which we are treated as subjects" (2008, p. 65). Relational events in which we are acknowledged as subjects accumulate as the ground for ongoing mutuality and a relatively stable yet flexible identity. This does not culminate in a conflict-free existence, however. The existential universals of death, loss, grief, pain, and anxiety regarding separation, dependency, coping with difference, and limits to control remain—what Freud called "common unhappiness"

ayton, 2004, p. 38). This is what I have referred to as first-order suffer-
g. Experiences of being treated simply as objects, which Layton equates
th Jessica Benjamin's "doer-done to" enactments, amount to relational
uma. Examples include "... shaming, humiliation, gross relational
predictability, and empathic ruptures that are consistently met with
taliation and withdrawal rather than with attempts at repair" (2008,
64). The accumulation of such experiences results in a division within
bjectivity: "The other's consistent or intermittent abuse of our vulner-
ility, mild or major, the other's consistent or intermittent misrecogni-
n—these are the events that fragment the subject and divide the subject
gically against itself" (p. 65). Layton asserts that "anxiety about the
ss of love" leads the subject to repress historically contingent features
experience, producing unconscious conflicts. These split-off elements
e then re-enacted as repetition compulsions, the essence of "neurotic
isery" (2004, pp. 36–40, 47–48). Although neurotic misery in other
storical contexts might simply appear as what I am calling second-order
ffering, I will now show that the neuroses Layton describes as typifying
oliberal subjectivity are hybrids of second- and third-order suffering.

What distinguishes Layton's theory and practice from most of her psy-
oanalytic contemporaries is that she locates herself in the stream of radi-
l psychoanalysis that began with the Berlin Free Clinic in the 1920s and
en flowed through the heirs of the Frankfurt School, such as Fromm.
us she refuses to limit subject formation to a process occurring in fami-
s treated as if devoid of social context. If psychoanalysis subjects itself to
moral familism," she argues, then it colludes with the individualism and
ivatism of today's capitalism (2009, pp. 117–118). Central to her theory
the idea of "normative unconscious processes":

> I call "normative" that aspect of unconscious process that works to uphold
> dominant ideologies, and I assume that the motive for doing so, even at the
> cost of much psychic pain, is to secure the love of intimates and the approval
> of one's social world. (2006a, p. 107)

The function of normative unconscious processes is to maintain the splits
at accord with the dominant ideologies of one's social context. Major
rces include the power hierarchies oriented around class, race, gender,
d sexuality: "Thus, social processes such as gendering, racing, classing,
d sexing are at the very heart of subjectivity and subjective trauma, not
cidental add-ons (as they are conceived to be in most psychoanalytic

theories)" (2008, p. 67). These hierarchies, in other words, constitute ". the power structures that establish norms of recognition" (p. 66). Layto is critical of theorists such as Žižek, however, for suggesting that the powers are imposed in some unmediated fashion. The family, she argue is only one of the cultural institutions that "... mediate between desi and the rules of capital" (2004, p. 37). Others include schools, the vario media, and religion. This mediation is a significant source of individuali The family, for instance, communicates "culturally inflected projection to children, which vary in emphasis, style, and intensity depending up the particular family and its precise social placement (2004, p. 38). (Th leaves aside, for the moment, ways a family might also introduce cou ternormative elements.) Another source of individuality, however small may be compared to the powers of cultural hierarchies and institution is individual agency. In Layton's words, this has to do with "... the ve ways the psyche operates on what is given socially" (p. 43). This ability sturdier, she emphasizes, for individuals who have enjoyed a greater su ply of experiences in which they have been treated as subjects rather th objects. I prefer to call this ability *improvisation*. It is suggested by tl psychoanalytic term identification, which refers to the idiosyncratic wa we "internalize" our experiences of others and the world.

Nevertheless, Layton argues that subjects forming under a particul social paradigm will display shared characterological patterns. She is ther fore able to describe a "neoliberal subjectivity" (2009, 2010). If this su jectivity had to do only with misrecognitions rooted in race, gender, cla and sex, we could assume that a rather straightforward social injustice is work, simply producing contemporary variations on second-order suffe ing. However, Layton cogently argues that there are other forces at wo in the dominant ideology of today's capitalism, forces that drastically alt the distress circulating around these misrecognitions. One is what she ca "attacks on linking," or "the unconscious pull to dissociate individua from their social context" (2006a). Layton is directly discussing here tl second type of unconsciousness that exemplifies third-order suffering- the lack of awareness of the social origins of one's distress. This necessari highlights the presence of another aspect of this genre of misery—tl privatization of suffering. Layton concludes: "Dominant ideology wor very diligently on a number of fronts to hide the systemic nature inequalities of all kinds, to make sure that an individual's problems see just that—individual" (2006a, p. 108). She objects to liberal suspiciou ness of the value of belonging to social movements and collectives, an summarizes the effects of neoliberal subjectivity in a way that resonates with what I have called the erosion of soul: "All of these processes unlink individuals from each other, from themselves, and from their social and natural world" (p. 109). Layton is an exceptional analyst, so throughout her work she uses case material to carefully lay out symptoms associated with this unlinking: the denial of dependency and vulnerability, lack of empathy, disavowal of complicity in the suffering of others, irrational exuberance, and retaliation toward and/or withdrawal from those who are marginalized by neoliberal rationality, including the working class and the poor (2006b, 2007, 2009, 2010). Most of these symptoms betray their origin in the entanglement between second- and third-order suffering.

Before moving to what a clinical reply might look like, and the clues it may hold for responding to third-order suffering, I should note that Layton does not, as far as I know, address the other sort of unconsciousness I have mentioned—suffering that is not aware of itself as suffering. Even a cursory treatment of how to respond to neoliberal subjectivity must include this admittedly confounding problem. Whereas the concerns Layton discusses are rooted in various identifications, the distress at issue here relies on what psychoanalysts have generally considered a more "primitive" defense—incorporation. Identification involves complex, nuanced internalizations upon which the individual has improvised. Incorporation, on the other hand, refers to the inclusion of something into subjectivity without it being metabolized or improvised upon. The entity in question is, as it were, "swallowed whole." The consequence is a reduction or, in the worst cases, a near erasure of subjectivity. For this I turn to Bollas's articulation of what he calls normotic illness.

Bollas (1987/2011) describes normotic illness as "... a particular drive to be normal, one that is typified by the numbing and eventual erasure of subjectivity in favour of a self that is conceived as a material object among other man-made products in the object world" (p. 22). He concedes that such an erasure may run from only partial to almost complete. In limited instances, the person may be "... aware of feeling empty or without a sense of self ..." and might speak of "... a pain that may only be experienced as a void or an ache" (p. 22). In full-blown cases the individual "... is fundamentally disinterested in subjective life and he is inclined to reflect on the thingness of objects, on their material reality, or on 'data' that relates to material phenomena" (p. 23). Such a person fills her life with agendas and acquaintances with whom to do things. But if you asked her what personal meaning a particular activity or associate held for her, she would be genuinely puzzled by the question. Bollas offers the example of a man who emphasizes he is going to a play for which he possesses season tickets, but is incapable of discussing the import of the play itself. Likewise, the normotic personality forms relationships and may even fall in love, "... without this ever making a claim on his subjectivity" (p. 24). She may display a keen wit, enjoy a laugh, or seem fun-loving, but is incapable of deeper emotions such as sadness or grief (pp. 24–25). Normotic individuals do not emerge from families who abuse them in the conventional sense of that term. Rather, the family "deflects the self" of the child (pp. 33–35). The parents do not mirror the child's affective states, engage the child's imagination, or make personal comments to the child. Ritual activities replace intersubjective encounters: "... the parents direct the child's psychological life outward into physical activity or into some structured and ritualized container, such as a television set or video game" (p. 29). In Layton's terms, this is a particular variant of treating the child as an object rather than a subject.

Bollas (1987/2011) does not historicize normotic illness or place it in a particular social context. However, his description of this condition clearly resonates with the rationality and practices of advanced capitalism. The normotic individual, by Bollas's own portrayal, is quite content in the fact-based world of production:

> It is truly reassuring to become part of the machinery of production. He likes being part of an institution because it enables him to be identified with the life or the existence of the impersonal; the workings of an institution or the products of a corporation. He is part of the team, he is at home in a committee, he is secure in social groups that offer in pseudo-intimacy an alternative to getting to know someone. (p. 24)

Furthermore, the normotic person's sense of isolation is softened by the presence of the familiar objects she consumes. These objects define her world, to the extent that she may become stressed while traveling until she comes upon a well-known commodity: "... the simple discovery of a familiar object, such as a Coca-Cola, can be greeted with an affection and celebration that other people reserve only for human beings" (p. 36).

I cannot think of a purer exhibit of neoliberal subjectivity and third-order suffering than Bollas's normotic personality. Not only does Bollas (1987/2011) describe the poignant isolation of such a person while immersed in a world of objects; he also notes that this condition "...

results in the de-symbolization of ... mental content" (p. 23). This individual uses language in such a repetitive and stereotyped way that it is evacuated of meaning (p. 35). Thus she is left unable to narrate her experiences and life. Consequently, she does not experience herself as suffering. What right then, we might ask, do we have to insist she is suffering nonetheless? Bollas makes clear that normotic persons do not feel their pain. Instead, they *enact* it. They do things that are starkly incongruous with what otherwise appears to be a busy, contented life. Bollas refers to this as "normotic breakdown" (pp. 29–31). Symptoms include substance and process addictions, psychosomatic disorders, eating disorders, and suicide attempts. If confronted with such incongruity, however, the individual appears sincerely clueless. Bollas points to his encounter with Tom, a young man who had made two serious suicide attempts:

> After five minutes of chat, I said to him that obviously he must be in great pain or else he would not have attempted to kill himself. He handled this comment as if I had not meant what I said. He politely rebuffed me with an 'OK'. (p. 32)

I find Bollas's descriptions of normotic illness persuasive, because I have come upon this in my own practice with growing regularity. Usually such persons do not bring themselves into therapy. Rather, they end up sitting with me because their family members are disturbed by their enigmatic, self-destructive behaviors. Not long ago, for example, I sat with a man whose spouse demanded he get counseling after she discovered he was in an affair. Before me was a successful professional who was gregarious and reported satisfaction with his marriage and his life. He was also a committed Christian and church attender. When I invited him to be curious about the incongruity between his affair and his stated beliefs and values, he stared at me as if I had just spoken in a language he had never heard. For me it was a profound experience of the uncanny, as I seemed to be containing the distress he was not feeling himself. I propose that normotic symptoms appear quite regularly in the normative unconscious processes of individuals living in neoliberal cultures, and represent an increasingly common type of the repetition compulsions otherwise described by Layton.

If normative unconscious processes push us to conform to the dominant culture—in this case neoliberal rationality and practice—how is it that we resist? The secret, Layton argues, lies within the sort of neurotic misery that arises in this sociohistorical context. As I have articulated in the preceding paragraphs, this misery appears as neuroses that either are entangled in third-order suffering or, in the case of normotic illness, collapse completely into third-order suffering. In the former instance, unconsciousness as unlinking predominates. In the latter, we see the double unconsciousness I mentioned at the outset of this chapter. In either case "... subjectivity is marked by unceasing conflict between those unconscious processes that seek to maintain the splits *and those that refuse them*" (Layton, 2008, p. 67, emphasis added). And these conflicts, to repeat, manifest as repetition compulsions: "For what one finds in repetition compulsions is precisely unconscious conflict between the pressure to internalize the norm and a *resistance* to internalization. This is certainly what one sees clinically, *a constant dialectical push-pull*" (Layton, 2004a, p. 42, emphases added). Layton identifies this refusal as "counternormative unconscious processes" (2008, p. 67).

From where might such counternormative forces emerge? Layton does not dwell on this question, except to suggest it may have two aspects. First, she postulates an innate sort of autonomy "... that consciously and unconsciously resists being bent to the will of the other" (2004a, p. 42). I prefer to think of this, along the lines of the new materialism, as a characteristic of the sort of agency resident within psychological systems. It is the ontological refusal of a subject to being totally transformed into an object. It appears, so to speak, as the natural immune system of soul. To this is coupled, Layton proposes, a persisting longing: "... that part of the subject that seeks mutuality in attachments" (2004, p. 42). I also see this as a dimension of psychological agency that is a given, the life-force of soul. Agency within psychological systems thus displays both a refusal and a desire. And this desire is buttressed, according to Layton and other relational psychoanalysts, by past and present encounters in which we are treated as subjects.

It is critical for us to notice that, without these counternormative forces, no second- or third-order suffering could arise. Rather, we would have only a harmonious existence with hegemonic powers. Given powers that are as overwhelmingly oppressive as they are under neoliberalism, this would entail the total erasure of subjectivity. This highlights that such suffering necessarily constitutes a dialectical resistance to oppression, even when it is nebulous or inchoate. In instances where dominant powers are internalized, this agony may be both experienced and enacted. Where they are primarily incorporated, as occurs in normotic conditions, the suffering is physically or behaviorally enacted, but not subjectively experienced.

Recognizing the dialectical significance of this type of suffering brings us to a critical juncture toward the practice of caring for soul. If we follow Layton's analysis, in which neurotic misery (as opposed to "common unhappiness") consists of a clash between normative and counternormative unconscious processes, then *practitioners of care do not have the luxury of refusing to take sides in psychological conflict.* Layton, like many other relational psychoanalysts, implicitly rejects the classical psychoanalytic insistence on "therapeutic neutrality," which demands that the analyst maintain an "evenly hovering attention" that involves observing and interpreting psychological conflicts without weighing in on them. Because normative unconscious processes are rooted in whatever is culturally dominant, adopting a neutral stance means these forces will retain their supremacy for the individual subject. In this case the therapy relationship itself re-enacts repetition compulsions, which includes a consent to powers of cultural hierarchy:

> Often enough, enactments in treatment involve an unconscious collusion in which patient and analyst, as members of the same culture subject to the same ideologically mandated splits, together shore up the very social norms that have brought about pain in the first place. (Layton, 2004, p. 46)

Such collusions, as noted before, will necessarily include the ways these splits are raced, gendered, sexed, and classed, as well as how neoliberalism mystifies their entanglements. It is the therapist's responsibility to be watchful for these enactments and to invite the patient to join her in vigilantly looking for how they may reproduce oppressive social norms within their relationship. Put another way, therapists must be committed to catching the ways they are implicated in their patients' suffering Layton, 2009). The upshot of all this is that psychotherapy is inherently political, whether the therapist is aware of this or not. And, under the conditions of neoliberal culture, caring relationships will give preferential treatment to counternormative psychological processes.

Importantly, this means that psychotherapy and other forms of self-care are not inevitably self-indulgent or individualistic. Layton (2013) contends that neoliberal culture traumatizes individuals, whose defenses against this trauma typically yield narcissistic disorders of either a grandiose or self-deprecating sort. Unfortunately, if psychotherapy fails to connect suffering with its social context, it modifies but does not relieve these narcissistic conditions:

> Indeed, a psychoanalysis that separates the psychic from the social is likely to collude with individualist trends and to produce healthier versions of narcissism, thereby failing to produce subjects who can see themselves in others outside the intimate circle of family and friends. (Layton, 2008, p. 69)

On the other hand, any psychotherapy that restores the linkage between distress and the cultural conditions of neoliberalism re-establishes interdependency, increases awareness of complicity with the suffering of others, and lays the ground for solidarity. In my judgment this aligns Layton with Sara Ahmed, a cultural critic in the United Kingdom. In recent blog post, Ahmed (2014), while herself critical of neoliberalism observes that some critics of neoliberalism representing the "white male left" have portrayed feminists as participating in an identity politics that is self-promotional and individualistic. Ostensibly, then, feminists are themselves co-opted by neoliberalism. Ahmed replies: "Neoliberalism sweeps up too much when all forms of self-care become symptoms of neoliberalism." She continues:

> Those who do not have to struggle for their own survival can very easily and rather quickly dismiss those who have to struggle for survival as "indulging themselves." As feminism teaches us: talking about personal feelings is not necessarily about deflecting attention from structures. If anything, I would argue the opposite: not addressing certain histories that hurt, histories that get to the bone, how we are affected by what we come up against, is one way of deflecting attention from structures .... Not the only way, but one way. (para. 25)

Self-care that is about survival, Ahmed contends, "... is not about one's own happiness. It is about finding ways to exist in a world that diminishing" (para. 23). The link between this struggle for survival and oppressive social structures "... is why in queer, feminist and anti-racist work self-care is about the creation of community, fragile communities assembled out of the experiences of being shattered" (para. 39). Ahmed sums all this up in a citation of Audre Lorde: "Caring for myself is not self-indulgence, it is self-preservation, and that is an act of political warfare" (para. 1). Might psychotherapy of the type Layton proposes, or that links individual suffering with social power structures, also constitute an act of political warfare? The people who arrive at my office today, though they may suffer narcissistic disturbances, do not seem fundamentally to be self-indulgent individuals. Rather, they come to me as nomads, wandering across a vast neoliberal desert in search of an oasis where they may experience a few minutes of communion with another human being who recognizes them as subjects in a world of objects.

Caring for souls in a neoliberal age, then, requires practices that reconnect the sufferings of individuals with the larger social, cultural, and political context. This does not mean, in psychotherapy, that we no longer address the precise ways that family dynamics, discrete instances of trauma, or relationship patterns alter psychological systems. Layton's case studies are filled with situations where she does exactly that. However, she also sees such events as existing in and shaped by a larger social reality, and she freely comments on the linkages between her patients' pain and specific features of the social context whenever this seems indicated. For example, Layton (2010) writes of her work with Sally, a professional woman in her forties who decided to work part time to care for her children. Sally feels marginalized by this decision. Whenever her husband's business seems threatened, "Sally spirals downward into a familiar despair about the possibility of ever getting what she wants: a bigger house" (p. 313). Working in the details of Sally's personal history, she and Sally come to regard this desire "… as a fetish object, a stand-in for a traumatic failure of social and individual caretaking" (p. 313). Despite their repeated joint efforts to explore the nuances of this meaning, Sally only becomes more desperate and depressed. Layton confesses: "Sitting with Sally's despair is quite difficult. Like so many of my patients, she can be brutal toward herself with scathing self-recriminations" (p. 314). As I noted at the beginning of this book, this has become a familiar scene in my own work. But, as with myself in similar circumstances, Layton continues listening to Sally as:

> … she measures herself against those of her friends who have the big house and wonders what the hell is wrong with her, why is she so weak and stupid. A good subject of bourgeois ideology in its neoliberal incarnation, no context, no history enters into Sally's thinking. Indeed, when she is in despair and railing against herself, there is little evidence of thinking. (p. 314)

Sally is clearly stuck, so Layton decides on a different approach: "And that tack was to supply the missing context, which, unanalytic as it may seem at first glance, I have come to regard as an important part of holding, containment and metabolization" (p. 314). Layton points out that Sally's inability to work full time while caring for her children is not a weakness. She tells Sally that one aspect of second-wave feminism "was a compromise with neoliberalism and patriarchy" that had "... merely placed middle-class women into the same psychic condition that had prevailed for men, one which demands a repudiation of capacities for nurture, emotionality and dependence and fosters an omnipotent kind of autonomy: the dominant version of neoliberal subjectivity ..." (p. 314). She informs Sally about the "care drain" that often occurs as women from developing countries are drawn away from their own families to care for the children of middle-class families in the United States whose work commitments leave them unable to provide such care themselves. This, she observes, is what allows many of her associates to have "the big house." This leads Sally to recall the number of times her friends have expressed regret at not having enough time with their kids. As it turns out, supplying this context allows Sally finally to begin mourning the care she had not received as a child. In addition, it "... gives Sally's unbearable despair new meaning, psychosocial meaning." Layton concludes that supplying the social context "... seemed to enable her to begin to internalize my voice as a soothing presence in a way she had not been able to do before" (p. 316). I must add here, and I believe Layton would agree, that the patriarchy embedded in neoliberal culture results in far more women than men staying home to care for children or aging parents. Nonetheless, the burdens now placed on middle-class families with dependents during an era of stagnant or falling wages lead us to recognize the difficult decisions faced by families dealing with the particularities of their own circumstances.

Given my own training in a rather classical psychodynamic attitude, I resonate with Layton's residual anxiety that some will regard her methods as "unanalytic." In its classical versions, providing the social or political context would be considered an "intrusion" into the therapy or, worse, an "enactment" of the therapist's countertransference. In contemporary relational psychoanalysis, however, everything that happens between the therapist and patient—indeed, in all human encounters—is understood as enactments (Wachtel, 2008, pp. 220–244). The emphasis here shifts from the cognitive knowledge yielded by the therapist's interpretations to the procedural knowledge that emerges from mutually experiencing and observing what is intersubjectively created within the therapeutic relationship (Natterson & Friedman, 1995). In this view, even therapist self-disclosures may move the process forward, as long as they are intended for the benefit of the patient and do no harm. Clearly, we are a long way here from the classical psychoanalytic insistence on "therapeutic neutrality." Layton (2010) suggests that relational psychoanalysis should be historicized. This school emerged in the United States during the 1990s, she observes, most likely to counter the neoliberal devaluing of dependency, love, and attachment (p. 318). At any rate, relational psychoanalysis has created an opening for recognizing the social and political context of both the therapeutic relationship and individual suffering. This leads to a revaluation of the classical injunction to always "follow the patient's lead." Responding to renowned analyst Jessica Benjamin's comments during a roundtable discussion, Muriel Dimen (2006) concludes:

> When, as Jessica pointed out, we follow the patient's lead, we are not likely to be led to politics. But even if a patient doesn't consciously want to talk about dependency or sexual desire, aggression or mourning, we are always listening for those leads to take us to these very important matters, aren't we? Might we do the same for civil life? (pp. 199–200)

This represents nothing less than a revolution in psychoanalysis. Suddenly everything explored in the clinical encounter, at least potentially, holds sociopolitical significance. As Layton (2006a) demonstrates, this is even true of dreams, once considered the most private and idiosyncratic of phenomena. Once we understand the parameters of neoliberal subjectivity, it is not that difficult to notice the social elements within many dreams, and even to entertain the probability that some dreams will provide commentary on the cultural surround.

So far Layton has helped us imagine how we might address one of the types of unconsciousness of third-order suffering—the lack of awareness of the link between individual suffering and social context. What about the other type, suffering that is unaware of itself as suffering, the distress evident in normotic conditions? Here we are, admittedly, on a more challenging terrain. How do we care for souls unaware of their pain? The more obvious path, considering that this suffering is enacted but not felt, is simply to point to the enactments and express our own curiosity about the behavior that is obviously so contrary to the person's life or well-being. I once worked with a successful businessman who denied feeling depressed or particularly distressed. In neoliberal terms he was a "winner," and he was quite disparaging toward addicts, depressives, and other "whiners." This man was referred by his physician because he was compulsively exercising several hours per day, to such a degree that he recurrently suffered stress-related injuries. He ultimately incurred an injury that sidelined his exercise regimen for several months. His only motive for following up on the referral, he said, was his inability to exercise, which had made him feel "down." I maintained a steady attitude of curiousness toward his behavior and, after developing a secure relationship based largely on intrigue and exchanges of wit, I suggested to him one day, in a jovial manner, that I did not see much difference between his self-injurious behavior and that of drug addicts. This somehow inspired his own curiosity, enough to keep him in relationship with me for some time after his injury had healed. Eventually his affect began to surface, followed by a personal narrative that included childhood trauma. Interestingly, this man ultimately brought politics into our conversations and began to question his hardened attitude toward "losers" and people who "lived off the government." He even tolerated my care for him after I confessed to being a "bleeding-heart liberal," and he built upon this tolerance to entertain the thought of befriending people who were not quite like himself.

However, I would consider this man to be an example of what Bollas would see as a "partial" case of normotic illness. Other cases, such as Tom, whom Bollas interviewed, seem incapable of curiosity about their enactments. Bollas (1987/2011) finally responds to Tom by talking about his own experience of adolescence. He muses: "When I started to talk about myself, he seemed more interested, but also more anxious and uncertain, as no doubt he was unaccustomed to hearing an adult talk to him about the ordinary fears and uncertainties of adolescence" (p. 33). Like Bollas, the only success I have had with such individuals, and that has been quite limited, is to disclose my own subjectivity. I might, for example, talk about an instance in my own life similar to one shared by the patient, noting what I experienced in that event. Lacking an analogous experience, I might suggest what I imagine I would feel if I were in the circumstance she just described. I sometimes report directly on what I am feeling, or what associations come to me through my own reverie, as the patient is speaking. Sometimes such self-disclosure appears to evoke some resonance from the patient, if only limited or for a fleeting moment. At other times, in desperation, I might simply guess out loud what the patient would be feeling if he were to have a feeling about whatever he is discussing. One does the best one can in the hopes of gaining something. Third-order suffering, in its purest forms, is a daunting and uncanny (non-)presence.

Dreams of the Depleted Soul

iile fully developed normotic conditions are not rare in my practice,
omplete versions, almost invariably coupled with combined personal
d cultural trauma, have become more the rule than the exception. Most
my work these days, in other words, requires me to immerse myself
the complex entanglements between second- and third-order suffer-
, that manifest in the particularities of individual lives. I have been
pressed with how often patients report dreams that ingeniously portray
se entanglements, dreams that also suggest an incipient resistance to
th the personal (familial and/or interpersonal) and cultural trauma they
ve experienced. Moreover, patterns of neoliberal subjectivity frequently
erge in these dreams with astounding clarity. Mutual work toward elu-
lating both the personal and cultural contexts of these dreams usually
lps the patient move forward by strengthening the counternormative
ments of their suffering. I will now present two such dreams, noting
w work around the dreams buttressed the patients' capacity for agency
d resistance. In the first instance I will provide clinical details of the
e. Circumstances surrounding the second case preclude offering spe-
ics about the individual's life or the therapeutic work, yet the dream
ne still allows some understanding of how the social surround appears
something as supposedly private and idiosyncratic as a dream.

The first dream appeared late in the work with Joan, a European-
nerican female in her mid-fifties, who engaged me weekly for pasto-
psychotherapy for a period of five years.[2] Joan initially presented with
nic attacks, which in due course she recalled usually occurred after driv-
g past a street that led to a location where she had been date-raped while
her mid-teens. She had never told anyone of the rape, and had since for-
tten the location where it had occurred. Upon making this connection,
wever, the panic attacks subsided. What then remained was a vague
lessness and emptiness that eluded description or interpretation. Joan
on began to describe a tragic history that seemed to explain why she had
ver told anyone of the rape. From about the age of nine until around
berty she had been treated for recurrent vaginal infections, which, as
e became aware, were related to having suffered repeated sexual abuse
om a close male relative. She had also never revealed this history of
use. In addition, she described a childhood spent playing in her room
ne. Both parents were markedly emotionally detached. The family lived
an affluent neighborhood and seemed to care only about maintain-
g an active social life and appearing happy and well-adjusted to other

members of the community. Joan had been well-schooled on how to ¿ speak, and dress to fit into this environment. As an adult she discontinu her own professional life after marrying a man who was moving up in corporate world. They had several children and settled in the same nei borhood in which she had grown up. Though chronically anxiety-ridd Joan reported finding satisfaction in being a mother and indicated t her husband was a good man with whom she had a reasonably accepta marriage. She carefully maintained a well-groomed appearance and che ful demeanor, as well as a busy social life, but admitted that she felt bor empty, and superficial. The two people with whom she felt most cc nected were one of her children, a very depressed young man who by late teens had already attempted suicide twice, and a former fiancé fr her college days with whom she had re-established a long-distance, nc sexual, but emotionally intense relationship. Joan found her feelings this man, an intelligent and reflective individual who was also a depres: alcoholic, quite puzzling. But she agreed her intense identification w these two people revealed her own chronic loneliness and a depressi that was well-concealed, including usually from herself. Eventually I spouse was transferred to a lucrative corporate position in another sta and this terminated the therapy. Several weeks prior to termination : shared a dream:

> In the dream I am in my home and there is a spinning something—like a tornado—*inside* my house. I am watching as it sucks everything into it—all my furniture and belongings—and I see it all spinning around in the twisting column. Then I notice my husband is also in the thing, turning round and round with everything else. And he says to me as he spins around: "Honey, I increased the business 75 % last year." Then the dream ends.

When I inquired as to what feelings she was having within the drea Joan paused, nonplussed, and finally said: "*Nothing. I felt nothing.*"

As is the case with dreams this one held several useful insights, and discussed as many as we could in the final weeks of the therapy. It seem to comment, for example, on her history of trauma—most of which h occurred within her home. It also appeared to be triggered by the imper ing move to an opulent home they were in the process of building, as w as in some way anticipating the termination of therapy. It rather ing niously portrayed both her family life in her childhood and her prese household life. Ostensibly everything looked great on the outside, b inside a storm was raging and chaos reigned. And as often seems the case with dreams, the dream-house in some way revealed the state of Joan's very self, her soul. On the outside all appears well, but inside she is being evacuated. Even her affect, metaphorically speaking, is sucked into the vortex. Despite the horrifying circumstances, in the end she can feel nothing.

The crucial import for our focus here, however, lies in the way this dream displays Joan's *sociopolitical* location. More to the point, it displays how self, personal relationships, and society are seamlessly and inevitably interwoven. In Fromm's words the dream illustrates the *social character* of these neoliberal times (1976/1997, pp. 109). Fromm also argued that what is unconscious is not simply personal but social, and therefore, even the dreams of individuals are penetrated by the society in which they live. Joan's dream reveals self, relationships, and society in the same vein. They are all *consumed*, stripped of any meaning beyond production and consumption, and deprived of affect. Indeed, some aspects of the dream seem to require a social construal. The consumerism implied in the dream is fairly evident. But most striking is the words spoken by the husband: "Honey, I increased the business 75 % last year." He does not say, "Honey, I love you," or "What are we going to do about this mess?" or even "Please help me!" This is not the language of dialogue or intimate personal relationships, but of *the market*. He essentially gives her a business report. The husband's importance is limited to his role as a *producer*, and this is implicitly accepted by the dreamer as well. (This interpretation was later confirmed by the response of Joan's husband when she told him about the dream: "Oh, I did much better than that!") All this is rendered more striking, within the dream, by the obliviousness of both the husband and the dreamer to the devastation in which they are literally enveloped. It seems unremarkable to them. In effect the world as they know it is ending, but they feel fine.

Finally, the social dimensions of the dream may legitimately be regarded as an unconscious commentary on the neoliberal society that is entangled in the dreamer's existence. From this standpoint the house in the dream signifies the greater "household" of contemporary life in the United States. (It is suggestive here to recall that the ancient Greek word for house, *oikos*, is also the root for the English word "economy.") The dream in this sense refers to a neoliberal culture in which relationships are reduced to the economy of the market, with their utility subject to cost-benefit analysis. It comments, moreover, on a society in which the most devastating effects for personal relationships are considered normal, and in which meaning outside the discourse of the market has been evacuated. The dream suggests a society devoid of deeper emotions, in keeping with Meštrović's provocative thesis concerning postemotional society (1997). Again, the house looks great and even opulent on the outside, but on the inside is hollow. Furthermore, the dream alludes to the gender hierarchy to which Joan has been subjected her entire life, sometimes violently so. She is reduced to the role of a helpless observer. Her husband, by contrast, exists contentedly within the source of power, though it proves to be a dominating force that consumes everything, including himself.

This dream, then, represents the normotic character of Joan's personality, her personal relationships, and her society as well. The emptiness it portrays points to the depression hidden within, a depression that has lost its mood and its self-awareness as well as its voice. It raises the appalling prospect that there are many depressed individuals today who would escape even the enormously expanded definitions of depression that currently hold sway. In effect, these people would be depressed if they were more aware, if they experienced feelings beyond those required by superficial living within contemporary social networks.

At the same time, the dream, by oddly juxtaposing a horrible threat and an absence of feeling, indicates a path forward. Rieger (2009) observes: "Resistance depends on the creation of alternative desires," but "… desires cannot easily be controlled and redirected at the conscious level" (p. 115), indicating that they are not subject to cognitive-behavioral interventions. However, he cites McFague's notion of "wild spaces" that do not conform to what a society accepts as "natural," such as occurs "when confronting clinical depression" (p. 115), as places where resistant desires may emerge or be revealed. Indeed, by simply noting the peculiar lack of feeling in the dream, Joan was able to recognize both who she had become and a desire to be otherwise. She experienced the dream as a portrayal of her empty depression and began to understand her depression as a desire for something different, a resistance to her abnormally normal life. The dream pointed to a desire within her that opposed the "natural" desire, also within her, shaped by living in a society that valued only production and consumption. Moreover, conversation about the social context arose organically as we discussed the dream. In Joan's words this helped her feel "less crazy" and made the formerly enigmatic features of her suffering seem "more meaningful," even though it raised troubling questions about her conformity to a society that had gone quite insane. Finally, the dream aided a process in which Joan moved from a nameless boredom to awareness of depression to an inauguration of giving voice to her depression—a process that appears to have continued beyond the termination of therapy.

The second dream appeared in the initial stages of my work with Robert, a male in his early adolescence.[3] Robert also presented with panic attacks and depression, as well as recurrent suicidal thoughts. I have suggested elsewhere in this book that individuals born after the neoliberal transformation tend to be more susceptible to its characteristic maladies, including third-order suffering. Robert's dream represents an instructive and poignant symptom of such vulnerability:

> I am walking toward my school, and I see several people huddled around a car in the parking lot. They are like giants, maybe nine feet tall. As I get closer I can see that they are rolling joints on the hood of the car. I walk past them and enter the building. Inside there are no students, only teachers wandering the halls. I head toward my English classroom. Teachers walk past me whispering to each other. I see they are holding wooden replicas of hand guns, and I realize they are discussing how they will kill themselves. I get to my classroom and sit down. I am the only person in the room. As I begin doing my assignment my English teacher walks in. Without saying a word, she puts the barrel of a real pistol into her mouth and pulls the trigger.

The very tall people, Robert said, reminded him of how small he feels in the world. Although he is rather tall himself, he experiences everyone else as somehow much bigger. Another association to this was to the actual "big people" in the world—adults. That these people were rolling joints, though he noted he has no particular opposition to marijuana use, made him think about how "big people" can be irresponsible and "messed up." When I asked whether this could also suggest something about the adult world, he nodded and observed: "Yeah, that makes sense. I think the whole world is really messed up." Noting the absence of other students in the dream, Robert flatly stated that is just how he feels—alone and isolated. He remarked: "It's weird. I have some friends and we do things, but it feels like there is some sort of membrane between me and other people. I can see them and hear them, but yet I'm not really connected to them." "What about the school?" I inquired. Robert replied that school is where his panic attacks are worse and more frequent. It is also the place where he is around the most people and, ironically, where he feels the loneliest and most detached. I observed, in the dream, there are only adults at the school, and wondered if that means it is part of the adult world. He remarked: "Yes. Well, it is a public institution. And it's where you go to learn to fit into the adult world." Discussing the teachers walking the halls in the dream, Robert described them as if they had a spectral quality—real, but at the same time ethereal. Their murmuring presence was tantamount to non-presence. Noting the terrible ending of the dream, I asked whether his English teacher seemed distressed. "No," he responded. "She just calmly walked in and did it." I probed to determine if the dream suicide was graphic. "Oh yes," Robert noted, "It was very realistic." As is my custom, I queried concerning affects within the dream. He confirmed that the dream contained no feelings at any point, but that he did awaken from the dream in a panic attack.

This dream may be shocking, but unfortunately is not that remarkable. I have heard similar dream reports from others, especially from young people. Our mutual collaboration on the dream, scattered over several sessions, led Robert and me to several insights. Robert's perceived smallness, compared to the "big people" in the dream and in the world, reflects, among other things, his diminished sense of self. The ghostly quality of the dream, together with a complete absence of emotion, depicts not only the emptiness he experiences daily, but also the hollowness of the social world he inhabits. Perhaps the most striking feature of the dream, and Robert's life, is the pervasive loneliness and detachment. The dream is virtually a cinematic depiction of normotic existence, a video clip of third-order suffering. And yet there is a sign of protest—Robert awakens from this horror flick in a panic attack. By working this dream and the manner of his awakening from it, Robert and I began to understand his panic attacks as symptoms of an irresolvable conflict between the pull to comply with the zombie existence around him, and his fervent but inchoate resistance to this pull. Panic looks and feels like emotion, but lacks the discernable texture or meaning of deep emotion. It is a stand-in for emotions one does not experience, a one-size-fits-all response to tragedy. I cannot say that this dream or its working-through brought Robert immediate relief from his panic attacks and ensuing depression, but it did give him some hope that his experience might hold some meaning, and enough courage to continue his work.

The Fragility of Psychotherapy

have raised the question earlier in this chapter, reflecting on Sara Ahmed's
(014) position on "self-care as warfare," whether psychotherapy may,
der some circumstances, constitute a form of "political warfare." This
ay be particularly applicable when the patient is trying simply to survive
the face of power hierarchies that marginalize and oppress them accord-
g to certain sexual, gender, racial, ethnic, class, ability, or age designa-
ons. This relates to Joan in the preceding section. It also pertains to
obert. As Henry Giroux (2008) has argued, the young are among those
ho have been demonized and placed under surveillance in neoliberal cul-
res (pp. 84–111). What I must now assert is that, if psychotherapy can
 a form of self-care that amounts to political warfare, it is nevertheless a
agile, transient, and limited form of political struggle. Broad-based and
urable campaigns to contain or repeal neoliberal rationality and prac-
ce cannot be mounted from the beachhead of psychotherapy and other
pes of individual care of souls. As this book makes clear, this is the case
rimarily because the power of the cultural and social surround is immea-
urably greater than that of isolated individuals and their caregivers. An
dditional reason is that, with reduced collective funding for counseling
rvices, at least in the United States, psychotherapy has become increas-
gly complicit with and dependent upon the neoliberal status quo. It
 more entrepreneurial than ever, and more reliant upon patients who
e able to pay for such services themselves. Very few therapists, myself
cluded, are immune to these pressures. Given the still-expanding degree
f economic inequality, I suspect this will mean that progressively more
ounselors will, in effect, be chasing a diminishing pool of people who can
ford their fees. Working for fees scaled to income level will likely do little
 ameliorate this situation. The probable outcome will be that psycho-
erapy becomes an increasingly class-based service, able to attract mostly
rofessionals and financial elites. I fear this is already the case.

Nevertheless, as I have attempted to show in this chapter, the focused
tention to suffering individuals afforded by the clinical context can
form a caring for souls that exceeds such limited boundaries. This con-
xt reveals that more encompassing acts of care must be able to address
e double unconsciousness of third-order suffering, as well as attend to
e growing isolation, narrative incapacitation, and fragmented subjectiv-
y that this suffering entails. While such an effort may seem ambitious
 the point of audaciousness, clinical practice also discloses impulses of

resistance within even the most unconscious, sequestered, and shatter individuals. This offers encouragement for a far-reaching care of souls th can only occur in collectives and social movements, which can hope discern and amplify a resonance within the hearts of distressed individua In the final movement of this book, I will turn now to these larger effoi to care for souls in a neoliberal age, summarizing features of the ca required during these times.

NOTES

1. The comparable organization in the United States is the Americ Psychological Association. A report published by the Briti Psychological Society (BPS) in 2014, titled *Understanding Psycho and Schizophrenia*, while acknowledging possible biological facto insisted that psychotic disorders were also shaped by material conc tions, such as economic inequality, and that these disorders held mea ing for the sufferer. Such a position stands in sharp contrast to t dominant opinion in the United States, which regards these types distress as the epitome of biologically determined mental illness. T BPS report may be downloaded free of charge at http://www.bps.oi uk/system/files/Public%20files/aa%20Standard%20Docs/unde standing_psychosis.pdf
2. This case first appeared in Rogers-Vaughn, B. (2014). Blessed are tho who mourn: Depression as political resistance. *Pastoral Psychology*, (4), 503–522. It is reprinted here with the permission of Springer, tl original publisher. Joan—a pseudonym—has given full consent to u this material. Although I have withheld some information to preser her anonymity, all the information presented here is accurate to tl best of my knowledge.
3. This is also a pseudonym. Robert and his legal guardian have given fi consent to use the dream here, as well as his associations to the drea that are relevant to understanding its cultural dimensions.

REFERENCES

Ahmed, S. (2014, August 25). Selfcare as warfare [Web log post]. Retrieved May 2016, from https://feministkilljoys.com/2014/08/25/selfcare-as-warfare/
Altman, N. (2015). *Psychoanalysis in an age of accelerating cultural chan; Spiritual globalization*. London: Routledge.

Bennett, J. (2010). *Vibrant matter: A political ecology of things.* Durham, NC: Duke University Press.

Bollas, C. (1987/2011). Normotic illness. In C. Bollas & A. Jemstedt (Eds.), *The Christopher Bollas Reader* (pp. 22–36). London: Routledge.

Carrette, J. (2007). *Religion and critical psychology: Religious experience in the knowledge economy.* London: Routledge.

Cazdyn, E. (2012). *The already dead: The new time of politics, culture, and illness.* Durham, NC: Duke University Press.

Connolly, W. E. (2010). Materialities of experience. In D. Coole & S. Frost (Eds.), *New materialisms: Ontology, agency, and politics* (pp. 178–200). Durham, NC: Duke University Press.

Connolly, W. E. (2013). *The fragility of things: Self-organizing processes, neoliberal fantasies, and democratic activism.* Durham, NC: Duke University Press.

Davies, W. (2015). *The happiness industry: How the government and big business sold us well-being.* London: Verso.

Dimen, M. (2006). Response to roundtable: Something's gone missing. In L. Layton, N. C. Hollander, & S. Gutwill (Eds.), *Psychoanalysis, class and politics: Encounters in the clinical setting* (pp. 195–201). London: Routledge.

Fanon, F. (1952/1967). *Black skin white masks: The experiences of a black man in a white world* (Charles L. Markmann, Trans.). New York, NY: Grove Press.

Fanon, F. (1963/2004). *The wretched of the earth* (Richard Philcox, Trans.). New York, NY: Grove Press.

Fenichel, O. (1945). *The psychoanalytic theory of neurosis.* New York, NY: W. W. Norton & Company.

Fromm, E. (1962/2010). The concept of mental health. In Rainer Funk (Ed.), *The pathology of normalcy* (pp. 81-99). Riverdale, NY: American Mental Health Foundation.

Fromm, E. (1976/1997). *To have or to be?* New York, NY: Continuum.

Giroux, H. A. (2008). *Against the terror of neoliberalism: Politics beyond the age of greed.* Boulder, CO: Paradigm Publishers.

Gold, J. (2002). The failed social legacy of interpersonal psychoanalysis. *Race, Gender & Class, 9*(4), 147–157.

Greenberg, G. (2010, September). The war on unhappiness. *Harper's Magazine,* 27–35.

Ingleby, D. (Ed.). (1980a). *Critical psychiatry: The politics of mental health.* New York, NY: Pantheon Books.

Ingleby, D. (1980b). Introduction. In D. Ingleby (Ed.), *Critical psychiatry: The politics of mental health* (pp. 7–19). New York, NY: Pantheon Books.

The Invisible Committee. (2009). *The coming insurrection.* Los Angeles, CA: Semiotext(e).

Jacoby, R. (1983). *The repression of psychoanalysis: Otto Fenichel and the political Freudians.* Chicago, IL: University of Chicago Press.

Keller, C. (2003). *Face of the deep: A theology of becoming.* London: Routledge.

Keller, C. (2015). *Cloud of the impossible: Negative theology and planetary entanglement.* New York, NY: Columbia University Press.

Kierkegaard, S. (1849/1980). *The sickness unto death: A Christian psychological exposition for upbuilding and awakening* (Howard V. Hong & Edna H. Hong, Eds. and Trans.). Princeton, NJ: Princeton University Press.

Kovel, J. (1981). *The age of desire: Reflections of a radical psychoanalyst.* New York, NY: Pantheon Books.

Lasch, C. (1991). *The true and only heaven: Progress and its critics.* New York, NY: W. W. Norton & Company.

Layton, L. (2004). A fork in the royal road: On "defining" the unconscious and its stakes for social theory. *Psychoanalysis, Culture & Society, 9,* 33–51.

Layton, L. (2006a). Attacks on linking: The unconscious pull to dissociate individuals from their social context. In L. Layton, N. C. Hollander, & S. Gutwill (Eds.), *Psychoanalysis, class and politics: Encounters in the clinical setting* (pp. 107–117). London: Routledge.

Layton, L. (2006b). Retaliatory discourse: The politics of attack and withdrawal. *International Journal of Applied Psychoanalytic Studies, 3*(2), 143–155.

Layton, L. (2007). What psychoanalysis, culture and society mean to me. *Mens Sana Monographs, 5*(1), 146–157. Retrieved May 17, 2016, from http://www. msmonographs.org/article.asp?issn=0973-1229;year=2007;volume=5;issue=1 ;spage=146;epage=157;aulast=Layton

Layton, L. (2008). What divides the subject? Psychoanalytic reflections on subjectivity, subjection and resistance. *Subjectivity, 22*(1), 60–72.

Layton, L. (2009). Who's responsible? Our mutual implication in each other's suffering. *Psychoanalytic Dialogues, 19*(2), 105–120.

Layton, L. (2010). Irrational exuberance: Neoliberal subjectivity and the perversion of truth. *Subjectivity, 3*(3), 303–322.

Layton, L. (2013). Psychoanalysis and politics: Historicising subjectivity. *Mens Sana Monographs, 11*(1), 68-81. Retrieved May 18, 2016, from http://www. ncbi.nlm.nih.gov/pmc/articles/PMC3653236/

Layton, L., Hollander, N. C., & Gutwill, S. (2006). Introduction. In L. Layton, N. C. Hollander, & S. Gutwill (Eds.), *Psychoanalysis, class and politics: Encounters in the clinical setting* (pp. 1–10). London: Routledge.

Loewenthal, D. (Ed.). (2015). *Critical psychotherapy, psychoanalysis and counseling: Implications for practice.* New York, NY: Palgrave Macmillan.

Malabou, C. (2012). *Ontology of the accident: An essay on destructive plasticity* (Carolyn Shread, Trans.). Cambridge: Polity Press.

Marcel, G. (1951/1978). *Homo viator: Introduction to a metaphysic of hope* (Emma Craufurd, Trans.). Gloucester, MA: Peter Smith.

Martín-Baró, I. (1994). In A. Aron & S. Corne (Eds.), *Writings for a liberation psychology.* Cambridge, MA: Harvard University Press.

Meštrović, S. G. (1997). *Postemotional society*. London: SAGE Publications.

Moloney, P. (2013). *The therapy industry: The irresistible rise of the talking cure, and why it doesn't work*. London: Pluto Press.

Natterson, J. M., & Friedman, R. J. (1995). *A primer of clinical intersubjectivity*. Northvale, NJ: Jason Aronson.

Parker, I. (2007). *Revolution in psychology: Alienation to emancipation*. London: Pluto Press.

Parker, I. (2015a). *Psychology after the crisis: Scientific paradigms and political debate*. London: Routledge.

Parker, I. (2015b). *Psychology after psychoanalysis: Psychosocial studies and beyond*. London: Routledge.

Rieger, J. (2009). *No rising tide: Theology, economics, and the future*. Minneapolis, MN: Fortress Press.

Rieger, J. (2016). Rethinking the new materialism for religion and theology: Why movements matter most. In J. Rieger & E. Waggoner (Eds.), *Religious experience and new materialism: Movement matters* (pp. 135–156). New York, NY: Palgrave Macmillan.

Rogers-Vaughn, B. (2014). Blessed are those who mourn: Depression as political resistance. *Pastoral Psychology, 63*(4), 503–522.

Samuels, A. (1993). *The political psyche*. London: Routledge.

Samuels, A. (2001). *Politics on the couch: Citizenship and the internal life*. New York, NY: Karnac Books.

Smail, D. (1997). *Illusion & reality: The meaning of anxiety*. London: Constable.

Smail, D. (2001). *The nature of unhappiness*. London: Robinson.

Smail, D. (2005). *Power, interest and psychology: Elements of a social materialist understanding of distress*. Ross-on-Wye: PCCS Books.

Wachtel, P. L. (1983). *The poverty of affluence: A psychological portrait of the American way of life*. New York, NY: The Free Press.

Wachtel, P. L. (2008). *Relational theory and the practice of psychotherapy*. New York, NY: Guilford Press.

Watkins, M., & Shulman, H. (2008). *Toward psychologies of liberation*. New York, NY: Palgrave Macmillan.

CHAPTER 7

Concluding Theological Postscripts

nay be misleading you by referring to the following reflections as post-
ripts. Often this term designates musings that amount to mere after-
oughts. In some letters, however, the postscript reveals the author's
ost candid or personal thoughts or feelings, or perhaps anticipates some
cisive future occurrence or follow-up activity. The latter is the better
scription for what I have to say in concluding this book. For some of my
aders, this book will not have seemed sufficiently religious or theologi-
l, while others may have patiently tolerated the frequency of religious or
eological content. As I have indicated all along, however, I see no clear
undary between the sacred and the secular, the spiritual and the mate-
il. So, for me, even when I have been writing about economic, politi-
l, interpersonal, or psychological matters without using overtly religious
nguage, the issues with which theology is preoccupied were always
immering in the background. If, as the theologian Paul Tillich (1957)
mously claimed, faith has to do with that for which we are ultimately
ncerned, then it is an orientation from which we relate to all that exists,
disposition that moves us to action in the material world. For many peo-
e, this does not take the form of theism or conventional affirmations of
anscendence. For example, commenting on the work of Gilles Deleuze,
w materialist thinker William Connolly (2010) observes:

The Author(s) 2016   209
Rogers-Vaughn, *Caring for Souls in a Neoliberal Age*,
OI 10.1057/978-1-137-55339-3_7

It may be surprising to some to hear an immanent naturalist embrace the spiritual dimension of life. But it is not surprising to those of us who at once contest faith in transcendence in the strongest sense of that word and appreciate the profound role that the quality of spirituality plays in public life. (p. 196)

Connolly proceeds to criticize those on "the democratic left" w presume "that to drop theism in favor of any version of materiali*means* to forfeit or go beyond spirituality." He concludes: "Those are t judgments I seek to contest" (p. 197, emphasis in original). Conno argues, on the contrary, that any effort for constructive change in c time requires "ontological affirmation," his word for faith: "Ontologi affirmation, the democratic left, and political militancy belong togeth in the late-modern era. It takes all three in tandem—in their theistic a nontheistic forms—to press for pluralism, equality, and ecological se sitivity" (p. 197). In basic agreement with Connolly, I will be assertir in these concluding reflections, that caring for souls in a neoliberal a requires a combination of social solidarity, political activity, and fai This remains true even if faith does not assume established religio forms.

Having acknowledged this, I offer the following postscripts in a mc personal, even confessional, vein. For me this will often mean referri to actual religious practices and explicit theological deliberations. Ma of these, congruent with my own religious home, will be particular Christian faith and practice. Some of my comments will be specific pastoral theology. In each case, these postscripts are intended to be su gestive rather than exhaustive. Indeed, each deserves its own book. F my readers who prefer not to think in frankly religious terms, or who hc religious commitments other than Christian, I welcome you to transl: these themes into your own context, wherever such translation seems pc sible. Although these final reflections range over a number of issues, th cluster into three general postscripts. Each of these denote a dimensic of care that will prove critical to both survival and moving forward this neoliberal era. As we will see, these dimensions are inseparable a interpenetrate. True to what we have seen throughout this book, they z entangled. If we removed one of them, the remaining two would nece sarily diminish. I address them in the following order: the cultivation a strengthening of collectives, the nurture and increase of soul, and the su port and amplification of hope.

CULTIVATING COLLECTIVES BEYOND THE MARKET

As I have observed throughout this book, neoliberalization is a process that is rapidly and effectively dismantling human collectives, particularly those cherishing values that may threaten the hegemony of the market. The consequent isolation of human beings is a central marker for third-order suffering. Challenging the effects of this sort of suffering, as well as the continuing forms of second-order suffering imposed by the practices of advanced capitalism, will require us to find ways to cultivate and sustain such communities. This will not be easy. The ethos of the academic and political left, the offspring of the emancipatory movements of the 1960s, tends to see all manifestations of conviction as dogmatism or rigidity, and obligations to groups or institutions as unwelcome limitations on personal choice and freedom. The passions that typify group loyalty, evident as assertions of dearly held beliefs and values, evoke suspicion. Thus Connolly (2010), commenting on "the democratic left," observes: "They fear that the nerve of critique will be severed if ontological affirmation is pursued" (p. 197). Jodi Dean (2009), likewise, states that "the academic and typing left" reacts to the vehemence of many conservatives and neoliberal ideologues "by rejecting dogmatism and conviction, advocating instead micropolitical and ethical practices that work on the self in its immediate reactions and relations" (p. 123). Not only does she believe this to be "politically suicidal" (p. 123), she contends it also means "we have been unable to give voice to values of collectivity, cooperation, solidarity, and equity strong enough to counter neoliberalism's free-trade fantasy" (p. 73).

Moreover, as the psychoanalyst Ian Parker (2007) notes, (post)modern psychology pathologizes dissent, largely by pathologizing collective activity (pp. 74–93). Psychology regards the "normal" individual as one who "engages in rational decision-making and is not unduly influenced by others" (p. 75). The pattern, notes Parker, was set in the late nineteenth century in Gustave Le Bon's classic *The Crowd*, and was continued in Freud's treatments of "mass psychology." Here crowds are viewed as inherently subject to being controlled by passions that are difficult to tame, urges that are unreasonable at best and dangerous at worst: "Collective activity is equated with irrationality, as if it were 'deindividuation'" (p. 82). The result, says Parker, is an inversion of Marx's concern. Marx worried that it was the isolation of individuals that lay at the root of social compliance and a herd mentality. The dominant view in psychology, on the contrary, "is that 'false consciousness' is something that kicks in when people work together" (pp. 83–84). As Phillip Rieff (1966/2006) has shown, psychology has played a critical role in the shaping of contemporary culture. One consequence is that anxiety about collective action has become pervasive. In the United States, for example, news media outlets commonly portray organized protests and labor strikes, if they are covered at all, as mobs inclined to violent behavior.

To make matters even more difficult, Meštrović (1997) discusses how the "postemotional society" of advanced capitalism has become adept at creating artificially constructed "communities," as well as carefully manufactured "authenticity." He calls this the "Disneyfication of community" (p. 76). Observing that the erosion of traditions and collectives has become a cause of alarm among present-day communitarians, such as Amitai Etzioni and Anthony Giddens, he argues that their response has been to call for "properly constructed" communities and intentional planning to build new traditions upon the ruins of the old. Meštrović sees such proposals as bureaucratic efforts to "derive a sense of community from individualism" (p. 96). He asserts that this amounts to "postemotional magical thinking," and concludes: "One could no more construct a community than one could construct a forest" (p. 96). Instead, as in traditional societies, genuine communities must spring up spontaneously. They emerge organically, or not at all.

So, if today's neoliberal cultures erode collectives, evoking suspicion toward collective activity even among those on the radical left who otherwise wish to oppose neoliberal agendas, and if we cannot intentionally build communities, how can we hope? I suggested in the sixth chapter that we cannot develop strategic anti-neoliberal psychotherapies to replace those that serve the interests of present-day capitalism. What we can do is *pay attention* to the individual sufferings and longings for connection that are *already there*, even when this pain has been de-linked from its social context, even in the most severe third-order conditions where people are not aware of their suffering. At an abstract level, new materialist thinking maintains that no systems are static. All systems are movements, entangled with the movements of all other systems. The very openness of all things leaves an opening for change, for hope. At a concrete level, the practices of relational psychoanalysis, as we witnessed in the sixth chapter, reveal the irrepressible desire of individuals for relationships in which they exist as subjects rather than objects, and implacable resistances to powers—social, interpersonal, and psychological—that would return them to the status of objects. Neoliberalism makes us into objects existing in a world of objects. However, as William Davies (2015) has noted, neoliberal rationality "gets stuck when it comes to love" (p. 90). And love, as we will see in the next section, points to soul. Thus attending to the movements of soul can lead us to be more hopeful than many of the totalizing critiques of neoliberalism might suggest.

In the sixth chapter, I avowed that individuality offers a window into the dialectics—the movements—of soul. I must now recall that soul is not contained within individual subjectivity. Soul inhabits a collective home. Indeed, individuality, because it is dependent upon soul, arises only in a communal context. Even so, not just any collective may house soul or give birth to individuality. The requisite community is one that recognizes suffering, both the pain that is shared and anguish that is as idiosyncratic as the individual sufferer. It is also a community where complicity in one another's suffering is acknowledged. Moreover, this means that moving from individuality in the sixth chapter to community in this postscript does not entail bridging a chasm between one type of thing and another. To support these observations, I will turn briefly to the important work of Sara Ahmed, particularly her book *The Cultural Politics of Emotion* (2015).

Ahmed (2015) argues that emotions do not arise from inside, nor are they constructed by society and then placed into individuals, nor are they contagions occupying the spaces between individuals, nor are they something we "have." Rather, they are circulations or movements that orient us to the objects in our world. To be even more exact, Ahmed affirms:

> I suggest that it is the objects of emotion that circulate, rather than emotion as such. My argument still explores how emotions can move through the movement or circulation of objects. Such objects become sticky, or saturated with affect, as sites of personal and social tension. (p. 11)

As such, "they are also about attachments or about what connects us to this or that." Because they concern attachments, they also concern "that which holds us in place, or gives us a dwelling place" (p. 11). In concurrence with Marx, Ahmed contends that emotions "accumulate over time, as a form of affective value" (p. 11). This, she says, is what can make social change so difficult, even in the face of collective resistance: "Attention to emotions allows us to address the question of how subjects become *invested* in particular structures such that their demise is felt as a kind of living death" (p. 12, emphasis in original). This affective stickiness may cause us to continue clinging, even when the attachment causes considerable pain. Such an understanding of emotional conflict and suffering is reminiscent of Layton's view of psychic conflict and repetition compulsion, which I explored in the sixth chapter.

While emotions in general are not the same thing as suffering, they are what make us both aware of our suffering and what orient our suffering in particular ways. This leads Ahmed (2015) to discuss "the sociality of pain" (pp. 28–31) as well as "the politics of pain" (pp. 31–39). Suffering does not achieve "the status of an event, a happening in the world" unless it is witnessed or recognized (pp. 29–30). She concludes: "Even in instances of pain that is lived without an external injury (such as psychic pain), pain 'surfaces' in relationship to others, who bear witness to pain, and authenticate its existence" (p. 31). This offers another way, I believe, to understand third-order suffering. This is a sort of suffering that has not surfaced. No one has borne witness to it. It has not been recognized or authenticated, even by the sufferer. Furthermore, Ahmed contends, politics come into play, as uneven flows of power determine whose pain is recognized and whose is not, to what extent, and in what way. For my purposes, I take this to indicate that third-order suffering and its entanglements are unevenly distributed according to complex interrelationships of sex, gender, race, class, and so on. Finally, and importantly for this postscript, Ahmed alleges that the surfacing of pain is critical to the formation and sustenance of genuine community. As suffering is recognized and authenticated by others, the sufferer and the witnesses are bound together. This reminds me of an unforgettable passage by the Spanish philosopher Miguel de Unamuno:

> For men (sic) love one another with a spiritual love only when they have suffered the same sorrow together, when through long days they have ploughed the stony ground bowed beneath the common yoke of a common grief. It is then that they know one another and feel one another, and feel with one another in their common anguish, they pity one another and love one another. For to love is to pity; and if bodies are united by pleasure, souls are united by pain. (1921/1954, p. 135)

To this, Ahmed would add significant qualifiers and clarifications. The sorrow to which Unamuno attests should not be sentimentalized as literally "the same," as a shared and uniform "fellow feeling." The suffering of individuals, if individuality is to have any meaning, is non-identical. In Ahmed's words: "Pain is evoked as that which even our most intimate others cannot feel" (p. 39). And yet suffering that surfaces as an event, that is authenticated, produces an ethical demand: "Our task … is *to learn how to hear what is impossible*. Such an impossible hearing is only possible if we respond to a pain that we cannot claim as our own" (p. 35, emphasis in original). This ethic yields

> a demand for collective politics, as a politics based not on the possibility that we might be reconciled, but on learning to live with the impossibility of reconciliation, or learning that we live with and beside each other, and yet are not as one. (p. 39)

This is a peculiar sort of solidarity, a common life rooted not in sameness, but on a deep respect, obligation to, and thus love for, the infinite and unique value of every individual. This is the solidarity that sustains soul.

Theologians Joerg Rieger and Kwok Pui-lan (2012) refer to this as "deep solidarity." They assert: "Solidarity in this context is not the support of people who are exactly like oneself but rather what we are calling deep solidarity. Solidarity is the support of others who are different yet experience similar predicaments" (p. 28). Drawing upon the Occupy movement's metaphor of "the 99 percent," Rieger and Pui-lan note that their unity "becomes stronger when they respect the diversities in their midst, in terms of race, ethnicity, gender, sexuality, and other markers of differences" (p. 30). In my judgment, this affirmation implicitly assumes Ahmed's concern that sufferings of individuals must be respected and not be made identical. We cannot blithely say "I know just how you feel" without doing violence to the other's unique pain. On the other hand, Rieger and Pui-lan seem to allow for much more commonality than does Ahmed's text. For example, they repeatedly contend that "solidarity now begins with an understanding that *we are all in the same boat*: we are the 99 percent, and we challenge the 1 percent to stop building their power and wealth at our expense and invite them to join us" (p. 79, my emphasis). What these theologians add to Ahmed's analysis is an emphasis on *class*. In a neoliberal era, when material inequality has become so extreme that millions more are suffering and dying every year, and when the environment of the planet is under siege, we are all in the same boat more than we might be aware. Thus our predicament is indeed shared—as the foregoing passage by Unamuno indicates—even though the ways we suffer these conditions will differ.

The collectives necessary for caring for soul during this neoliberal age, therefore, are those that are not only brought together by the communal recognition and authentication of suffering, but also take sides in class struggle. As I discussed with regard to intersectionality in Chap. 5, this does not mean the importance of class should be elevated above other markers of difference. As I stated there, however, oppressions circulating around race, gender, sexuality, and ethnicity cannot be understood, much less resisted, without appreciating how they are entangled with class conflict. Any form of identity politics that ignores class, therefore, will be fated to support the ongoing domination of neoliberal interests. As Cedric Johnson (2016) has maintained: "Respect for difference is valued in today's multicultural milieu, but the mobilization of different sub-strata of the working class against one another has long been a cherished strategy of capital" (para. 46). Communities that strive to redress the current neglect of class issues will likely face strong opposition, as many on the left may fear that this will come at the expense of diversity, while those on the right decry all efforts to put class on the cultural map. This represents an additional challenge for cultivating collectives beyond the market.

Rieger and Pui-lan's work (2012) highlights yet another feature that will prove essential to forming collectives that can resist neoliberal power hierarchies—the importance of the symbolic function. In this book, I have discussed the ways third-order suffering arises from the inability to identify and articulate pain within a symbolic framework. For Christian congregations, addressing this suffering and its entanglements will require a critical retrieval of tradition. According to theologian Edward Farley (1975), these congregations embody what he calls ecclesia: "Theologically expressed, ecclesia is that form of corporate historical existence whose origin and continuation is made possible by Jesus Christ" (p. 127). Likewise, Rieger and Pui-lan cite Rita Nakashima Brock, who "affirms that the Christian community is an incarnated body to continue the movement that Jesus started" (pp. 122–123). Drawing upon Hardt and Negri's metaphor of "the multitude," Rieger and Pui-lan repeatedly delve into biblical text and especially the gospels, for narratives to describe what a "church of the multitude" might look like. For example, they observe:

> At the heart of the Jesus movement was not what has often been referred to as the *demos* of the Greeks, the assembly of privileged citizens from which the word "democracy" comes. At the heart of this movement were the *laos* and the *ochlos*, both of which describe the common people in contrast with

the privileged citizens of the empire or of the religious elites. (p. 60)

Thus, whereas Wendy Brown (2015) is concerned about how neoliberalism is "undoing the demos," Rieger and Pui-lan, relying upon the founding texts of Christianity, are far more troubled about how it is undoing those who are not privileged by class power. Not surprisingly, they repeatedly appeal to passages in the gospels that demonstrate Jesus's lower-class status and emphasize his overriding concern for "the least of these." Elsewhere, Rieger (2007) has written at length about how Christianity, even in its imperialist forms, never quite eradicated the anti-imperial image and message of Jesus as it articulated its Christological dogmas and claims.

Meanwhile, I must confess to my bemusement at what I perceive to be a relative disinterest in Jesus by some within Christian theological schools these days. Such indifference, where it exists, stands in marked contrast to the ongoing ardor for Jesus in congregations, particularly those of the working class. Might this contrast be a symptom of class differences? The last time I heard a sermon that took seriously the text of Matthew 19:24—"Again I tell you, it is easier for a camel to go through the eye of a needle than for someone who is rich to enter the kingdom of God"—was at Welcome Hill Baptist Church, a rural congregation near Fort Payne, Alabama (USA). I had to have been less than 12 years of age, and the preacher had no more than a secondary school education. I suspect research dedicated to the class differences between theological schools and the majority of Christian congregations would yield some fascinating results.

I have said that forming Christian communities of resistance will require a "critical retrieval" of this tradition. Like Edward Farley (1998), I am deeply suspicious of recent calls for "traditioning" or "retraditioning" in Christian faith and practice. Such efforts are often conservative reactions to the erosion of religious collectives I have discussed in this book, and frequently amount to no more than uncritical knee-jerk obsessions with doctrinal formulas and prescribed liturgical practices. Sometimes this takes on sophisticated forms in the theological academy, as in the "Radical Orthodoxy" movement that emerged recently in the United Kingdom. "On the other hand," Farley remarks, "it's clear that there can be no religious faith without a sense of tradition. Without tradition, religion would disappear in a generation" (1998, p. 113). The issue here is that we must take a critical posture toward tradition, on the lookout for how it serves hierarchies of power while retaining its potential for disruption of the social and political status quo. As a student of Farley during the 1980s, I frequently heard him ask, as we reviewed some theological text, "What is retrievable here?" This question, of course, assumes a lively and fluid exchange between the texts and practices of a tradition and the social context of a particular time and place. Traditions, at their best, are not stale repetitions of the past, but living engagements with the entangled and fragile movements of all things.

One reason that the retrieval of Christian tradition must remain critical is that, in many of its contemporary forms, it is decidedly complicit with present-day capitalism. William Connolly (2008) has carefully documented this complicity in his book, *Capitalism and Christianity, American Style.* It is also rigorously examined by Rieger and Pui-lan (2012), who contend that the "top-down theism" assumed in most Christian collectives and in the public imagination, especially in the United States, serves the interests of capital (pp. 83–109). They declare, for example: "The all-controlling God who acts from the top down, alone and without inviting the participation of the people and without the need to listen to anyone, is not the God of Jesus Christ or the people of Israel" (p. 58). In keeping with this popular theology, Rieger and Pui-lan note that Christian denominations and churches in North America and Europe have been patterned upon "the capitalist ruling class" (pp. 112–117). The average Christian in the United States attends a church that is propertied, contained inside walls, functions generally like an exclusive club, and operates according to prevailing business models.[1]

What if we were to re-imagine religious congregations, following Saskia Sassen's (2014) argument that neoliberalism constitutes a global system of expulsion, as communities of the expelled? In the final paragraph of her book, Sassen states: "I want to conclude with a question: what are the spaces of the expelled? These are invisible to the standard measures of our modern states and economies. But they should be made conceptually visible" (p. 222). Though largely unnoticed, she contends they nevertheless exist: "They are many, they are growing, and they are diversifying. They are conceptually subterranean conditions that need to be brought aboveground. They are, potentially, the new spaces for making—making local economies, new histories, and new modes of membership" (p. 222). From a theological perspective, I believe this is precisely what Rieger and Pui-lan (2012) put forward as "the church of the multitude" (pp. 111–132). These theologians ask us to envision church as "beyond walls," and to focus on "doing" or "forming" church rather than "going" to church (pp. 118–119). Such a church, they assert, would look more like the

Occupy movement, or the base Christian communities of Latin America. I want to suggest that much religious life, even in the United States, is closer to this vision than we might think. In the rural congregations of my youth, all attended by fewer than 100 people—all working class and mostly without education beyond secondary school—I was consistently told that *the people* were the church. So this is not a new or radical idea, nor is it confined to the early movements that circulated around Jesus. Even today, the average religious congregation in the United States is about the size of those in my childhood.[2] And this leaves out the growing number of people participating in house churches. In 2009, a Pew Forum survey estimated that close to 10 % of Protestants in the United States only attend home services.[3] If we add to this Michael Zweig's (2012) conclusion that the working class makes up 63 % of the labor force in the United States, and that this group is disproportionally female, black, and Hispanic (pp. 32–36), we can assume that the typical congregation looks quite different "on the ground" than it might from the hallways of the theological academy. With the dramatic increases in material inequality under neoliberalism, it is quite likely that more and more of these gatherings are coming to resemble Sassen's "spaces of the expelled." On the other hand, some studies are indicating that religious participation has been declining among the working class faster than the middle and upper classes.[4] This portends a worrisome possibility that religion is fast becoming a rather bourgeois activity.

Nonetheless, it is clear that religious collectives and the traditions that support them are far from dead. My former colleague at Vanderbilt, theologian John Thatamanil, has asserted that religious congregations may be one of the last remainders of face-to-face communities that can serve as intermediaries between individuals and families, on the one hand, and corporations and governments on the other (personal communication; spring, 2011). In a recent interview, Noam Chomsky (2015), a social critic not known for his optimism, was asked whether he thought the Occupy movement had made a lasting impact. He replied:

> It's a very atomized society. There are very few continuing organizations which have institutional memory, that know how to move to the next step and so on.
> This is partly due to the destruction of the labor movement, which used to offer a kind of fixed basis for many activities; by now, practically the only persistent institutions are the churches. So many things are church-based. (para. 7–8)

Comments such as these call upon those of us who are theologian and religious leaders not to lose heart. We have neither the time nor the luxury to despair. If Thatamanil and Chomsky are correct, the erosion of collectives by neoliberalization leaves us standing upon one of the few places from which to mount a resistance. However, as Rieger and Pui-lan (2012) have shown, we have some serious work to do. We will need to retrieve from our religious heritage the elements of faith and practice that run counter to the faith and practice of the market. We have the resources and congregations have taken on similar missions before. During the first Gilded Age, in the early twentieth century, churches combined forces with labor groups to struggle against material inequality and economic oppression (Carter, 2015). This kind of collaboration extended throughout the era of the New Deal (Cantwell, Carter, & Drake, 2016). There are some signs that a retrieval of the Social Gospel is underway, such as the 100th anniversary release (1907/2007), including responses by contemporary religious leaders, of the Walter Rauschenbusch classic, *Christianity and the Social Crisis*. Several contemporary thinkers and activists are working to reconnect theology and religious studies with class-based analyses (Rieger 2013), as well as to revive collaborative efforts between congregations and labor (Rieger & Henkel-Rieger, 2016). There are also a number of scholars who are revising liberation theology toward the repudiation of neoliberal culture (Míguez, Rieger, & Sung, 2009; Sung, 2007, 2011). I must also add to this the many voices of today's feminist, mujerista, womanist, black, queer, and postcolonial theologians—whose works are far too abundant to document here—who are speaking from the margins and thus offer valuable tools for examining and opposing global neoliberal imperialism. Using the resources at our disposal, we are left now to fashion alternatives to what Johann Baptist Metz (1977/2013) has identified as bourgeois religion and bourgeois theology. Metz calls us to a religion and theology that forms "solidarity with the dead and the vanquished" (p. 67) precisely those who neoliberal powers have forgotten and expelled.

This brings me full circle back to Ahmed's work, which reminds us that much of the work before us does not fall comfortably into either intellectual or activist categories. Rather, collectives are critical to the *affective* work that will be required to adequately address third-order suffering. It is not enough for us to be convinced, taught, or guided into proper action. We must also be *moved* or *touched*. Because third-order suffering is invisible and often not even felt, it is highly resistant to cognitive or behavioral interventions. And because it relies on isolation, it requires subject-to-subject relationship to break its hold. In the sixth chapter, we saw how the clinical context of psychotherapy offers clues about how this can occur. The problem, as I noted at the end of that chapter, is that psychotherapy is far too limited and fragile to achieve a broader antidote to third-order suffering. Ahmed (2015), however, offers a way to understand how particular types of human collectives might be able to reverse the double unconsciousness of this form of suffering. Collectives that embody the care of soul, that bear witness to individual as well as corporate pain, involve a circulation of affect that is capable of calling third-order suffering out of its seclusion and unconsciousness. In the poetic words of the Hebrew Bible, "deep calls unto deep" (Psalms 42:7). The power of collectives to circulate affect means that they have more potential to address such suffering—including bringing it to consciousness—than all the psychotherapy in the world. This, then, is the solidarity needed in the neoliberal age, a solidarity that can do the deep emotional work necessary to reach the recesses of today's normative suffering.

For pastoral and practical theologians, this means that cultivating and strengthening religious collectives is the single most important thing we can do to offer pastoral care in our time. I have said, however, that this holds true only if a community embodies the care of soul. With this in mind, I turn now to the second postscript.

Caring for Soul

What I have asserted in the foregoing postscript should not be taken as a blanket endorsement of all human collectives, or a reification of the notion of community, or a general sentimentalizing of religious congregations. As I noted earlier in this book, neoliberalism itself depends on giant, international collectives to accomplish its economic and political agendas. The banking and finance industries, large corporations, and the governments now largely controlled by them are prime examples. Moreover, the cultural processes of neoliberalization, as we have seen, co-opt even the most traditional collectives, such as schools, religious bodies, labor unions, and civic organizations. These mainstays of societies are increasingly adapted to conform to neoliberal practices, and even its governing rationality. Not even the most intimate communities are immune. These tend to succumb over time to the individualistic and highly competitive ethos of neoliberalism, which assumes there will be winners and losers. This increases an us-versus-them mentality that fears those who are marked as different. Thus, despite the formal promotion of diversity and multiculturalism by neoliberal interests, we are now seeing a broad increase of oppressions based on the intersections of race, gender, class, sexuality, religion, ethnicity, and so on. If we combine these developments with Ahmed's (2015) analysis of how emotions circulate among groups and entire cultures, we can appreciate why Le Bon's and Freud's concerns about the crowd mentality and mass hysteria were not entirely misplaced.

Clearly, not just any collective will do. This is why Rieger and Pui-lan (2012) have emphasized "deep solidarity" as the character of the requisite communities and religious congregations. Their use of this term generally points to the inclusivity of a "church of the multitude." This sort of church makes diversity not simply a policy, but a calling: "The fact that we live in the complex intersections of race, class, gender, and sexuality should not be a cause of frustration, but a call to develop less oppressive and more productive relations." They conclude: "There is no going back to some primordial unity without diversity (p. 66)." Later on, Rieger and Pui-lan extend this inclusivity to religious differences. The type of church they envision leaves behind the triumphalism of Christendom and embraces conversation with other religions. Truth is not seen as something any religious tradition possesses, but "is to be discovered in dialogues with one another and in working together in deep solidarity" (p. 128). These theologians envision a "polydoxy" that appreciates the diversity within the Christian tradition, as well as between the religious traditions. The result is not a uniform or universal religion, but an ongoing dialogue and collaboration that allow people to be simultaneously more faithful and more critical toward their own religious heritage (pp. 128–129).

I am in agreement with what Rieger and Pui-lan have envisioned. What I wish to add is a line of thought that I suspect these theologians might accept as congruent with their proposals. Linking back to the insights of Ahmed (2015) and the warnings of Meštrović (1997) in the preceding postscript, deep solidarity does not arise from intentional planning or by being "properly constructed." It cannot be manufactured. Rather, this solidarity emerges, if at all, from a recognition that is simultaneously both cognitive and affective, or perhaps even affective prior to arising into cognition—an appreciation that we are all profoundly entangled with one another. *In other words, it is rooted in an experiential comprehension of sor* This is not a comprehension that simply occurs within individuals, who then come together based on their shared insight. Rather, as Ahmed work would suggest, it emerges organically from a circulation of affect bodies come into contact with each other, and as these bodies together encounter objects that "become sticky, or saturated with affect, as sites of personal and social tension" (2015, p. 11). In other words, comprehension of soul does not first originate within individuals. It grows out of social–material movements. However, as I observed in passing in the sixth chapter, soul is not simply the ontology of entanglement. Rather, soul is a posture, an activity, a way of existing within this entanglement. And it is evoked, called out, by the particular sufferings circulating within this entanglement. *Wherever the response to this pain is care, there is soul.* Soul, then, exists in the form of this call-and-response. This assertion beckons for a critical retrieval of this quite traditional term, "soul." I will say more.

In historical Christianity, pastoral care has been understood within the tradition of the care of souls.[5] Lately, the term "soul" has appeared to fall into disregard, leading pastoral theologian Herbert Anderson (2001) to ask: "Whatever happened to *Seelsorge* (the care of souls)?" (p. 32, emphasis in original). While Anderson attributes the disappearance of the term from contemporary theology to its association with dualistic (body versus soul) thinking, I suspect it also involves the current aversion to essentialist thought. For many, as I mentioned in the introduction to this book, soul connotes a substance or essence of the human that is eternal, universal, and beyond history. I share the opinion that dualistic and essentialist views of soul are no longer helpful. However, throughout this book, as indicated even in its title, my conviction that the idea of soul warrants retrieval has been quite apparent. First, in a very practical vein, the term remains in broad use in cultural literature, both in popular (Moore, 1992) and academic (Rose, 1999) settings. This presents an opportunity for theology to improve its standing as a public discourse. Second, salvaging the notion of soul, as I have been arguing, may help counter the radical individualism within the neoliberal paradigm, including the individualistic assumptions that currently appear to swirl around alternative terms such as "spirit" and "spirituality." Third, this reframing might oppose neoliberalism's complete suppression of the category of transcendence, the conviction that there may be a value more ultimate than the agendas and rationality of the market. Finally, the critical retrieval of the notion of soul that I am proposing does not simply make suffering an object of care. It restores voice to the suffering that, under neoliberalism, has been silenced and privatized.

Throughout most of this book, I have focused on *soul*, using the singular of this term, as a material sociality. But, as in the sixth chapter where I discussed individuality as a window into the dialectics of soul, I do not understand individuality apart from soul. Thus I sometimes use the plural, *souls*, when referring to the appearance of soul from the perspective of subjectivity. Self, or subjectivity, may be considered generally as individual self-consciousness and agency. Observed from the perspective of individuality rather than sociality, soul appears as a dimension of self, namely the capacity or, better, the *activity* or *movement*, of self-transcendence. But what sort of transcendence is this? Theunissen (1977/1984) identifies two strands within Western philosophy that attempt to account for relationship between self and other. Each implies, in my judgment, a quite different idea regarding self-transcendence. The first, which Theunissen calls "the transcendental project" (pp. 13–163), originates in Descartes and finds articulation in Husserl's philosophy. Here, self-transcendence is both *rational* and *individual*. It is a movement in which the individual, in an imaginative act of reason, exits herself and observes her own thoughts, feelings, and processes. It is thus objective and *objectifying*. Relation to the other is then mediated through an idea or image of the other constructed within this act of reason. My belief is that this project is congruent with understandings of knowledge as dependent on vision or "insight," which Ihde (2007) refers to as the "visualism" that has dominated Western philosophy since the ancient Greeks (pp. 6–13). In this instance, self-transcendence appears as an activity of solitary individuals and is fully compatible with the neoliberal paradigm.

An alternative understanding of self-transcendence is suggested in what Theunissen (1977/1984) calls "the philosophy of dialogue," most completely developed in the thought of Buber (pp. 257–344). Here, self-transcendence is dialogical and intersubjective. It arises within what Buber (1947/2002) identifies as "the between." Self-transcendence occurs not from some neutral standpoint within an individual's rational act, but *from the standpoint of the other(s)*. It appears as a form of knowledge or experience that is intrinsically relational or social and, according to Ihde's (2007) typology, is *auditory* rather than visual, depending on *listening* and *speaking*. This self-transcendence is an intersubjective, *social* act and cannot be achieved by isolated individuals. It lies outside cost–benefit calculations and concerns for efficiency and thus is fundamentally incompatible with neoliberal culture.

This is apparent in what theologian Robert Johann (1966) calls "disinterested love." "When love is interested," observes Johann, "when the attraction is based on a motive of profit or need, it has no difficulty in finding words to justify itself" (p. 19). Disinterested love, however, cannot explain itself: "Why do I love you? Because you are—*you*. That is the best it can do. It is indefensible" (p. 19, emphasis in original). It is this sort of love, not the "interested" attachment of romantic love, mere affection, or desire for benefit, that forms the heart of authentic soul. Rieger and Pui-lan (2012) have been careful to not describe the relationality of the multitude solely in terms of love, fearing this can easily dissolve into bourgeois forms of self-serving attraction or affection. They therefore propose: "the notion of love needs to be tempered with the notion of justice" (p. 80). In Johann's understanding of love as disinterested, however, the ethical dimension—justice—is already present. I believe this to be congruent with Ahmed's assertion that such a sociality involves "learning that we live with and beside each other, and yet are not as one" (2012, p. 39). In my terms, soul is always-already-there whenever the response to the call of non-identical, particular sufferings is care. The activity of soul is intrinsically an ethical activity.

This sense of soul as ethical activity is steadily worn away by neoliberal interests. Attributing the erosion of dialogue to "the totalizing capacity of modernity-cum-capitalism," Walter Brueggemann (2012) concludes:

> The loss of dialogic articulation, rendered impossible in modernist rationality, has led to complete abdication of dialogic capacity …. Either *cold absoluteness* or *totalizing subjectivity* leaves no possibility of mutual engagement of the kind that belongs to dialogic speech and life. (pp. 26, 29, emphases in original)

Similarly, Dufour (2003/2008) argues that life under a neoliberal regime seeks to eliminate transcendence and non-utilitarian relationships (pp. 64–70). He contends that it is so efficient in this reduction that it has created a "historic mutation" of human life (p. 13), a mutation that I have called third-order suffering.

This suggests that soul is endangered, perhaps as never before. This should be of grave concern to any who are inheritors of the care of souls tradition. The human values, capacities, and experiences that were once the foci of care, pastoral or otherwise, have become dispersed, diffuse, and at times even absent. Are we now increasingly caring for souls that are threatened with extinction? Have we not now become T.S. Eliot's "hollow men" (1925/1930–1970), zombies of our former selves? Indeed, whereas Haraway (1985) once celebrated the cyborg as a version of liberated humanity, it seems now to have become the mindless, machine-like fate of vacuous servitude to capitalist consumption and flex worker production. Thus Turkle (2011) laments: "We are all cyborgs now" (p. 152). Both self and other are commodified and reduced to an object, an "it." As Bollas (1987/2011) said of normotic personalities, they are objects in a world of objects. What remains is a relationship Buber might not have imagined: not an "I-Thou" or even an "I-it" relationship, but an "it-it" relationship.

If we combine the first postscript with this one, the necessary response to neoliberal hegemony comes into clearer focus. There will be no path forward that does not involve the strengthening of collectives that nurture and maintain soul. Such collectives must be welcomed wherever they appear. Not all of them will identify themselves as religious. Nor will all forms of the care of souls be identified as pastoral. At the same time, if the observations by Thatamanil and Chomsky cited in the previous postscript are credible, then religious institutions and congregations will play a critical role in this journey. But this can only be the case if religious bodies can critically reclaim the radical elements of their ancient origins. The theologian Nicholas Lash (1996) claims that what have been called religions are best regarded as schools, "whose pedagogy has the twofold purpose—however differently conceived and executed in the different traditions—of weaning us from our idolatry and purifying our desire" (p. 21). Today the historical communities embodying such a pedagogy will strive to expose the ways that contemporary capitalism has redirected our hearts onto idols that demand our souls as sacrifice, and to replace the cravings of the market with the desires of soul.

There is an additional emphasis within these schools that will prove necessary to resisting the soul-killing effects of neoliberal hegemony. All of them endeavor to remember, honor, and grieve the dead. As Goss and Klass (2005) have documented, this is a dimension of religious traditions that established powers often find most threatening to their control, and thus work to either co-opt or eradicate. As we saw in Chap. 4, Bauman (1997) establishes that neoliberal interests operate to either hide death and grief or render them banal. Likewise, Goss and Klass (2005) observe that, in the culture of advanced capitalism, grief is simply psychologized. It therefore holds no power to relativize or oppose the desires of the market, or reveal anything that might lead us to question the status quo. "When grief is conceptualized as a psychological process, it is painful but ultimately not meaningful. Grief is a part of life but has no special truth-value" (p. 256). There is no room in a world ruled by competition entrepreneurship, exchange, and debt for communities and traditions that cherish the dead. Commenting upon the erosion of tradition in this age, Metz (1977/2013) asserts:

> Perhaps this substantive loss of tradition shows itself most clearly in the relation to the dead. When it comes to the dead there is no exchange relationship, no *do ut des*. The love that mourns for the dead is that form of love ... that cannot be taken up into a consumer society's exploitation structures. In line with this, the community of feeling with the dead dwindles away ... it is blocked, trivialized, and inevitably privatized. (p. 51, emphasis in original)

Metz concludes: "A symptom of this is the fact that ... men and women are forbidden any mourning or melancholy" (p. 51).

If soul is coterminous with a love that permeates our entanglement with all others and all things, then it is continually marked by grief and mourning. For, as I have said elsewhere (Vaughn, 2003), grief is nothing but love under the condition of absence. Moreover, because it lives within this entanglement in the mode of love, soul suffers the loss or anguish of even one individual. It is in this spirit, I believe, that Derrida, in his final lecture, could claim that the death of the individual was the death of the world (2003/2011, pp. 259–260). Finally, soul manifests a temporality as well as materiality. It is not confined to the present. It is historical. It extends not simply through entangled spaces, but times. Soul is lived as memory, both individually and socially. Putting all this together, I must agree with Metz (1977/2013) that Christian praxis is not only social but *mathic* in structure. Collectives that nurture and sustain soul, in other words, are communities of memory characterized by a peculiar solidarity: a solidarity that is an openness to past suffering; a solidarity, thus, that looks backward': *a solidarity with the dead and the vanquished*" (p. 67, my emphasis). In an age of "radical interiorization and privatization," in a culture of "a growing sense of apathy," Metz argues that such a solidarity represents a powerful form of resistance.

In my judgment, the "deep solidarity" advocated by Rieger and Puin (2012) entails this "solidarity with the dead and the vanquished." It encompasses, as well, those who are no longer useful to neoliberal systems, those who Sassen (2014) calls "the expelled" and Bauman (2004) designates "human waste," in addition to the vast populations that continue to be materially exploited and subjugated. This solidarity must also embrace the many people Cazdyn (2012) has termed "the already dead."

Among these are individuals who may not appear afflicted, yet have undergone a kind of spiritual death. They are enduring what I am calling third-order suffering. Their misery has been so privatized, silenced, and fragmented that it may no longer look like suffering. We do not yet fully understand how to establish deep solidarity with the already dead. This is a new challenge for our time, one toward which this book makes only tentative first steps.

I have suggested that collectives that sustain soul are deep solidarities that are historical. They thus live by memory, in continuity with the past. But historical communities also anticipate the future; they live in hope. And this brings us to the third and final postscript.

Amplifying Hope

The rhetoric of neoliberalism is incorrigibly optimistic. It heralds and celebrates creativity, industriousness, efficiency, best practices, infinite growth, technological triumph, globalization, human flourishing, multicultural harmony, equal opportunity, positive psychology, and authentic happiness. Many have therefore latched onto Fukuyama's (1992/2006) assertion that, following the apparent demise of all the world's socialist experiments, today's capitalism represents the fulfillment of the Enlightenment project and the "end of history." If this were only true, we would have little need for hope. Derrida's (1994) response to Fukuyama's declaration, however, is devastating:

> For it must be cried out, at a time when some have the audacity to neo-evangelize in the name of the ideal of a liberal democracy that has finally realized itself as the ideal of human history: never have violence, inequality, exclusion, famine, and thus economic oppression affected as many human beings in the history of the earth and humanity. Instead of singing the advent of the ideal of liberal democracy and of the capitalist market in the euphoria of the end of history, instead of celebrating the "end of ideologies" and the end of the great emancipatory discourses, let us never neglect this obvious macroscopic fact, made up of innumerable singular sites of suffering: no degree of progress allows one to ignore that never before, in absolute figures, never have so many men, women, and children been subjugated, starved, or exterminated on the earth. (p. 106)

In keeping with Derrida's reminder, we have seen, throughout the book, that the age of neoliberal capitalist expansion is an age of unimaginable anguish. Thus for those suffering under the current regime capitalism to be told, in the infamous words of Margaret Thatcher, "there is no alternative," is to receive a fate of unmitigated despair. Consequently, we have never needed hope more than we do today.

Accompanying the macroscopic suffering to which Derrida points, I have argued throughout this project that neoliberalization also produces unprecedented microscopic suffering, evident in interpersonal relationships and within the individual subject. The most obvious signifier of this is not depression, which still holds some residue of resistance (Rogers-Vaughn, 2014). At the depth of contemporary despair lies a profound apathy. I have witnessed this repeatedly in my clinical practice. It appears not as a wish to die, but as a relative lack of concern whether one lives or dies. It is evident as an absence of feeling other than the ephemeral emotions manufactured and served up for consumption by the market (Meštrović, 1997). Metz (1977/2013) claims that we are living in "a golden age of apathy" (p. 81). He associates this with the steady erosion of a sense of self: "With this experience of a more fragile identity a new culture is in the offing; its first name is apathy, the absence of feeling" (p. 26). This loss of self appears to be accelerating, and is virtually invisible. Many years ago, conducting his own analysis of despair, Kierkegaard (1849/1980) anticipates how stealthily this demise transpires:

> The greatest hazard of all, losing the self, can occur very quietly in the world, as if it were nothing at all. No other loss can occur so quietly; any other loss—an arm, a leg, five dollars, a wife, etc.—is sure to be noticed. (pp. 32–33)

And he notes that the despair of this lost soul is likewise imperceptible:

> Now this form of despair goes practically unnoticed in the world. Just by losing himself this way, such a man has gained an increasing capacity for going along superbly in business and social life, indeed, for making a great success in the world ... He is so far from being regarded as a person in despair that he is just what a human being is supposed to be. (p. 34)

Kierkegaard is describing here a form of despair that is now becoming normative. It is the despair of the neoliberal subject, the normotic personality, the individual afflicted by third-order suffering.

This returns us once again to the dialectics of suffering, in this case to Marcel's (1951/1978) observation "that there can strictly speaking be no hope except when the temptation to despair exists" (p. 36). Similarly,

Kierkegaard (1849/1980) stresses: "Precisely because the sickness of despair is totally dialectical, it is the worst misfortune never to have had that sickness" (p. 26). He continues:

> Compared with the person who is conscious of his despair, the despairing individual who is ignorant of his despair is simply a negativity further away from the truth and deliverance. Despair itself is a negativity; ignorance of it, a new negativity. However, to reach the truth, one must go through every negativity, for the old legend about breaking a certain magic spell is true: the piece has to be played through backwards or the spell is not broken. (p. 44)

For the necessary change to come about, insists Kierkegaard, "there must first be effective despair, radical despair, so that the life of the spirit can break through from the ground upward" (p. 59). Playing things through backwards, he suggests, will first mean returning despair to consciousness. In my terms, it requires a reversal of the double unconsciousness of third-order suffering. First, we must become aware of suffering, then reconnect it to its social origins. Under the conditions of neoliberalism, the consequence of this renewed awareness produces what Cazdyn (2012) calls "the already dead." This sort of consciousness, in turn, is the seed for the emergence of a new, spontaneous community: "Since one is already dead, the fear of death ... works differently and opens up a relationship to death and dying that is not wholly contained by personal struggle" (p. 200). I will return to this presently.

First, I must highlight something implicit in this dialectic, an important matter that could easily be overlooked. And that essential truth is this: wherever there is despair, there is hope. In the radical despair of third-order suffering, hope may be reduced to a virtual silence. Yet it is there, even though as a still, small voice—or perhaps an inchoate resonance. This holds true whether we regard despair individually or collectively. Many times, when sitting with psychotherapy patients who appeared completely hopeless, I have pointed out to them that they would not be talking with me, nor would I be listening to them, unless we both were entertaining some sort of hope, however minuscule it might seem to be. Our very presence to one another indicated an embryonic hope that only appeared to be absent. On a number of occasions, these individuals would later report to me, sometimes after months or even years, that hearing those simple words had helped them imagine the possibility of a better life. I must now add to this the likelihood that this hope could only emerge in the context of a communion that began to take shape during those initial conversations. As I noted in the foregoing postscript, soul is a self-transcendence that occurs within dialogue, in the form of the call-and-response of relationship. Whenever we speak, whether through words or through gestures of our bodies, we must wait for the other's response. We cannot know in advance what this will be. In that precise moment, the future is open, undetermined. This waiting, as Marcel affirms, is a marker of hoping. We might say that this pause, this space, between speaking and responding is the birthplace of hope. And, as the relational psychoanalysis I discussed in the sixth chapter demonstrates, if the response is then directed to a subject rather than an object, this hope is nurtured and grows. This happens, in other words, if the dialogue embodies something of the ethic Johann (1966) calls "disinterested love." Marcel (1951/1978) concurs: "Now it is precisely where such love exists, and only where it exists, that we can speak of hope, this love taking shape in a reality which without it would not be what it is" (pp. 57–58). This leads Marcel, in the same essay, to this final statement about the meaning of hope:

> we might say that hope is essentially the availability of a soul which has entered intimately enough into the experience of communion to accomplish in the teeth of will and knowledge the transcendent act—the act establishing the vital regeneration of which this experience affords both the pledge and the first-fruits. (p. 67)

If we place this alongside the understanding of soul I outlined in the second postscript, we can now see that soul exists within the entanglement of all things in the mode of hope. If the body of soul is love, then hope is its breath.

The outcome of all this is that we are not in the position of having to create hope ex nihilo. Instead, our task is to amplify the hope that is already there, even in the depths of third-order despair. This amplification takes place, as we have just seen, whenever we respond to each other as subjects rather than objects. However, if this is limited to dyadic relationships or to intimate circles, what remains will continue to be a small voice. As I noted in the conclusion of the sixth chapter, the benefits of psychotherapy, for instance, are tenuous and fragile in the face of the global challenges of neoliberalization. This holds true for all interpersonal relationships. This does not mean that hope at this level is without value. As Sara Ahmed (2014) has asserted, even these microscopic forms of care

are nevertheless acts of resistance: "It is about finding ways to exist in a world that is diminishing" (para. 23). Still, the macroscopic portrait of suffering painted by Derrida at the beginning of this postscript begs for hope on a much larger scale. The macroscopic and the microscopic are indelibly entangled. Fortunately, hope is not entirely eradicated in this dimension either. As feminist theorists such as Lauren Berlant (2011) and J.K. Gibson-Graham (1996/2006, 2006) have argued, no hegemony is total. There are always cracks in any hegemony, spaces where resistant longings seep up, creating alternative movements and communities. This is just as true of neoliberalism, they observe, as any former hegemony. And these marginal factions, though scattered and local, portend the possibility of large-scale political activity.

Similarly, Cazdyn's (2012) notion of "the already dead," as I am appropriating it, consists of those who have been expelled by neoliberal systems, as well as those afflicted with third-order suffering, who have subsequently become both conscious of their suffering and also aware of "the larger structure of power" (p. 200) that has excluded or subjugated them. Cazdyn then asks: "But what does one do with this awareness? Make a revolution, since awareness changes nothing." The critical question, he declares, can be posed succinctly: "How will the already dead transform into a collective political subject?" Cazdyn concludes:

> The already dead, however, do not constitute a political movement in the traditional sense. They, rather, evince a political consciousness that can inspire and inform political movements. The already dead already inhabit revolution—that is, a revolutionary consciousness informed by a certain way of living in time and with the future. (p. 200)

But, how are the already dead to make the turn from political consciousness to activity? Cazdyn addresses this only obliquely, especially in his allusions to the work of Ernst Bloch (pp. 185–186), but I believe this will require a critical retrieval of the utopian imagination. Without inspiration from visions of a better world, social and political movements rarely if ever, gain traction.

In the neoliberal age, openly utopian discourse has fallen upon hard times. A confluence of streams has made it almost impossible to embrace dreams of "the Good Society" anymore. One such stream is the post modern suspicion that any sort of grand narrative will prove to be inherently exclusive and oppressive. But postmodern skepticism merges with earlier currents in twentieth-century thought. Historian Russell Jacoby (2005) observes that for the "liberal anti-utopians," such as Karl Popper, Isaiah Berlin, and Hannah Arendt: "Totalitarianism became the catchall for utopianism as well as Marxism, Nazism, and nationalism." He concludes: "Today the liberal anti-utopians are almost universally honored; their ideas have become the conventional wisdom of our day" (p. xiii). Finally, the freedom movements that sprang up globally during the 1960s shared a general distrust of institutions and obligations to collectives. We have seen, in the second chapter of this book, how neoliberalism co-opted these libertarian sentiments. Most of today's political powers, both conservative and liberal, at least in the United States and Europe, are heirs to these currents of anti-utopianism.

There are two problems with contemporary anti-utopianism, and they are related. First, the utopian impulse appears to spring up spontaneously, even where it is most maligned. Hayek's post-World War II best seller, *The Road to Serfdom* (1944/2007), a major contribution to what was to become neoliberal ideology, decried utopian thinking as much as the writings of Popper, Berlin, and Arendt, and was far more popular. Like these thinkers, as Jacoby (1999) has noted, Hayek equated all utopian ideals with totalitarianism (p. 43). And yet, in ways Hayek could not have possibly imagined, neoliberalism has evolved into a utopian movement. In the neoliberal utopia, the unencumbered functioning of markets, which is avowedly both natural and scientific, will (eventually) solve all human problems that are capable of being solved. This utopian impulse hidden within neoliberalism is becoming widely recognized. Kunkel (2014) observes: "neoliberal 'post-ideology' resembled nothing so much as a caricature of Marxist historical determinism. It merely substituted liberal capitalism for communism in claiming that here we beheld the final form of human society" (p. 137). Similarly, Žižek (2009) contends: "the very notion of capitalism as a neutral social mechanism is ideology (even utopian ideology) at its purest" (p. 25). Later on, he concludes:

> Far from proving that the era of ideological utopias is behind us, this uncontested hegemony of capitalism is sustained by the properly utopian core of capitalist ideology. Utopias of alternative worlds have been exorcized by the utopia in power, masking itself as pragmatic realism. (p. 77)

What we now have, in other words, is one utopian project eradicating its competitors. An implicit recognition of the utopian character of neoliberal capitalism, complete with its own secular theology, is also evident in the recent work of several theologians, including Cobb (2010), Rieger (2009), and Thistlethwaite (2010). The issue before us, then, as the preceding quote from Žižek suggests, is not whether to pursue a utopian spirit, but rather which sorts of visions are truly just and warrant our support. This will require serious ongoing theological analysis and critique, in order to counter the inevitable idolatrous tendencies of utopian dreams.

The second problem with anti-utopianism is the evisceration of any political effort that might actually alter the existing system in a meaningful way. In his book *The End of Utopia: Politics and Culture in an Age of Apathy*, Jacoby (1999) agrees with Fukuyama that utopianism has become obsolete. Unlike Fukuyama, however, Jacoby believes this has had devastating consequences. We are now deprived of large-scale visions of alternatives to the existing capitalist order, dreams of the possible that are necessary to fund genuine social and political change. "Instead of championing a radical idea of a new society," remarks Jacoby, "the left ineluctably retreats to smaller ideas, seeking to expand the options within the existing society" (p. 13). This has occurred, he observes, even among socialist parties the world over, as well as among the remaining theorists who still dare to wear the Marxist label: "At the *fin de siècle*, Marxism seeks an afterlife as a more perfect capitalism" (p. 23, emphasis in original). Jacoby concludes: "Can liberalism with a backbone exist if its left turns mushy? Does radicalism persist if reduced to means and methods? Does a left survive it abandons a utopian hope or plan?" (p. 25).

As I have noted in Chaps. 2 and 5, part of the success of neoliberalism consists in how effectively it has co-opted the spirit of the 1960s. As have documented, it accomplished this by driving a wedge between social justice efforts focused on economic fairness and those emphasizing cultural identities. Henceforth, social justice, even among most progressives has been identified with the elimination of discrimination and oppression based on sex, gender, race, ethnicity, and so forth. Meanwhile, the insistence on economic justice has been virtually abandoned. However, as have argued, removing an awareness of the entanglement between class conflict and oppressions rooted in race, gender, and other markers of difference has only made the daily lives of the vast majority of women, minorities, and other marginalized people immensely worse. It has also had the untoward effect of making the struggles of working-class whites invisible. One consequence of this, in the United States, is the backlash evident the support of the racist-inflected presidential campaign of Donald Trump by the white working class. Similar reactions are now evident in the support of conservative political parties and politicians all over Europe.

Jacoby sees this problem as well, and thus is highly critical of neoliberal multiculturalism, which emphasizes diversity while leaving out the realities of class struggle (1999, pp. 29–66). The resulting emphasis on inclusion means simply gaining access to the rewards of capitalism. Ironically, this produces an actual decline in diversity, as cultural differences are flattened out, reduced to stylistic variations of living in a consumer society. As I mentioned in Chap. 5, this is also a theme in Paul Gilroy's W.E.B. Dubois Lectures at Harvard (2010). Gilroy bemoans the African-American embrace of equal opportunity, while leaving behind the revolutionary dreams of leaders such as Martin Luther King, Jr., Angela Davis, Malcolm X, Frantz Fanon, and Bob Marley. Referring to this type of inclusion as cultural conformity, Jacoby concludes: "Multiculturalism spells the demise of utopia" (1999, p. 40).

This brings us back to the main points of these postscripts. If caring for souls in a neoliberal age requires collectives that nurture soul, it is now apparent that these collectives must also amplify hope in a time of pervasive conformity and despair. And amplifying hope in the social dimension will entail a critical retrieval of the utopian spirit. But what sort of utopian spirit is required? Jacoby (2005) discerns two streams of utopian thought: "the blue print tradition and the iconoclastic tradition" (p. xiv). "The blueprint utopians," he notes, "map out the future in inches and minutes" (p. xiv). These are the utopians of the planned economies and controlling states, and they are in the majority. This utopianism, Jacoby claims, was the variety so rightly reviled by Popper, Berlin, and Arendt (pp. 37–82). Ironically, neoliberal utopianism generally falls into this vein. The iconoclastic utopians, on the other hand, are an overlooked minority. These are "those who dreamt of a superior society but who declined to give its precise measurements" (p. xv). Jacoby summarizes:

> Rather than elaborate the future in precise detail, they longed, waited, or worked for utopia but did not visualize it. The iconoclastic utopians tapped ideas traditionally associated with utopia—harmony, leisure, peace, and pleasure—but rather than spelling out what could be, they kept, as it were, their ears open toward it. Ears and eyes are apposite, for insofar as they did not visualize the future, they listened for it. They did not privilege the eye, but the ear. (p. 33)

I cannot read these words without recalling, as in the second postscript, that soul consists in hearing, in dialogue, rather than in seeing. Jacoby, a historian, traces the iconoclastic current of utopianism to the Jewish tradition, and specifically to the Hebrew Bible, with its refusal to make graven images depicting the Divine (pp. 113–144). The contemporary expressions of this utopian spirit are found in the writings of "the Weimar utopian Jews—intellectuals such as Ernst Bloch, Gershom Scholem, T. W. Adorno, and Walter Benjamin" (p. 127). I must also remind those of us who are Christians that Jesus of Nazareth—a faithful Jew—stood firmly within this tradition. In the Gospels, he is recorded as preaching "the Kingdom of God," a reversal of earthly kingdoms, a realm of peace, love, and justice. In keeping with this utopia, the prayer that bears his name asks: "And forgive us our debts, as we also have forgiven our debtors" (Matt. 6:12). This is clearly a different place from the one we now inhabit.

The deep longing of the iconoclastic utopians for a world they refuse to portray is in keeping with Marcel's description of hope. Hope, insists Marcel, "tends inevitably to transcend the particular objects to which it at first seems to be attached" (1951/1978, p. 32). Optimism depends upon calculation, and is narcissistic, the object being desired for oneself. Hope, by contrast, is open to a future it cannot control, and what is longed for is "for us" (pp. 32–34, 60). By these measures, Marcel would no doubt claim that blueprint utopians are optimists. They have no need of hope, for they are busy designing the future. The interests behind neoliberal systems are eternally optimistic. Any who attempt to turn the neoliberal tide will have to rely instead upon hope.

The hope needed today is not a dreamy-eyed longing locked within the individual subject. If the analyses in this book are anything close to accurate, this will not do, even for individual subjects. Soul inhabits a collective body, a body that exhales hope. This hope, once exhaled, expands to enfold our precious, entangled world, only to take it back in again. It has economic and political aspirations and inspirations. Just because it is expansive, however, does not make it abstract. It exists in material form, the form of love and justice. The utopian spirit of soul must exceed neoliberal blueprints for multiculturalism and diversity. Without economic justice, there will be no inclusivity that makes a great difference in human lives. The mere appreciation of racial, gender, and sexual diversity will not relieve the oppression that is fueling destruction and genocide on a global scale. At the same time, economic justice will not matter unless all

CONCLUDING THEOLOGICAL POSTSCRIPTS   237

are included. While workers seizing control of the means of production would not in itself end sexism, racism, or heterosexism, neither can an end be brought to any of these without addressing class struggle.

These postscripts finally converge. Collectives that nurture soul will be spiritually utopian and politically active, working toward economic and social justice. A pastoral care that is not rooted in such communities will, however unintentionally, serve the interests of a global system that produces the suffering it seeks to assuage. Caring for souls while giving up on striving toward a better world is, at best, a betrayal of our best traditions and, at worst, a hypocritical and cynical activity. I have said that, in interpersonal relationships such as psychotherapy, hope emerges in the pause between speaking and responding. This is surely no less true in the social world. If human collectives give voice to the suffering within them and listen intently to the suffering in the world—including that of the dead and the vanquished—a large-scale hope may yet be born anew. Deep calls unto deep.

NOTES

1. See the 2015 report by the National Congregations Study (NCS), available at http://www.soc.duke.edu/natcong/Docs/NCSIII_report_final.pdf. The study found that while the average religious congregation in the United States is very small, the average participant attends a large, propertied, and relatively well-funded church.
2. The previously cited study by the NCS confirms that the average religious congregation in the United States in 2012 had 70 active participants (p. 5).
3. As reported in a *USA Today* article titled "'House churches' keep worship small, simple, friendly" (July, 2010). Available at http://usatoday30.usatoday.com/news/religion/2010-07-22-house-church21_ST_N.htm
4. See W. Bradford Wilcox, "Why so many empty church pews? Here's what money, sex, divorce and TV are doing to American religion," *The Washington Post* (March 26, 2015). Available at https://www.washingtonpost.com/news/acts-of-faith/wp/2015/03/26/why-so-many-empty-church-pews-heres-what-money-sex-divorce-and-tv-are-doing-to-american-religion/
5. This paragraph and the succeeding five paragraphs first appeared, with minor differences, in Rogers-Vaughn, B. (2014). Blessed are those

who mourn: Depression as political resistance. *Pastoral Psychology, 63* (4), 503–522. This material is repeated here with the express permission of Springer, the original publisher.

REFERENCES

Ahmed, S. (2014, August 25). Selfcare as warfare [Web log post]. Retrieved May 7, 2016, from https://feministkilljoys.com/2014/08/25/selfcare-as-warfare/

Ahmed, S. (2015). *The cultural politics of emotion* (2nd ed.). New York, NY: Routledge.

Anderson, H. (2001). Whatever happened to *Seelsorge*? *Word & World, 21*(1), 32–41.

Bauman, Z. (1997). *Postmodernity and its discontents.* Cambridge: Polity Press.

Bauman, Z. (2004). *Wasted lives: Modernity and its outcasts.* Cambridge: Polity Press.

Berlant, L. (2011). *Cruel optimism.* Durham, NC: Duke University Press.

Bollas, C. (1987/2011). Normotic illness. In C. Bollas & A. Jemstedt (Eds.), *The Christopher Bollas Reader* (pp. 22–36). London: Routledge.

Brown, W. (2015). *Undoing the demos: Neoliberalism's stealth revolution.* Brooklyn, NY: Zone Books.

Brueggemann, W. (2012). In the "Thou" business. *Journal for Preachers, 35*(4), 21–30.

Buber, M. (1947/2002). *Between man and man* (Ronald Gregor-Smith, Trans.). London: Routledge.

Cantwell, C. D., Carter, H. W., & Drake, J. G. (Eds.). (2016). *The pew and the picket line: Christianity and the American working class.* Urbana, IL: University of Illinois Press.

Carter, H. W. (2015). *Union made: Working people and the rise of social Christianity in Chicago.* New York, NY: Oxford University Press.

Cazdyn, E. (2012). *The already dead: The new time of politics, culture, and illness* Durham, NC: Duke University Press.

Chomsky, N. (2015, September 22). History doesn't go in a straight line. *Jacobin* Retrieved May 24, 2016, from https://www.jacobinmag.com/2015/09/noam-chomsky-bernie-sanders-greece-tsipras-grexit-austerity-neoliberalism protest/

Cobb Jr., J. B. (2010). *Spiritual bankruptcy: A prophetic call to action.* Nashville TN: Abingdon Press.

Connolly, W. E. (2008). *Capitalism and Christianity, American style.* Durham NC: Duke University Press.

Connolly, W. E. (2010). Materialities of experience. In D. Coole & S. Frost (Eds. *New materialisms: Ontology, agency, and politics* (pp. 178–200). Durham, NC Duke University Press.

ies, W. (2015). The democratic critique of neo-liberalism. *Renewal 23*(3), 86-92. Retrieved May 22, 2016, from http://www.renewal.org.uk/articles/ he-democratic-critique-of-neo-liberalism

n, J. (2009). *Democracy and other neoliberal fantasies: Communicative capitalism and left politics.* Durham, NC: Duke University Press.

rida, J. (1994). *Specters of Marx: The state of the debt, the work of mourning and the new international* (Peggy Kamuf, Trans.). New York, NY: Routledge.

rida, J. (2003/2011). *The beast & the sovereign* (Vol. 2) (Geoffrey Bennington, Trans.). Chicago, IL: University of Chicago Press.

Unamuno, M. (1921/1954). *Tragic sense of life* (John Ernest Crawford Flitch, Trans.). New York, NY: Dover Publications.

Four, D.-R. (2003/2008). *The art of shrinking heads: On the new servitude of the liberated in the age of total capitalism* (David Macey, Trans.). Cambridge: Polity Press.

ot, T. S. (1925/1930–1970). The hollow men. In T. S. Eliot (Ed.), *Collected poems, 1909-1962* (pp. 77–82). New York, NY: Harcourt, Brace & World.

ley, E. (1975). *Ecclesial man: A social phenomenology of faith and reality.* Philadelphia, PA: Fortress Press.

ley, E. (1998). Toward theological understanding: An interview with Edward Farley. *The Christian Century, 115*(4), 113–115 149.

kuyama, F. (1992/2006). *The end of history and the last man.* New York, NY: Free Press.

son-Graham, J. K. (1996/2006). *The end of capitalism (as we knew it): A feminist critique of political economy.* Minneapolis, MN: University of Minnesota Press.

son-Graham, J. K. (2006). *A postcapitalist politics.* Minneapolis, MN: University of Minnesota Press.

roy, P. (2010). *Darker than blue: On the moral economies of Black Atlantic culture.* Cambridge, MA: The Belknap Press of Harvard University Press.

ss, R. E., & Klass, D. (2005). *Dead but not lost: Grief narratives in religious traditions.* Walnut Creek, CA: AltaMira Press.

raway, D. (1985). A manifesto for cyborgs: Science, technology, and socialist feminism in the 1980s. *Socialist Review, 80,* 65–107.

yek, F. A. (1944/2007). In B. Caldwell (Ed.), *The road to serfdom: Text and documents, the definitive edition.* Chicago, IL: University of Chicago Press.

le, D. (2007). *Listening and voice: Phenomenologies of sound.* Albany, NY: State University of New York Press.

oby, R. (1999). *The end of utopia: Politics and culture in an age of apathy.* New York, NY: Basic Books.

oby, R. (2005). *Picture imperfect: Utopian thought for an anti-utopian age.* New York, NY: Columbia University Press.

ann, R. O. (1966). *The meaning of love: An essay towards a metaphysics of inter-subjectivity.* Glen Rock, NJ: Paulist Press.

Johnson, C. C. (2016, February 3). An open letter to Ta-Nehisi Coates and liberals who love him. *Jacobin*. Retrieved February 28, 2016, from http: www.jacobinmag.com/2016/02/ta-nehisi-coates-case-for-reparations-be sanders-racism/

Kierkegaard, S. (1849/1980). *The sickness unto death: A Christian psycholo exposition for upbuilding and awakening* (Howard V. Hong & Edna H. H Eds. and Trans.). Princeton, NJ: Princeton University Press.

Kunkel, B. (2014). *Utopia or bust: A guide to the present crisis*. London: Verso

Lash, N. (1996). *The beginning and the end of 'religion'*. Cambridge: Cambri University Press.

Marcel, G. (1951/1978). *Homo viator: Introduction to a metaphysic of hope* (En Craufurd, Trans.). Gloucester, MA: Peter Smith.

Meštrović, S. G. (1997). *Postemotional society*. London: SAGE Publications.

Metz, J. B. (1977/2013). *Faith in history and society: Toward a practical fu mental theology* (J. Matthew Ashley, Ed. & Trans.). New York, NY: Crossroad Publishing Company.

Míguez, N., Rieger, J., & Sung, J. M. (2009). *Beyond the spirit of empire: The and politics in a new key*. London: SCM Press.

Moore, T. (1992). *Care of the soul: A guide for cultivating depth and sacredne everyday life*. New York, NY: HarperCollins Publishers.

Parker, I. (2007). *Revolution in psychology: Alienation to emancipation*. Lon Pluto Press.

Rauschenbusch, W. (1907/2007). *Christianity and the social crisis in the 21st tury: The classic that woke up the church*. New York, NY: HarperOne.

Rieff, P. (1966/2006). *The triumph of the therapeutic: Uses of faith after Fr* (40th anniversary ed.). Wilmington, DE: ISI Books.

Rieger, J. (2007). *Christ & empire: From Paul to postcolonial times*. Minneap MN: Fortress Press.

Rieger, J. (2009). *No rising tide: Theology, economics, and the future*. Minneap MN: Fortress Press.

Rieger, J. (Ed.). (2013). *Religion, theology, and class: Fresh engagements after silence*. New York, NY: Palgrave Macmillan.

Rieger, J., & Henkel-Rieger, R. (2016). *Unified we are a force: How faith and l can overcome America's inequalities*. St. Louis, MO: Chalice Press.

Rieger, J., & Pui-lan, K. (2012). *Occupy religion: Theology of the multit* Lanham, MD: Rowman & Littlefield Publishers.

Rogers-Vaughn, B. (2014). Blessed are those who mourn: Depression as polit resistance. *Pastoral Psychology, 63*(4), 503–522.

Rose, N. (1999). *Governing the soul: The shaping of the private self* (2nd e London: Free Association Books.

Sassen, S. (2014). *Expulsions: Brutality and complexity in the global econo* Cambridge, MA: Belknap Press.

Sung, J. M. (2007). *Desire, market and religion.* London: SCM Press.

Sung, J. M. (2011). *The subject, capitalism, and religion: Horizons of hope in complex societies.* New York, NY: Palgrave Macmillan.

Theunissen, M. (1977/1984). *The other: Studies in the social ontology of Husserl, Heidegger, Sartre, and Buber* (Christopher Macann, Trans.). Cambridge, MA: MIT Press.

Thistlethwaite, S. B. (2010). *Dreaming of Eden: American religion and politics in a wired world.* New York, NY: Palgrave Macmillan.

Tillich, P. (1957). *Dynamics of faith.* New York, NY: Harper & Row.

Turkle, S. (2011). *Alone together: Why we expect more from technology and less from each other.* New York, NY: Basic Books.

Vaughn, B. (2003). Recovering grief in the age of grief recovery. *The Journal of Pastoral Theology, 13*(1), 36–45.

Žižek, S. (2009). *First as tragedy, then as farce.* London: Verso.

Zweig, M. (2012). *The working class majority: America's best kept secret* (2nd ed.). Ithaca, NY: Cornell University Press.

Index[1]

---

[1] Note: Page numbers with "n" denote notes.

© The Author(s) 2016   243
B. Rogers-Vaughn, *Caring for Souls in a Neoliberal Age*,
DOI 10.1057/978-1-137-55339-3

Printed in Great Britain
by Amazon